"The passion and the sharp intellect which inform this volume, make it required reading for all those who seek to lead our nation in the twenty-first century. Ullman concisely reviews how we got to our current troubled state—both internationally and domestically—and offers several challenging thoughts on overcoming a particularly perilous time in our history. Many of his suggestions will be controversial, but his admirable goal is to force us to restore America's promise, at home and abroad."

—Ambassador Frances D. Cook

"Ullman wisely addresses our national problems at home and abroad. He explains the historical setting and most importantly gives us cogent suggestions for reform and improvement. Universal voting for the people, better coordination and accountability in our government, and international cooperation for our friends and neighbors are at the heart of his changes. Are you concerned about the current condition? Read this book for critical insights, constructive ideas and strategic solutions."

—Ambassador Thomas R. Pickering

America's
Promise
RESTORED

America's
Promise
RESTORED

PREVENTING
CULTURE, CRUSADE, AND PARTISANSHIP
FROM WRECKING OUR NATION

HARLAN ULLMAN

CARROLL & GRAF PUBLISHERS
NEW YORK

AMERICA'S PROMISE RESTORED
Preventing Culture, Crusade, and Partisanship from Wrecking Our Nation

Carroll & Graf Publishers
An Imprint of Avalon Publishing Group, Inc.
245 West 17th Street
11th Floor
New York, NY 10011

AVALON
publishing group incorporated

Copyright © 2006 by Harlan Ullman

First Carroll & Graf edition 2006

Library of Congress Cataloging-in-Publication Data is available.

ISBN-13: 978-0-78671-758-3
ISBN-10: 0-78671-758-0

9 8 7 6 5 4 3 2 1

Interior Design by Maria E. Torres
Printed in the United States of America
Distributed by Publishers Group West

Contents

PART III: RESTORING AMERICA'S PROMISE

"For a window on politics and all its failings, consider the current fight over pension reform. It's a fight that reveals the cowardice of the Bush administration and the venality of Congress. It demonstrates the *government's inability to grapple seriously with public policy*—even when the case for action seems too obvious to ignore."

—*Washington Post* Editorial,
October 17, 2005
[italics added]

"Americans expect others to reason like us or to be in need of education to bring them up to our level."

—Stanley Hoffmann, 1967

"Today's crisis of confidence in political leaders is in large part a crisis of competence at home and abroad. The American people are learning the hard way that visions are not plans and hope is not a strategy."

—William Galston and Elaine Kamarck,
October 2005

"The people . . . have been led in Mesopotamia into a trap from which it will be hard to escape with dignity and honor. They have been tricked into it by a steady state of withholding of information. The Baghdad communiqués are belated, insincere and incomplete. Things have been far worse than we have been told . . . a disgrace to our . . . record and may soon be too inflamed for any ordinary cure. We are today not far from a disaster."

—T. E. Lawrence, *Times* (London),
August 22, 1920

"Invention of novel solutions to tough problems of governance is relatively easy. But satisfactory implementation is likely to prove impossible."

—Ullman's Paradox, 2005

Introduction

IF YOU ARE INCREASINGLY CONCERNED, worried, or even angry about America's future and what it may hold, I urge you to read on. The United States is in trouble, and for two major reasons. First, our federal government is currently unable to deal with the plethora of problems facing it. Second, Americans do not fully understand the nature or the depth of the dangers that confront us or the consequences of deferring action until it is too late.

If you disagree with this warning or understandably question why America is at great risk today, probably greater than in the past, I also ask that you read further.

Iraq and the Global War on Terror are the most visible and immediate dangers. But even if Iraq magically turns into an oasis of stability and global terror miraculously fades away (and neither will), America still faces a spate of very tough issues and challenges that place its future safety, well-being, and security in jeopardy.

Put simply, America's national government is foundering. Correcting this condition extends beyond the responsibility of the executive and legislative branches and ultimately rests with the American public. If the public does not become engaged and demand action, then it will get the government it deserves. The same, however, cannot be said for future generations, who will inherit a broken republic if we do not act quickly and effectively.

Today, the White House and much of Congress are fixated on and even obsessed with Iraq and the war on terror. Trenchant questions about the handling of Iraq must be answered. Why, for example, did George W. Bush's[1] administration conclude that Iraq's weapons of mass destruction (WMD) posed a "grave and gathering" threat, meaning an imminent danger, when in fact it turned out that those weapons did not even exist? Why were plans for the peace in Iraq so woefully deficient? How did the administration allow its definition and treatment of enemy combatants to turn into a national disgrace and a diplomatic nightmare? And was the administration's decision to bypass specific laws in authorizing electronic surveillance of suspected terrorists legal? Full public disclosure and accountability are sorely needed. But those inquiries must not prevent or defer action on other critical problems and dangers.

The answer to the question of why the United States is in trouble is clear and stark and forms this book's thesis. Government, and the people elected to populate it—no matter how noble or gifted—have been stymied in finding workable, effective, and—in a few crucial instances—even legal solutions to this array of tough issues. Our government is not working; it has become dysfunctional.

The indictment of the House of Representatives majority leader Tom DeLay, the criminal activities and plea-bargain of disgraced former super-lobbyist Jack Abramoff, and the investigation of possibly improper financial transactions by Senate majority leader Bill Frist, while not new in terms of Congressional scandals and wrongdoings, are further symptoms of the state of politics and government today. In the building ground swell to "reform" any and all ills, to the degree that history is a guide, it is a good bet that the process of government will be made worse.

At the same time, our principal adversaries, mislabeled as terrorists, target the "fault lines" of society, meaning our major political, psychological, social, and economic vulnerabilities, which if successfully attacked, will do great damage to the nation and to our citizens. Terror, ideas, and ideologies are these adversaries' main weapons, not armies and navies, and therefore cannot be defeated by conventional military means alone.

The reasons why government is not working are also clear and stark. The challenges, crises, problems, and issues that the United States faces at home and abroad have been accumulating in number, complexity, and difficulty of solution. None has an easy answer. Many are intractable. And some, beyond Iraq, can no longer be deferred without incurring unaffordable costs and/or risks in the future.

The war on terror; the rebuilding of Iraq; real or possible nuclear proliferation in North Korea, Iran, and elsewhere; the election of what we have declared to be a terrorist organization, Hamas, to govern Palestine; a resurgent Asia; soaring debts and deficits and skyrocketing expenses for retirement plans and especially health care; these are a few of the many vexing issues that must be resolved. The fiscal reality is that long-term government revenues will fund only part—perhaps only a small fraction—of the expectations and commitments promised by government and obligated by statute. Unless economic growth defies the laws of gravity or the nation has the political capacity to make truly tough and painful choices, the gap between obligations and resources will destroy the American Dream and its promise.

Some of the dysfunctional performance of government stems from the Constitution. The Constitution is based on a system of divided government and checks and balances that contain inherent contradictions and tensions among the three branches. Disputes over the division of responsibility and authority between Congress and the White House have traditionally arisen over war powers, the conduct of foreign policy, and the spending of appropriated monies. These points of conflict have expanded and become more contentious just in the past few years, such as the controversy over terrorist surveillance, called "domestic spying" by critics.

More of this dysfunctionality comes from the strength and growing influence of special-interest groups and lobbies that often represent political extremes and narrow constituencies that exist outside the mainstream of America.

And an increasingly large measure arises from a destructive alchemy catalyzed by ingredients combining the best and worst of America's unique culture, its preference for crusade and the emergence of highly destructive partisanship.

To make matters worse, the excessively "adversarial" nature of government has driven political discourse beyond the bounds of civility and reason, devolving into a nearly continuous cycle of attack campaigns and negative advertising that produce dangerous levels of hostility and acrimony.

The causes of this condition will not be corrected quickly. But the destructive aspects of culture, crusade, and partisanship can be remedied if we put our minds and our will to that task as a first step in restoring our government's ability to function.

Failure to act will guarantee not only a government incapable of providing for the common welfare, but one that too often will do real harm to the nation's best interests. A survey of American politics at work today captures the symptoms of a dysfunctional government and should shock the reader.

When the president of the United States signs a bill into law, most Americans would expect that Congress has carefully crafted and reviewed that legislation. The fact is that nowadays few, if any, congressmen have even read the bill before or after voting on it (in most cases, the bills have not even been circulated beforehand, in direct contravention of Congressional rules that require advanced distribution at least twenty-four hours prior to a vote); and the practice of lumping together many pieces of pending legislation into monster "omnibus" bills that are thousands of pages in length precludes any review. And, more than occasionally, amendments and add-ons known as "earmarks" are inserted *after* the vote and without the knowledge of the members.[2] A CEO in the private sector would be fired for far less, and might face legal proceedings over such practice. Many other egregious examples follow in future chapters.[3]

Remedies will be impeded by another simple truth. Most of the choices facing the nation, sadly, are not between good and bad. The choices will be between bad and worse. Treatment of suspected terrorist detainees is the striking example of a tough choice that ended up destroying American standing within and even beyond the Arab and Muslim worlds. Similarly perplexing dilemmas and lack of good choices are common to too many of the other issues on which government must act. Fortunately, that statement of fact is not totally bereft of hope.

The challenges and crises that we face will not fade away or ease with the passage of time. Our adversaries will exploit our "fault lines" ruthlessly and with cunning. Nor can Americans assume that a "great leader" will emerge to show us to the promised land. What can be accomplished, however, is twofold. First, we can relieve, repair, or reverse the destructive effects of culture, crusade, and partisanship that have made and are making our government dysfunctional. Second, these and other actions can defeat the external dangers that threaten us, making the nation safer.

Two broad remedies are prescribed. The first is a strategic vision or construct, much as containment, deterrence, and alliances worked in the Cold War. Second is the means to reengage the public in their governance through a step so simple and obvious that it may prove too shocking to implement. The vision offered is one of "peace, partnership, and prosperity" and is applied at home and abroad.[4] The reason for greater public engagement is taken from the Declaration of Independence:

> "Governments . . . deriving their just Powers from the Consent of the Governed, that whenever any Form of Government becomes destructive of these Ends, it is the Right of the People to alter or to abolish it and to institute new Government."

The cry is not for revolution but for restoration of our promise.

PART I

THE FAULT LINES

Why We Are at Risk

THERE IS NO WAY TO soften the argument or to minimize the extent of the danger. Powerful fault lines permeate the fabric of American society, threatening to shatter our democracy and well-being, taking with them much of America's promise. The greatest vulnerability is caused by the incapacity of our government to deal with the array of problems and issues confronting the nation. The next danger is the potentially catastrophic consequences of the war in Iraq and the global struggle against the jihadist extremists,[5] an adversary we still do not fully comprehend. Third is the huge and growing disparity between government obligations for social and entitlement programs, including health care and retirement, and the revenues to fund them.

Internationally, the end of the Cold War, the powerful forces underlying the attacks of September 11, 2001, and the global reach of jihadist Extremists have created, supercharged, and multiplied many challenges exerting huge pressure on the fault lines in our society. The irony is that during the Cold War, America countered and overcame an enemy possessing tens of thousands of nuclear weapons and prodigious military strength, all without bloodshed. But how can an adversary—lacking a standing army that can be beaten by our overpowering military—that uses ideas, ideologies, and terror instead, ever be defeated?

At home, faced with structural economic and social change that is shifting the bedrock on which American promises for prosperity and greatness have rested for decades, the crux of the challenge is to make the transition to whatever lies ahead without shattering America's social cohesion. Structural economic changes, in part induced by globalization, must be accommodated as debts, deficits, and liabilities escalate. Energy, environmental, and immigration issues must also be resolved.

The graying of the population places huge strain on social security, health care, and pension schemes. In late 2005, outbreaks of avian flu in Asia and Europe raised the specter of a global pandemic. While all of these crises will not boil over simultaneously, if at all, failure to address them compounds the costs and difficulties of deferring action. A further dilemma is that almost all likely solutions to these issues will not muster a large or even a majority consensus, making decisions harder to take.

For much of her history, America was protected by two oceans. The fault lines of earlier times could be overcome by virtually unlimited resources that enabled us to speed our way clear of disaster. World War II was the most noteworthy example of the virtues of a big wallet. But those advantages no longer hold. And many Americans do not realize the potential danger that lies ahead.

Consider two cases of fault lines failing catastrophically. Because of fault lines that could not be contained by the incredibly dysfunctional Soviet political system, the USSR shattered and disappeared. Thankfully, that implosion ended a cold war that could have metastasized into the nuclear destruction of much of mankind. However, as World War I begot World War II and World War II begot the Cold War, although the West won, the end of the Cold War and the demise of the Soviet Union created a new world order, but not one devoid of dangers and risks.

On a less global level, President Lyndon Johnson's Great Society, along with much of the American Dream, was shattered when the fault lines in America's Vietnam policy split apart. The Tet offensive in January 1968, and the failure to find a way to end the war, ultimately broke LBJ's will to govern, and he did not seek election for a second term as president. Seven years later, as South Vietnam finally fell, America suffered its first outright defeat in war, losing 58,000 of its citizens while killing hundreds of thousands of North Vietnamese and Vietcong in the process.

Unlike the Vietnam War, the struggle in Iraq and against jihadist Extremists does have vast strategic consequences irrespective of who leads the nation. And the United States is not going to implode. America is many things, but it is not the Soviet Union in its latter days. However, the consequences of ignoring where the nation is headed, and how the dysfunctionality of government is driving us in directions that put our society at great risk of collapse, will be far more profound than merely ending a presidency or losing a war that turned out to have no real geopolitical importance for America's security and safety.

Many Americans are uncomfortable or concerned about the future, sensing that, both at home and abroad, things are amiss. I have chosen to employ the terms "American Dream," "culture," "crusade," and "partisanship" as shorthand for the chain reactions and effects caused by these realities and forces that threaten to damage the nation.[6] Through a combination of strategic and historical analysis, this book will assist readers in better appreciating how and why America's future is especially at risk and what must be done to mitigate the dangers.

But what is really new in the 230 years since the Declaration of Independence proclaimed why Americans were revolting against the harshness and unjustness of British rule? Are these current warnings credible? Critics, skeptics, and those who are merely curious will rightly observe that America has earlier been in grave difficulty in wars, depressions, and crises. There have even been times when malaise and pessimism seemed inescapable. But we survived, and we will continue to survive. On the other hand, will we thrive? Iraq might turn out a success and al Qaeda might be destroyed. Sometime in the future, America's gross domestic product will reach higher double-digit figures and the Dow Jones will grow well into the five-digit range. Critics will rightly note that the warnings I am sounding must square with all our myriad prospects and possibilities.

What is most striking, distinguishing today from other periods in American history, is the simultaneous accumulation and deepening of the fault lines in our society, accelerated by the destructive impact of culture, crusade, and partisanship. Yes, America has the capacity for self-correction; but we also have the capacity for self-deception, as we painfully discovered in Vietnam and are relearning today in Iraq. Whether corrective action will occur before irreparable damage is done should self-deception and complacency win out is a question that begs for an answer. Consider the danger signs and symptoms again.

As will be argued and demonstrated, America's system of government, based on checks and balances, has become unstable and unresponsive to its duties and responsibilities to govern the nation competently and effectively. Our government was never perfect, but if "muddling through" once worked, those days are now over.

Gradual but steady corruption of political culture has accelerated the growth of the destructive elements of government. Highly ideological, well-funded interest groups and constituencies with agendas that often depart from the broader common welfare grow in number and in influence, drowning or crowding out much of mainstream America.[7] Both the Republican and Democratic parties have become polarized and more hostile and adversarial to one another.

Accountability of government has virtually disappeared, except when misconduct has unmistakably criminal implications. Proof of the absence of accountability is vividly in view. No high-level heads have rolled over Iraq and the erroneous certainty of the presence of WMD; for the unconscionable abuse of enemy combatants in the war on terror; or for the failed response to Hurricane Katrina. And, equally stunning, Congress's lack of oversight has produced not a whit of public outrage.[8] Meanwhile, politics have become consumed with continuous campaigns staffed by political operatives who find attack and negative ads the most effective means of defending or defeating almost all issues, from health care to confirmation of Supreme Court justices.[9]

In this culture, truth and fact have become subordinated to ideology and beliefs. At the end of the day, it made little difference whether or not Saddam Hussein had WMD. The Bush administration had embarked on a course for war against Iraq, and Congress was simply not going to block the executive branch in achieving its objective. In many (or all) aspects of government, truth and fact are increasingly less relevant to actions and decisions. Too many politicians prefer the world as they would like to see it, not as it is, turning Descartes on his head ("I wish, therefore I am"). The absence of ground truth and fact also applies to spending bills and budgets that routinely underestimate costs and future cost escalation, usually by large margins.

In addition to culture, the appeal of crusades to redress social ills, crises, and threats—often pursued with a "missionary zeal"—has put the nation at further risk. In the case of Vietnam, it took years to recover from that crusade. Iraq's future is still a festering question. However, because of the stakes involved in the Greater Middle East and South Asia over oil, terror, political disputes, and WMD and their proliferation, Iraq will have profound strategic consequences, whether the goal of democratization proves viable or unattainable.

Even with one party controlling Congress and the White House, because few domestic issues can be resolved with a majority or even a sizable plurality of support, gridlock often occurs. When it does not, legislation is often very diluted or badly drafted, such as the Medicare Prescription Drug Bill, in which millions of American seniors could not understand how to obtain their medications, making the situation worse, not better. Thus, given these realities, contemporary government has a much harder task than ever before.

Partisanship has always been present. But today, partisanship has become excessively bitter, eroding and breaking down many of the barriers protecting ethical practices and reasoned judgment. The pervasive and pernicious use of negative and attack advertising directly aimed at impeaching the character of opponents is symptomatic of the current excesses of partisanship. Winning has become the goal, no matter the means that must be employed. The destructive character of partisanship is fueled by an around-the-clock media that creates a poisonous political atmosphere inimical to effective governance.

A further sign of ill health is that, based on anecdotal evidence, many good people are choosing not to serve in the government or are being discouraged from service by the often ludicrous and intrusive clearance procedures, the nightmarish set of rules and ethical standards, and the pernicious politics through which even the tiniest political scratch can become septic. At the same time we face these destructive political forces at home, society's vulnerabilities have become the explicit targets for jihadists, whose weapons of ideology, ideas, and terror are inherently more difficult to counter than would be enemies with large standing armies.

Looming over the dangers of what the Bush administration steadfastly calls the Global War on Terror, tectonic change is sweeping the world, raising new challenges and testing the ability, relevance, and influence of the United States as a world leader. Indeed, from the perspective of many foreign capitals and virtually all opinion polls, America's policies and standing are in near free-fall abroad.[10] It is difficult to calculate the intensity of, or understand the passion and collective resentment of, Arabs and Muslims over U.S. policies in the Middle East. In particular, despite the Bush administration's support for a two-state solution that recognizes Palestine, Arabs and Muslims see the United States as Israel's permanent guardian. The animosity created is huge and is not helped by what is viewed as further American hypocrisy in its support of authoritarian regimes also in the Middle East.

The president and Congress are charged with the responsibility for governing the nation. It is worth a moment to examine the role of each. The main responsibilities of the president—the chief executive, head of state, and commander in chief of our armed forces—are to lead and act in the name of the nation. However, it is interesting to inquire on what basis a president is elected to that office. And if the expectation is that a "great" leader will ultimately emerge, is that hope a basis for actually choosing a president? In the private sector, a chief executive officer is elected by a board (in a public company), in large measure based on prior qualifications and experience. That person may or may not be a great man or woman. But that person will at least have shown some suitability for the assignment. That does not always hold true for presidents.

The specific qualifications and experience that new presidents bring to the job are rarely up to its demands. Obviously, presidents are expected to have political skills, intuitive judgment, and the ability to pick good people for key jobs rather than vast personal experience. Harry Truman's presidency is a good example of character overcoming inexperience. Franklin Roosevelt refused to inform Truman, his own vice president, on many key affairs of state, including the development of the atomic bomb. Later, as president, Truman also suffered from horribly low approval ratings in opinion polls and was savagely and regularly attacked in the press for poor leadership.

The White House is not the corporate world, and the conduct of politics is not the conduct of business. However, few entities in the private sector would promote individuals to their most senior ranks with the same degree of lack of prior experience as those who are elected president of the United States. And the fact that a president may choose the "best and brightest" to serve him is no guarantee of success. Vietnam and Iraq are cases in point.

Regarding national security, within living memory most of our presidents entered office lacking the experience to deal with current issues.[11]

Hence, presidents had to learn on the job. Future presidents are likely to be no different. A great leader, should one emerge, would be the exception. The predicament is that given the nature of current challenges and threats, the luxury of allowing presidents ample time to settle into the job may no longer be possible or sensible.

By itself, though, experience is not sufficient to assure a successful presidency. Over the past thirty years, only two—Richard Nixon and George H. W. Bush—seemingly had the requisite experience for the office as part of their earlier résumés. Yet Nixon was forced to resign and Bush was not re-elected. The others, all governors—Jimmy Carter, Ronald Reagan, Bill Clinton, and George W. Bush—had neither the formal experience nor theoretical skills demanded by the presidency and the nature of the times, but possessed strong instinctive passions and broader values about what was right and what was wrong.

Administrations rise and fall on more than the president. Events and personalities obviously count. So does luck, a much discounted factor. However, for good or ill, administrations take on the character of the sitting president. In that regard, one individual matters greatly. Too often, however, presidents and administrations do not rise above the negative elements of culture, crusade, and partisanship, thus allowing their influence to dominate policy. John F. Kennedy assumed office running on a missile gap that did not exist, but did so because politically it made his opponent, Vice President Nixon, seem weak on defense. Kennedy then embraced the "domino theory," on which involvement in Vietnam was rationalized. Similarly, Bush 43 saw the current war in Iraq to remove Saddam as the opportunity to "transform the strategic landscape of the Middle East," a judgment that will prove as flawed as the domino theory.

The only requirements for president are to be a native-born American citizen, over thirty-five years of age, resident for at least fourteen years in the United States, and receive a majority of votes in the Electoral College. The requisite experience is in the eye of the beholder. But what happens when on-the-job training fails or a president is severely tested immediately upon entering office? What happens when contemporary problems and challenges cannot be solved by campaign promises, and real thought must be given to effective solutions? There is little time for this to happen during the campaign or the transition period after the election. Yet our system of government allows no alternative.

Second, requirements for election to Congress are even less stringent (age and citizenship along with winning the vote) than those for president. By charter, Congress is slow to act and has no executive capacity to manage. Compromise is necessary to govern. As both parties become more partisan, adversarial, and polarized, Congress obviously follows suit. Hence, compromise becomes harder to obtain in an atmosphere poisoned by ideological differences and huge divides between Republicans and Democrats that make a workable melding of diverse opinions virtually impossible.[12] As with presidents, there seems to be an absence of "great men"; fewer members of Congress reach the stature of some of their predecessors, in large part because those who could rise to that level tend to fall outside the more extreme wings that control their parties and are often regarded as "mavericks."

Presidents and members of Congress hire staff with experience and expertise to help run government. It is not surprising that most so-called policy "experts" cluster around and operate within the two political parties. Few "independent" or non-partisan experts achieve high political office without party affiliation. Those in office must advocate and advance the administration's agenda. Those out of office await the day when they will return to power. However, as politics no longer stops at the water's edge and as political differences of opinion become more polarized, objectivity, reason, and balanced criticism are lost. The "loyal opposition" has become the enemy, further compounding the difficulty in obtaining good government.

At a time when political, social, economic, and ideological forces are transforming the world and when the *modus operandi* of our adversaries cannot be defeated by traditional means, the United States desperately needs a government that can function with competence and judgment. This is not the case at present. The failure of government to perform, possibly tolerable if the stakes were small, is made starker by the following proposition.

The United States may be in the gravest danger at any time in its history since the Civil War, an assertion that may be hard to accept at first—or at any—glance.[13] The danger is not the outright destruction of the nation, as was the case during the Cold War, when thermonuclear war would have obliterated society. Instead, today, we face a twofold crisis. The first is the emergence of a political rival wrapped in the ideology of jihadist extremism, which can metastasize into a current-day form of Bolshevism or Nazism. The symptoms extend far beyond September 11 and terror. Indeed, twin revolutions are sweeping through the Arab and Islamic worlds with the potential force of what happened in France in 1789. Much more will be said about these revolutions.

At the same time, the failure of government to govern poses a direct danger to the American Dream and the expectations most Americans have about their lives, futures, and standards of living. While American governments have always faced seemingly irreconcilable economic, fiscal, and social issues, the cascading effects of their growth and accumulation now mark a major break from the past. The long-term explosion of economic and fiscal debts and deficits and obligations to cover pensions, social security, and health-care programs as Americans age in increasing numbers cannot continue forever.

For the past few years, low interest rates have encouraged consumer borrowing, principally through home mortgages; and cheaper foreign goods have fueled the economy as foreign creditors, flush with U.S. dollars from trade surpluses generated by cheaper labor wages or windfall profits from oil, continue to invest in America. At some stage, unless the laws of economics are repealed, this circular flow of goods, services, and cash will come to a crashing stop. Unless government has intervened beforehand or an economic miracle has been performed, we are headed for a major economic readjustment, if not a calamity.

The corollary is also bitter medicine. If Americans do not demand major action to address this precarious position and deal with these dangers and realities sensibly, the alternative of leaving the future to chance is reckless in the extreme. At that stage, after waiting for destiny to determine America's fate, it will be too late. To make this case, strategic and historical analysis is essential.

Strategic and historical analysis is neither complicated nor abstract. It is simply a method for getting to what Franklin D. Roosevelt's chief confidant Harry Hopkins described as the "heart of the matter," whatever subject may be under review. The heart of the matter in this analysis focuses on uncovering the major fault lines that put the nation at risk.

In this process of making America safer and more secure, history counts. What has happened in the past cannot predict the future. However, history is very helpful in showing and explaining both the positive and pernicious effects that this alchemy of culture, crusade, and partisanship has had on the United States. From that examination, the case for reversing the damaging aspects of culture, crusade, and partisanship becomes self-evident.

But life has a dark side. Because of the huge wealth and power the United States has accumulated and enjoyed for well over a century, it is not surprising that Americans grew to believe in the superiority and universality of America's values from business to rap music, to reality television programs, and McDonalds' ubiquitous arches. The same attitude and arrogance affected and afflicted foreign policy, dating back at least to the administration of President William G. McKinley more than a century ago.

McKinley is an interesting reference point for today. Not only did he begin forging an American empire with the defeat of Spain and the annexation principally of Cuba and the Philippines in 1898, but with the able assistance of Senator Mark Hanna, McKinley also built a Republican governing coalition that lasted until the Great Depression, despite the interlude represented by the loss of the presidency to Woodrow Wilson from 1912 to 1920.

The combined impact of culture and crusade would become inseparable. Crusade was not merely directed at deposing dictators and villains abroad. For good or ill, crusades were launched at home, and often on both sides of the same issue, from prohibiting consumption of alcohol, drugs, and cigarettes to limiting or expanding social issues including abortion, gun control, and the insertion of religion into public life. Because of the impact of culture and crusade, inherently social issues became so politicized and polarized as to make them recurring flashpoints, without permanent solution.

How America waged its wars is an excellent example of the effects of culture and crusade. American idealism and selflessness are central to its culture and the inclination toward crusade. In defeating enemies in two world wars and a rival superpower thereafter, America made no territorial claims in victory except for the small plots of ground to bury our war dead. This idealism was crucial in harnessing wisdom, foresight, and compassion to help rebuild the defeated enemy in 1945 and turn those states into vibrant and peaceful democracies.

Most of our wars have been conducted as crusades against evil empires, from the Kaiser to Khrushchev, or so we believed, with the appealing if not simplistic black-and-white view of good against evil, imbued with a blend of piety and righteousness and the presumption of the superiority of our ideas. But when hubris and arrogance overcame good judgment, such as in Vietnam, the crusade failed disastrously. In almost every case, crusades were launched with bipartisan support across both political parties.

Today, when change is sweeping across the world, the United States is preoccupied with the war on global terrorism. To some observers such as former National Security Adviser Zbigniew Brzezinski, the understandable reaction to the attacks of September 11 and the necessity to punish the terrorist perpetrators has made many Americans ignore or downplay other realities of the international environment. Regarding the Global War on Terror and the interventions in Afghanistan and Iraq, Americans did not at first realize that the Bush administration had embarked on a crusade to transform the entire geostrategic landscape of the Greater Middle East.

Ironically, as the United States remains engaged in the Global War on Terror against jihadists, "crusade" takes on meanings centuries old. Religious fundamentalism, from the far Christian right to Jewish and Islamic extremists, is a driver of how states and entities often attempt to impose their dreams on others. In this most recent of crusades, however, there is no Jerusalem to conquer, one of many differences that make this war all the more difficult to ever bring to any conclusion.

At the outset of each, the war on terror and the forays into Afghanistan and Iraq mustered considerable bipartisan support. But the White House's plans for waging these wars did not disclose the Wilsonian expectations and idealism of making the world not only safe but safer through *democracy*—a very real crusade. Some of the so-called "neo-conservatives" responsible for creating this vision would later complain that the strategy of democratization was not Wilsonian but a commonsensical and pragmatic counterweight to the very real threats emanating from the Greater Middle East.

Iraq is the test case for that line of thinking, and how well or badly this crusade will fare in imposing or nurturing a democracy is still very much in doubt. However, while there was debate over going to war with Iraq, there was absolutely no debate over whether the path of democratization was feasible or even desirable. The initial argument for waging war was "regime change." When that rationale failed to garner sufficient support, the case for war shifted to ending Saddam Hussein's violation of United Nations resolutions forbidding Iraq WMD (weapons that, it turned out,

Saddam no longer possessed), and mandating an intrusive UN inspection regime to ensure and verify compliance.

The fixation with Iraq concealed key strategic realities and fault lines in American actions and assumptions. Al Qaeda and jihadist extremism were and are the primary international adversary, not Saddam Hussein and the Baathists, no matter how villainous they were or how much they lusted for WMD. jihadist Extremists are out to do great harm to the United States and others in pursuit of political ambitions as expansive as that of Lenin and the Bolsheviks a century ago and Hitler and his Nazi thugs after World War I.

But the shocking reality is that these extremist groups may not pose the greatest danger to the United States. Clearly, terrorists might get their hands on chemical, biological, or radioactive agents. Perhaps, one day, a nuclear weapon might fall into their possession. The possible scenarios are frightening, and an actual event far beyond the reach of the attacks of 2001 could surely do great damage to the nation.

As catalysts, however, jihadists can also unleash powerful and less visible destructive forces capable of destroying the fault lines of American society. Should that happen, the promise that has made America great and that has been at the heart of American society and politics could be broken. If those and other fault lines snap, much of the damage will be self-inflicted.

The handling of enemy combatants constituted self-inflicted assaults on our values and concept of due process of law. The consequences of the decision to authorize domestic surveillance outside the specifications of the Foreign Intelligence Surveillance Act (FISA) of 1978 are not yet visible. But what the Bush 43 administration calls "terrorist surveillance" and opponents call "domestic spying" raises potentially profound Constitutional clashes between the law of the land passed by Congress and signed by the president and the de facto power of the presidency to bypass or ignore the law. Whether or not genuine concern among Republicans and Democrats in Congress that the president is overreaching his Constitutional authority—including other spying programs that may exist but have not yet been disclosed—leads to a bitter legal struggle resolved only by the Supreme Court, the possibility is real. And the last thing the nation needs, given the spate of other problems, is a Constitutional donnybrook between those two branches of government.[14]

The principal danger today begins with the direction in which the political system is taking the nation and the question of whether a corrective function will be found to put us on a sounder footing. Absent the safety of geography, limitless resources, and a well-defined enemy to rally us, the only avenue to achieve these goals is through citizens willing to act with courage and commitment to demand the necessary changes to fix the dysfunctional and unsatisfactory performance of government. Unless the public engages, there is no other imperative forcing us into an effective response.

The result of losing our system of checks and balances will not necessarily produce a more autocratic government or anarchy. Instead, the possible results may be either a trend to implement extreme policies that do not reflect the attitudes of a majority of Americans, or a gridlock in which deferral of action makes future decisions even more difficult. The consequence will not be an America that is merely in decline or one that is "overtaken" by rising states such as India or China; instead, the consequence will be a profound societal transformation that could very well do more than erode our standard of living and way of life: It could change America into something that most of us Americans would not like to see—a nation that is incapable of dealing with the rigors and necessities of the twenty-first century.

The danger is entirely different from the pessimism about historical progress expressed by the German historian and philosopher Oswald Spengler (1880–1936, in *The Decline of the West*) and the British historian Arnold J. Toynbee (1889–1975, in *A Study of History*). States may rise or fall, and routs and rallies may mark history. For the foreseeable future, America will remain the most formidable economic and military power on the globe. But just as theologians believe that the soul is what distinguishes humankind from all other species, America needs a viable dream and a realistic vision to sustain itself. Without optimism about the future and the inherent worth of humanity, America can no longer be America.

What would take its place is unknowable. However, the chances are very great that this transformed America will not be the same force for freedom and progress that it has been for more than two hundred years. Worse, distorted by the tawdry aspects of culture, crusade, and partisanship, America could very easily undo much of the good it has done and stood for, both at home and abroad.

Most Americans are unaware of, or indifferent to, these fault lines and the destructive power of the pernicious aspects of culture, crusade, and partisanship. For those who are uncertain about these arguments or who disagree with them, a few minutes pondering these anecdotal pieces of evidence, stated as parliamentary questions, might prove useful.

What has happened to accountability in government? There has been no crusade for accountability in government, unlike the crusade against corporate misdeeds. Who was held accountable, punished, or chastised for going to war in Iraq over weapons that did not exist, or for massively mismanaging the reconstruction of Iraq, unlike CEO's of failing companies and those who may have broken the rules slightly (Martha Stewart) or massively (Kenneth Lay of Enron, Dennis Kozlowski of Tyco, and Bernard Ebbers of WorldCom)? Yet, aside from elections that rarely remove incumbents, and the rarer impeachment of presidents, members of Congress, and judges, public officials are rarely taken to task. It is tempting to return to Katrina and hope that the dereliction of duty was so great that legal charges will be filed. That is a hope that will never become reality. But if any CEO presided over a similar level of incompetence, shareholders and boards of directors would not be as passive. One of the recommendations that follows suggests how to return accountability to government and shore up this gaping fault line.

Second, why has Congress been so absent from duty for so long? The great humorist Will Rogers once remarked about Congress that every time it wanted to make a joke, it passed a law; and every law it passed became a joke. In this day of instant and massive communications and the Internet, why does the public remain so complacent about the pathetic performance of that body (even though E-mailing a member of Congress is far easier and quicker than using the post ever was)? Congress has offered virtually no oversight on Iraq and its reconstruction. Until the last months of 2005, Congressional oversight of the war on terror, and of the performance of the executive branch from Homeland Security to the FBI, had been similarly missing in action. (It did find enough time, however, to pass a nonbinding resolution regarding Terry Schiavo, the brain-dead woman kept alive for years by a feeding tube— a singularly ill-conceived and thorough waste of its precious time.) Congress seems constitutionally incapable of fiscal responsibility, and while "pork" may only reflect a few percentage points of spending, there must be a better way of balancing national and constituent interests.

A cynical conclusion is that mediocrity—or worse—is the standard by which government is allowed to operate, another fault line. Whether the FISA and torture controversies will provoke greater oversight or not, as 2006 progresses, is now unknowable, especially given that it is also an election year for Congress.

Third, why are more and more Americans turned off by the prospect of serving in government? And is it coincidental or instructive that parts of American culture seem in serious decline, indicated by an absence of civility (perhaps a byproduct of destructive partisanship), not only among the political classes but much of America, as well characterized by road rage and growing national impatience over the niggling aspects of society; the emergence of bad taste in stunningly popular "reality" television; and a bulging national waistline in which nearly one in three Americans is obese? Do these trends suggest values and standards for personal conduct far different than even a decade ago? If those anecdotal trends are representative, the conclusion is clear, and these fault lines regarding the direction of culture must be addressed.

Finally, the symbiotic yet ambivalent relationships among politics, culture, and the media have profound influence in shaping debate and opinion. Politics and the media are mutually dependent. Hence, at a time when the media increasingly has been absorbed by large corporations whose legitimate business interests focus as much on the bottom line as on fair and balanced reporting, how can the nation ensure that a free press really is free to carry out its traditional reporting and investigative duties?

America's Promise Restored is a warning and a prescription for Americans. The collapse of our promise and aspirations is under way. As most polls show, America's relevance and influence abroad are in free-fall. That America was opposed by virtually all of our allies in invading Iraq was a point of no return in this decline.

Corrective action must occur soon to keep America secure, vibrant, free, and able to pursue its promise as productively in the future as it has in the past. Curiously, perhaps, the solutions and cures rest in Americans. It is we the people who have the power and the responsibility to restore the system of checks and balances. There are solutions. One such solution seems so simple that many will wonder why it has been overlooked for so long. This recommendation could indeed transform the political system by forcing it to become more responsive to the people, restoring the balance in government rather than succumbing to small and powerful constituencies. Simultaneously, much of the excess and bitter partisanship and nonsense that has infected government for too long could be reduced.

While the national security policy aspects of this collision of culture, crusade, and partisanship are emphasized in the chapters that follow, the destruction of the American Dream and the demise of its promise have neither boundary nor border. The United States is running out of time to correct and repair the fault lines that threaten us all. The answer rests in one phrase—reinventing democracy through a vision of peace, partnership, and prosperity and restoring accountability in and for government through greater involvement of its citizenry. These may appear as deceptively simple solutions. But they are not, and they may prove too difficult to achieve, though achieve them we must.

History Matters:
Past Fault Lines

Strategic Analyses

Fault lines are present in every human society and activity. Americans need to know what these fault lines are, what forces can cause these fault lines to crack or to shatter, what can be done to protect or repair these potential weaknesses, and what the consequences can be if these fault lines fail—either partially or catastrophically. This line of inquiry has been the basis for strategic analyses down through the ages, from Sun Tzu to Clausewitz and beyond.

The geopolitical situation in Asia in 1941 provides a good example of strategic analysis and shows what can happen when assumptions turn out to be fatally flawed. By the late 1930s, Imperial Japan was expanding throughout Asia. The Greater East Asian Co-Prosperity Sphere was, in effect, nothing but a glib name for rationalizing military conquest. With its armed attack and intervention into China and, later, throughout Southeast Asia, Japan and its war machine were entirely dependent on external natural resources, particularly oil, rubber, and steel. Suffering under the American 1940 iron and steel embargos and believing that the U.S. Navy's Pacific Fleet presented the only credible military threat to Japan's expansion in East Asia, Tokyo explored various strategies to eliminate that impediment. Well aware of America's isolationism and introspection, manifested by close-run votes to approve Lend-Lease and extend the draft, the General Staff concluded that America lacked the stomach for war.

Roosevelt's focus on Europe and the transfer of part of the Pacific Fleet to the Atlantic further suggested an American unwillingness to fight a war in Asia. Japanese strategic thinking reasoned that if the United States could be dealt a severe military blow, the shock would reinforce its isolationist and pacifist views. America would seek to negotiate a diplomatic settlement, allowing the Japanese a free hand in Asia. On that logic, the plan to strike Pearl Harbor and destroy the Pacific Fleet was approved.

Sunday morning, December 7, 1941, just before eight o'clock local time, swarms of Japanese torpedo and bomber aircraft struck the naval base at Pearl Harbor, T.H. (Territory of Hawaii). The surprise attack worked perfectly. Battleship Row was hit and the damage was vast—but principally to old battleships only. Fortunately, the U.S. aircraft carriers were at sea and Japan ignored the submarine base a few miles away, so no carriers or submarines were lost.

But Japan's strategic assumptions could not have been more flawed. The fault line was clear. America obviously did not turn tail and play dead. Quite the opposite: Pearl Harbor awakened a sleeping giant, just as Admiral Isoroku Yamamoto, the architect of the attack, predicted. American apathy and isolationism turned into patriotic rage. War was declared; and three years and eight months later, some of the very battleships that had been sunk in the shallow waters of Pearl Harbor and later raised and repaired steamed into Tokyo Bay to accept Japan's unconditional surrender. An added bonus for FDR was that two days after America declared war on Japan, Germany unceremoniously and gratuitously followed suit and declared war on the United States, thus ending Roosevelt's fear of taking on the Japanese in the wrong war in the wrong place and against the lesser danger. Hitler had always been Roosevelt's priority target, in company with his closest ally (Britain) and his opposite number (Winston S. Churchill). Clearly, the fault lines in the Japanese strategy and assumptions proved Tokyo's undoing.

American strategic thinking today beyond Iraq suggests a parallel with Japan's logic in 1941. Clearly, the Bush 43 administration assumed that the post-war period in Iraq would go smoothly and, following the remarkable defeat of the Iraqi Army, American physical presence would not be needed for the long term or in large numbers. But what is the strategic thinking of this administration regarding other geopolitical challenges? The Arab and Islamic worlds are in the middle of profound change. North Korea and Iran seem determined to pursue nuclear ambitions. China's future as friend or foe is uncertain, and the result could impose huge pressure on Japan to rearm. Much of Africa remains a strategic wasteland. With the elections of Hugo Chavez in Venezuela, Evo Morales in Bolivia, and, of course Fidel Castro in Cuba, South America could be seen as moving to form an "axis-ito of evil" in its policies toward the United States. And Europe, America's traditional ally and NATO, its most important alliance, appear to have less strategic importance for the Bush 43 administration.

By virtually every opinion poll, America, as opposed to Americans, is viewed far more negatively abroad than at any time since Vietnam—and, in some cases, with greater cynicism and dislike. Polls can change, and perhaps international opinion is not important. However, the polls do at least send a message that all is not well abroad for America. But who in the United States is listening? And who is taking action? A good parallel is with an annual physical. When medical tests indicate that something is abnormal or wrong, does the patient ignore those findings? In the case of the nation's security, while the government recognizes some of the fault lines, it has not pursued the necessary remedies. The reasons are historical and current.

In order to evaluate the dangers and challenges of today, examination of past fault lines—when the nation was severely challenged or at grave risk—provides useful insights in understanding what enabled the United States to succeed or to fail. This evaluation covers existing conditions at home and abroad, the state of the American Dream, and the effects of culture, crusade, and partisanship on the ability of the political system and its leaders to navigate a safe course. From that perspective, better understanding of the challenges and dangers of today and remedies and corrective actions follow.

The American Dream

There is no single definition of the "American Dream." It has matured and changed from generation to generation and from crisis to crisis. There is, however, one common basis. From the first settlers—who arrived on these shores four hundred years ago to escape religious, political, or economic persecution—to today's immigrants, life, liberty, and the pursuit of happiness would become beacons for those "huddled masses yearning to breathe free." Since the beginnings of this nation, the operative presumption/myth was that ability, hard work, and persistence were the ingredients for success and that better-off Americans would look after those less fortunate.

Unstated in the Declaration of Independence and the Constitution were guarantees of racial, ethnic, and gender equality, none of which came quickly. All men may have been created equal—provided they were white and of some means. Women were not counted in that lot. For more than a hundred years, the vote was the near-exclusive domain of white male landowners. Women would not get that right until early in the twentieth century. And the fight against discrimination still persists. That a black man from the Bronx (or a black woman from Alabama) could rise to the positions of national security adviser to the president, chairman of the Joint Chiefs of Staff, the nation's most senior military officer, and secretary of state with an opportunity to become president, was powerful proof that these dreams were still real—or at least seemed to be.

As America matured and its influence extended beyond its own shores, the American Dream and its concomitant idealism would permeate foreign policy. The implicit assumption was that American values had universal appeal—a notion that reflected a degree of arrogance and cultural superiority, whether intended or not. Indeed, nationalism led to a preference for crusade; it was inherent in "manifest destiny" as the nation moved west to settle and expand the frontier from sea to shining sea in the mid-nineteenth century, and would become a permanent part of the culture.

William McKinley went to war with Spain in 1898 on a crusade, in large measure to lift the yoke of Spain's oppression and allegedly horrific treatment of Cubans. Woodrow Wilson took the nation into World War I "to make the world safe for democracy." Franklin Delano Roosevelt's famous four freedoms extended the dream to defeating Nazism and fascism unconditionally and then turning the enemy nations into allies and democracies. Harry Truman, followed by Dwight D. Eisenhower, took the dream into the battle against the Soviet Union and communism, a battle ultimately won four and a half decades after the end of the Second World War.

Long after the Civil War bloodily settled the Constitutional ambiguities over states' rights and the federal government's power, the American Dream was basic to the nation's culture. Most of the famous robber barons and families of great wealth of a century ago were self-made and conformed with the initial expectations of the dream, until profligate spending and opulent lifestyles brought excess to new levels. The Great Depression that began in 1929—and did not end until entry into World War II mobilized the nation and propelled it out of economic despair—battered the dream senseless. However, FDR and his "New Deal" offered hope, as well as the beginning of a social safety net to protect the nation and its citizens.

World War II accelerated the dream immensely. The nation was united as never before. The GI's who won the war came home to a GI Bill that provided them with a college education and degrees, putting America on a trajectory that would grant nearly universal access to universities. Low-interest GI mortgages had the same effect on the housing markets. Home ownership and the industry it would generate became new additions to the dream.

It is tempting to believe that yesteryear was idyllic in all respects. It was not. But in retrospect, life seemed easier. Crime was less visible. Illegal drugs, from marijuana to heroin and cocaine, were less prevalent or plentiful. Still, the middle class had ceilings and floors and social mobility was not guaranteed. Polio and other diseases struck fear into parents until Jonas Salk invented his vaccine. The Russians scared us and Joe McCarthy tried to panic us. But when Sputnik went up, Americans were not daunted. Ike challenged the nation to respond; and with the term "National Security" as the predicate, Congress passed bills covering the construction of highways and expanding education, each seen as vital to protecting the nation and its security. And in those heady days, athletes, particularly baseball stars, could be heroes, usually behaving civilly in public (with some exceptions) and were known for consuming hotdogs and booze rather than steroids as a means of reaching new levels of performance.

John F. Kennedy asked not what the nation could do for Americans but what Americans could do for the country during his short and expectation-filled tenure that was christened by the media as "Camelot." It was King Jack and the Knights of his Round Table who would slay all the dragons that threatened the kingdom. Camelot became the stage for Lyndon B. Johnson's Great Society after bullets cut the young president's life short on that day sparkling with sunshine and optimism in Dallas—November 22, 1963.

Vietnam surely was a nadir in the trajectory of the American Dream. Kennedy promised that America would "pay any price and bear any burden" to defend freedom. Thus started the long and unhappy journey in Southeast Asia. We could not and did not make good on Kennedy's promise. Trapped in Vietnam and then Watergate, Richard Nixon's demise turned the dream into a national nightmare. Jimmy Carter could not undo the damage, and the righteousness he projected did not sit well with the public.

It might not have been "morning in America" for everyone, as President Ronald Reagan declared. However, his challenge to Soviet President Mikhail Gorbachev to "take down that wall" that divided Berlin between east and west certainly accelerated the centrifugal forces that ultimately disintegrated the "evil empire." Followed by the short war to eject Saddam Hussein from Kuwait in 1991, it would have seemed that America was at the top of its game. President Bill Clinton very much was the beneficiary of the Bush 41 administration, as budget deficits turned into surpluses and the "economy stupid" mentality achieved record low levels of unemployment.

The economy began contracting well before the Bush 43 administration assumed office in January 2001. The election was highly contested and ultimately decided by the Supreme Court. Because Bush lost the popular vote, the transition was more difficult in at least two ways: First, Bush needed to establish his legitimacy; and second, the new team lost over five weeks in beginning the critical appointment-selection process.

September 11 literally changed the world—or, more precisely, brought into focus forces that would challenge America. The combination of terror, the political ambitions of our adversaries, and the pernicious aspects of American culture, crusade, and partisanship provided the ingredients that now threaten to shatter America's dreams and promises.

It doesn't take a cynic to observe that these dreams were at best myths—idealized expectations of the way the country *should* be, not true pictures of America as it was or is. At home, the political system invented by the best minds of the eighteenth century continued to struggle with the realities and demands of the new millennium. Increasingly polarized by politics that were partisan to the core and buffeted by the intrusion of values and beliefs that might best be left to individuals and courts rather than to politics and government, the nation foundered in coping with the rigors and contradictions of modern society.

The roots of these challenges lie deep in the past. What is strikingly different today is that, paraphrasing the great Prussian general and philosopher Carl von Clausewitz and his observations on war, politics consists of the simplest activities—each one of which, in the heat of battle, can prove impossible to achieve. But politics is hard-pressed to accomplish even the simplest of things.

The dream reflected—and was reflected in—the culture peculiar to America. Culture has many definitions. For our purposes, "culture" implies the structure and perception of the values and standards of a society, including political, moral, religious, ethical, and work-related beliefs. There is no more a single version of culture than there is a single average American. It is the composite of how society tends to react and respond to stimuli that partially measures culture. And from culture arose the capacity for crusade.

For those who believe in predetermination of events, that is not the *deus ex machina* at work. At any given time, societal fault lines can fail. Every society and political system has strengths, weaknesses, and vulnerabilities. Up until now, the United States has been able to overcome these vulnerabilities and fault lines. The question is whether history has finally caught up to the United States. One means of answering that question comes from learning from the past, as well as using that knowledge to avoid similar mistakes in the future. Strategic and historical analyses provide useful insights.

Consider some "snapshots" taken at various points in American history: 1789 and the election of Washington; 1860, the Civil War, and the aftermath; 1918 and the end of World War I; 1935, the Great Depression, and the rise of fascism and communism; and 1945 and the end of World War II. These are only snapshots meant to portray a flavor, not the complete picture of the attitudes and times.

1789: A Revolutionary Year

On April 30, 1789, George Washington took the oath of office in New York City as America's first president. Three months and fourteen days later, revolution would sweep through France, bookends to two of the more significant events in history. The two events were obviously related.

American strategy during the Revolutionary War (1776–83) against Britain presaged the North Vietnamese campaign 185 years later. Britain was fighting France and her allies in what was then a world war. The colonists' revolt was peripheral to Britain's main objectives, which lay in Europe. Hence, American strategy implicitly was based on outlasting the British and ultimately winning by not losing. Victory in battle was less important than keeping the war going. And the Americans were assiduous in recruiting France to support the effort and shift the strategic balance to the colonists.

With Benjamin Franklin as America's able ambassador in Paris, one single military victory was imperative in order to convince the French that it was in their broader interest to ally with the Americans. Franklin patiently bided his time, impressing the French court with his wit, brilliance, and sophistication. On October 17, 1777, the Battle of Saratoga in central New York state was joined. British forces commanded by General "Gentleman" Johnny Burgoyne were bested by General Horatio Gates. That victory tipped the scales for the French. Paris decided that a de facto alliance with the rebels was in France's best interest in its broader war with the British. Four years later at Yorktown, Washington faced General Charles Cornwallis. And the French were there, both on the ground and at sea.

The Marquis de Lafayette and Admiral Francois DeGrasse provided Washington with the military muscle to force Cornwallis to surrender and withdraw from the colonies, literally ending the Revolution in 1781. It took eight more years for the original thirteen colonies to move from Articles of Confederation to become the United States of America and for the ratification of the Constitution, a duration that should not be forgotten as Iraq grapples with its transition to democracy. The colonies, now the United States, were, however, still very vulnerable. Despite abandoning the colonies, the British still had strong strategic, economic, and commercial interests in America as it continued the fight against France. Spain had colonies throughout much of North America—at least until Napoleon changed that. And, while supporting the Revolution for reasons of self-interest, French friendship was never meant to be permanent.

American strategy, as Washington would phrase it eight years later in his farewell address as president in 1797, was to steer clear of "foreign entanglements." In other words, the United States would balance off the great powers of the day as the best means of ensuring its independence, a strategy that worked well despite later clashes with France, its former patron, and the War of 1812 against Britain. The strategy enabled the colonies to consolidate into a single nation. At the core of Washington's policy was self-interest: the survival of the still-fragile nation.

In 1789, white male landowners dominated America politically. The American Dream was largely defined by the Constitution and the Bill of Rights, provided that one fit the correct racial and gender profile. Benjamin Franklin, at the end of his life, would describe America as a good place for those who wanted to become rich. It was also, according to Franklin, a haven for the poor as "nowhere else are the laboring poor so well fed, well lodged, well clothed and well paid." And it was a country where a "general happy mediocrity prevails."

The former northern colonies were mercantile. The South was agrarian, and its primary product—cotton—was to become "King" after Eli Whitney's cotton gin coronated it. While the term "manifest destiny" had not yet been coined, pioneers were moving west into the Ohio Valley and beyond. Compared to today, in 1789 it took several days, at eighteen hours a day, to travel by horse-driven carriage between New York and Boston.

A spirit of crusade had not yet emerged. The Revolutionary War had been exhausting. Americans were more concerned with improving their own lot than with becoming involved with larger powers abroad on whose favor the nation's future and security rested. However, partisanship was alive, well, and fierce.

The Founding Fathers and the Federalist Papers had warned against political parties as "factions" that would not serve the public interest. But parties indeed would flourish. Two of the Founding Fathers from whom the current-day Republican and Democratic parties would evolve and who would be among the most important personalities in our history were entrusted with key cabinet positions. Thomas Jefferson, author of the Declaration of Independence and founder of the University of Virginia (as well as minister to France), was secretary of state and leader of the new Department of State that succeeded the old Department of Foreign Affairs established under the Articles of Confederation. The brilliant and youthful Alexander Hamilton, who by a series of bold financial maneuvers, revived the moribund body of American credit and finance, became the first secretary of the treasury.

But Hamilton and Jefferson had repeatedly and harshly clashed, and would continue to do so. In fact, at one stage each had acquired control of a newspaper to attack the other in print. This was the first and perhaps the most famous incident of intra-cabinet warfare in our history, reflecting the irreparable differences in philosophy, outlook, and policy between these two formidable, brilliant, highly experienced, and passionate believers in the superiority of their positions.

Jefferson was a strong liberal, highly intelligent, fluent in several languages, sophisticated across many subjects. He especially admired France, its people, its civilization, and its philosophers. Jefferson believed in the virtues of government and freedom and of the individual. Hamilton was a mirror image. Deeply conservative, Hamilton favored strong central government. Despite the war with Britain, Hamilton admired English institutions and believed that closer relations with Britain, not France, would best serve American interests.

From these profound differences over crucially important issues, two political parties emerged during Washington's first term. Hamilton led the Federalists, and the Democratic-Republicans were formed under Jefferson. The latter party would drop the democratic part of its name and become Republicans until Andrew Jackson renamed the party Democratic, as it is still known today. The Federalists were reincarnated as National Republicans, then became Whigs in 1834 and, in 1854, turned into today's Republican Party under the leadership of Abraham Lincoln.

Partisanship was bitter. The first years of the new nation were tumultuous, largely because of trade disputes with Britain and France. In 1794, after John Jay, chief justice of the Supreme Court, had negotiated a treaty with England over trade issues that had carried the United States to the brink of another war, one rabid Jeffersonian called Jay "the arch traitor" upon hearing that he had bowed to the queen and kissed her hand, and cried "seize him, drown him, burn him, flay him alive." The treaty, requiring a two-thirds majority, was passed by just that, 20–10, in the Senate. And John Randolph, one of the signers of the Declaration of Independence, made the celebrated toast "Damn George Washington" over the treaty.

This and other incidents are reminders that politics was always rough, and in many ways physically rougher than today, when misdeeds may be criminalized rather than resolved by fisticuffs or duels. John Adams, Washington's vice president, called the president "Old Muttonhead" (remember that the president and vice president were the top two vote-

getters in the presidential election, and therefore often of different parties), and Hamilton referred to the father of the country as the "great
booby." Hamilton was killed in a duel with Aaron Burr in 1804, himself
Jefferson's vice president who was tried and acquitted in 1807 of charges
of treason—interesting times! However, the arguments and battles were
usually drawn over issues of gravitas and great importance to the nation,
something that must be borne in mind. As it turned out, Jay's treaty had
important byproducts, such as reducing friction with Spain. Yet both the
stakes and the politics were sharp and harsh, and differences of opinion
were often vast and irreconcilable in terms of philosophy. Still, geography and the pressure-relief valve of moving west sealed off these major
fault lines.

What can be learned from this broad analysis? First, the nation was
fragile and vulnerable to foreign intervention, both economic and military. Protecting those fault lines became the centerpieces of policy.

Second, government may have been of the people and for the people,
but it certainly was not *by* the people. The ruling circles were small. In
fact, the only positions that were directly elected by the people were
the representatives in the House. Senators were appointed by the
states and the president elected by the Electoral College, the latter still
the Constitutional means for selecting the chief executive, a lesson
dramatically and catastrophically brought home in the 2000 Bush–Gore
election.

Third, as Washington noted in his farewell address, for more than a
century and a half, the United States would stay clear of permanent
alliances. Self-interest, described as noninvolvement, would be American policy, absent a few exceptions at the turn of the next century. Noninvolvement was not isolationism, wrongly attributed to Washington, but
meant that America would attempt to remain independent from European powers. That policy reinforced America's isolationist instincts
stemming from earlier colonial days when the settlers, fleeing some form
of persecution, wished to be as far from Europe as possible and would
become part of the political culture. But from that point on, until World
War II intervened, isolationism was to be a major, if misunderstood,
foundation stone of U.S. foreign policy. It would take two world wars to
change American thinking about continuous international involvement,
fanned by a sense of crusade beginning at the dawn of the twentieth century. And even today, in some Republican circles, geopolitical variants of

lessening our international involvement persist. George W. Bush entered office rejecting the need for nation building, a philosophy since rejected.

1860, the Coming of the Civil War, and the Aftermath

Over the next seventy years, America experienced explosive growth across every sector. Population, both homegrown and through immigration, soared from 4.5 million in 1789 to 31.4 million in 1860. With the Louisiana Purchase in 1803 (and the Lewis and Clark expedition), and the Gadsden Treaty of 1848 that confirmed the annexation of Texas, the United States had expanded to the Pacific. The Gold Rush of 1848, and the extraordinary resources that would be discovered in California and elsewhere, would make the United States the richest country in the world well before the Civil War.

Religion was spreading aggressively, and flourishing. The Second Great Awakening, starting at the end of the eighteenth century, brought evangelism to the frontier. Revivalism was part of many Christian sects, including Presbyterians, Baptists, Seventh-Day Adventists, Mormons, and Methodists, and became the basis for today's fundamentalism. Faith healing and the First Church of Christian Science would emerge, along with religious-utopian communities, especially of German origin. Catholics and Jews continued to settle in America and began to experience integration into the broader community, but not without fits and starts and bouts of anti-Catholicism and anti-Semitism.

The existence, number, and size of these sects, along with the larger religions, raised the question of how the religious toleration guaranteed in the Bill of Rights could square with a republican society. The boundaries between church and state from the beginning were ones over which debate and controversy would not cease. Indeed, in the future, religious controversy would encompass Islam and its views toward polygamy and the role of women that run counter to U.S. values and interests.

Major fault lines ran through the Constitutional, political, economic, and social fabric of the nation. Collisions between states' rights and the power of the federal government ultimately led to the Civil War. Southern states claimed that the theory of nullification granted states the power to "nullify" federal laws that did not conform to those states' interests. The Constitution was ambiguous by not specifying the authority of the federal government, and slavery was the specific issue that would cause this fault line to fail.

The abominable Supreme Court decision in the Dred Scott case of 1857, which declared slaves chattel and private property that could be legally moved across all state lines, simply deferred answering the most profound moral question over the existence of slavery. However, the universal commercial demand for cotton for clothing, the economic dominance cotton played in the South, and the reality that slavery was essential to filling those demands, meant that there was no easy or peaceful alternative solution. Even if slavery were to be abolished without war, the South lacked the resources and the means to continue producing cotton, a further example of how tough choices can elude decision until some forcing event occurs.

Slaves also provided political clout for the South, making abolition difficult. The Constitution apportioned the "Three-Fifths Rule," in which slaves would be counted for electoral purposes as 60 percent of whites. As the number of slaves increased from 750,000 in 1789 to about four million in 1860, the electoral clout of slave-holding states increased, a Constitutional contradiction that could be resolved only by force of arms.

These and other fault lines shattered on April 12, 1861, when Confederate General P. G. T. Beauregard trained his guns on the Union's Fort Sumter in Charleston, South Carolina and the Civil War began. The war would ultimately be an unfair fight. The North had seven times the manufacturing capacity of the South, and about two and a half times the population, with 22 million compared to 9 million of whom about 3.5 million were slaves. The North possessed a far better rail and transportation system and a vastly superior navy and merchant fleet, and had a central government already in place. Further, the North retained the advantage and legitimacy of remaining "the United States," making foreign support for the rebel Confederacy difficult, as it would violate international law. The vaunted superiority of Southern generalship would only go so far, once the North finally learned how to wage an effective war.

Abraham Lincoln was an extraordinary leader, even though it took him several years to find competent generals. General Winfield Scott, age seventy-two and so heavy that he could not mount a horse, was the first commander. Ultimately, in Grant and Sherman, Lincoln found two generals who would win the war. For all of his virtues, Lincoln was forced to curtail civil liberties. Suspension of the writ of habeas corpus was deemed a necessity of war, and the pendulum understandably swung from Constitutional protection to defense of the Union itself.

The transition from the Civil War to the peace and Reconstruction that followed is highly illustrative in the understanding of fault lines and their consequences. The Civil War created political animosities and hatred, among the so-called Republican radicals controlling Congress, that would become manifest long afterward. Lincoln intended that once the war ended, political justice must be served, including making former slaves free men (and women). Lincoln also intended to return the South to normal and local government as soon as practicable, a commitment that was central to his famous and arguably best address—the Second Inaugural, stating "with malice towards none and charity for all." Lincoln proposed a general amnesty for the South, based on an oath to abide by the Constitution. And his prescience in wanting to "make voters" of the former enemies "before we take the troops away" so the ballot will be "their only protection after the bayonet is gone" would have played well in Iraq. Yet post-war planning for Reconstruction was very much unfinished business, a characteristic that has proved not unique to that time.

On April 14, 1865, John Wilkes Booth ended Lincoln's life with a bullet to the head. Vice President Andrew Johnson, on whose shoulders fell Reconstruction, succeeded Lincoln. Johnson fully agreed with Lincoln's views on restoring the South as part of the Union. Johnson had what seemed the perfect résumé for that mission. He was a Southern Democrat, the only Southern senator to remain in Washington after the South seceded. Born in Raleigh, North Carolina, his modest background and profound belief in democracy made him a latter-day Jacksonian Democrat. But Johnson would become cannon fodder for the Congressional Republican radicals led by Senator Charles Sumner and Representative Thaddeus Stevens, chairman of the House Ways and Means Committee, as he (Johnson) would be seen as too willing to bring the South back into the Union fold.

The radicals argued that the South had to be punished to the maximum, having lost any Constitutional authority and rights by virtue of secession. A second Republican group was less hateful, but still agreed that the South had lost its political standing and it was up to Congress to determine the pace and timing of any restoration of political rights. Finally, there was the Lincoln–Johnson wing of the party, favoring clemency.

Lincoln had advocated ending slavery well before finally doing so. However, Lincoln wrestled with the critical matter of how blacks would be treated once freed, believing that emancipation would pose enormously difficult and not necessarily reconcilable problems for the short term regarding the reaction and attitude of former slaveholders and the culture of the South toward blacks. Johnson inherited that dilemma. Initially, Reconstruction was based on returning the Southern states to normality as soon as possible. But blacks still faced discriminatory and restrictive laws that made certain that none would be treated as equal citizens. As a result, Northern abolitionists and Republican radicals in Congress were irreconcilably opposed to the handling of Reconstruction, but for different reasons. Abolitionists fumed over treatment of blacks, radicals over allowing too much clemency for the defeated Rebels.

Fanned by Stevens and Sumner, revenge against the South was a dominant emotion when Congress reassembled in December 1865. All senators and representatives from the former Confederate states were excluded from Congress. Other legislation for Reconstruction, including extending the so-called Freedman's Bureau—the first U.S. federal welfare institution, created for helping, feeding and protecting blacks—was passed. Johnson vetoed the bill. Congress retaliated to strengthen the rights of blacks at the expense of Southern whites, passing a Civil Rights bill intended to alter the "Black Codes" that had been enacted, which relegated blacks to second-class status. Johnson vetoed that bill, and Congress overrode the veto with a two-thirds vote. This was the first time in U.S. history that a presidential veto had been overridden on an issue of importance.

The breach between the president and Congress over Reconstruction was irreparable. Johnson had no mandate or authority, as he had not been elected president, and was determined to treat the South with greater leniency than the radical Republicans in Congress. Congress was determined to assume the political leadership of the country. By 1867, Congress had prevailed and wrought a second and harsher form of Reconstruction. Failing to win political allies in the South through logic, Congress turned to the next best weapon—the law, passing a bill to ensure that blacks would cast their new votes for Republicans and not Southern Democrats (a precursor of the current controversy over the constitutionality of redistricting in Texas that added five Republican members to the House). Congress also moved to limit presidential authority by removing his powers to summon Congress in emergency session; to dismiss officials appointed by the president and confirmed by the Senate (the Tenure of Office Act); and to give legal orders to the military as commander-in-chief. Much of this legislation was unconstitutional. However, Congress intended to enforce it before the Supreme Court could strike it down.

These laws and programs smacked of American fundamentalist idealism in its extreme and unworkable form. The radicals had their ideological views of what was right and what was not, and would manipulate government to those ends. Predictably, the result was a political savagery unprecedented in American history. Excessive partisanship and bitterness led to the impeachment of President Johnson over the Tenure of Office Act.

Johnson believed that the Tenure of Office Act was unconstitutional. He ignored it by dismissing Secretary of War Edwin Stanton, whom Johnson viewed as an extremist who employed the Union Army to intimidate and repress the South and impose a stricter form of Reconstruction. Impeached by the House, after a three-month trial in the Senate, Johnson was acquitted on May 26, 1868 by a vote of 35–19. However, his presidency was effectively over.

The Reconstruction effort ultimately collapsed, with dire consequences. The story is well known: Northern carpetbaggers, scalawags, and blacks assumed unfettered power awash in a sea of corruption. The South became united in hatred of imposed state governments and harsh Reconstruction, and struck back. The Ku Klux Klan, vigilantes, and other terrorists exacted revenge. By the end of the 1860s, the white majority would reassume political power. The blacks had been freed, but it would be a century before the Civil Rights Act of 1965 would be passed, ending the restriction of blacks to second-class citizenship. In the 1860s, most Americans did not care about the freed blacks. Social responsibility was not a pressing issue across America. Engaged in settling the West and in an extraordinary economic boom that would continue through a world war until the late 1920s, expansion kept the most seminal event in the nation's history, the Civil War, from being fully and finally concluded.

The parallels with Iraq today are relevant. There simply was little or no planning for the post-war period in the South. Once Lincoln was gone, the Republican Congress was ideologically inclined toward treating the South with equal measures of revenge and harshness. That ideology was misplaced, but was a product of the times.

Crusade was less in fashion until Reconstruction began with a vengeance. The North was out to impose a harsh peace on the South. In terms of partisanship and polarization, that period was the most vicious in American history.

Reconstruction failed to bring equality and justice to the South. Whites maintained about an 80 percent majority. Over time and given the hostile environment, the political outcome was evident. Blacks remained second-class citizens, and the legacy was racial tension and occasional violence. Whether history will repeat in Iraq with the Shia and Kurdish majority and the Sunni minority remains to be seen. However, the tyranny of the majority is a powerful political force.

Finally, both the American West and the economy ultimately were stimulated by the Civil War. Southern Democrats in Congress had persistently blocked legislation that would have assisted settling the West, on the grounds of threatening the balance of free and slave states and the Southern economy. Their demise eliminated that obstacle. The Homestead Act of 1862 ceded 160 acres of land to enterprising farmers for a modest sum, creating a marvelous engine of economic growth. Despite periods of economic depression and trouble, business and prosperity became driving forces in American culture after the Civil War. Left were the fault lines between South and North and black and white that would take decades to close.

1918 and the End of World War I

The United States had been the richest nation in the world for more than half a century as World War I ended. By the 1890s (the Roaring or Gay '90s, as they were called), rogue capitalism had produced vast wealth. Railroads, steel, shipping, manufacturing, and soon thereafter automobiles joined agriculture, mining, and banking as key industrial sectors. At the turn of the century, the distribution of wealth was perhaps even more unbalanced than it is today. By some figures, more than 20 percent of the American population lived in or close to poverty.

This abundance of wealth was matched by rampant corruption. The press exposed great social evils across America, including forced child labor, atrocious and dangerous food preparation, and the tyranny of "machine politics" that circumvented the ballot box and thereby prevented a truly elected government. Exposés by the so-called muckrakers of the day were frequently published in leading publications, such as *The Saturday Evening Post*, *McClure's*, and *Ladies' Home Journal*, and

included Ida Tarbell, who exposed the inner workings of John D. Rocke-
feller's Standard Oil monopoly; Lincoln Steffens, who exposed big-city
corruption; and Upton Sinclair, whose novel *The Jungle* made the
country aware of the scandalous practices of the meat-packing industry.
These and other stories promoted a clamor for reform and for rectifying
the evils and excesses of American capitalism.

The result was reform-driven platforms of the Progressives and, most
significantly, of Teddy Roosevelt. "Trust-Busting" Teddy went after business monopolies. Reforms were implemented to overcome corrupt and
entrenched political machines, and included direct primary elections,
referendums, recalls, ballot initiatives, and the Seventeenth Amendment
(approved in 1913), which provided for direct election of senators. Large
monopolies in banking and beef production were broken up in 1906, and
Standard Oil was "trust-busted" in 1911. The Federal Reserve System
was created in 1913 to oversee banking practices, loans, and borrowing
practices, and to prevent failures and panics. While far from perfect, it is
easy to forget how progressive and reform-minded that period was, an
instructive lesson for today.

There was, of course, a short war with Spain, ostensibly provoked by
the sinking of the USS *Maine* in Havana Harbor on February 15, 1898.
Authorized, not declared by a joint resolution of Congress, the measure
passed four months and four days after the *Maine* went down and was
signed by President McKinley on April 25, after an official court of
inquiry (wrongly) concluded that the ship had been sunk by a mine.
Sixty years later, a study by Admiral Hyman Rickover, the acerbic father
of U.S. Navy nuclear power, concluded that an internal explosion in her
coaling bunkers had sunk the USS *Maine*.

The war was largely the result of American jingoism inflamed by press
barons William Randolph Hearst in the *New York Journal* and Joseph
Pulitzer in the *New York World*, and the "yellow press." The spirit of crusade was ubiquitous following the sensationalist yellow-press reporting
of war atrocities allegedly committed by Spain against the Cubans. The
short, splendid war ended on August 12 with the ceding to the United
States of Cuba, Puerto Rico, the Philippines, Guam, and the Marianas in
the Pacific. America's empire was founded.

The United States was also well ensconced in China. With McKinley's
assassination in 1901, Vice President (and former "Rough Rider" hero
from the Spanish War) Theodore Roosevelt assumed the presidency, and

his "speak softly but carry a big stick" policy shaped American diplomacy. In 1904, the Senate approved the Hay–Bunau–Varilla Treaty
annexing the Panama Canal. The Great White Fleet had already circled
the globe; and later, under Woodrow Wilson, U.S. Marines would begin
keeping the peace in Central America for three decades. In fact, the U.S.
Army under General John J. ("Black Jack") Pershing dashed into Mexico
in pursuit of the Mexican bandit Pancho Villa, who had made small raids
in the southwestern United States. Pershing never caught Villa.

A sense of nationalism was sweeping throughout the country, based
on economic prosperity and the growing power of American industry.
Americans felt confident of themselves and the increasing importance of
the country. However, while activism had been a hallmark of U.S. diplomacy, prior to Teddy Roosevelt, the United States had not aggressively
sought a role as world leader. It had indeed played a major role, but presidents and cabinet officers had not aspired to become global leaders.

When the guns of August 1914 boomed the start of World War I, the
United States remained neutral. American public opinion was evenly
divided between support for Germany and Britain. Neutrality was
Wilson's policy. But propaganda—the information warfare of the day—
was used by both the Central and Allied powers to influence United
States opinion. The British would prove the more successful in that form
of warfare. Germany continued to wage unrestricted submarine warfare
even after Wilson attempted to negotiate a peace in Europe between the
warring states following his re-election in 1916. The initiative failed.

In 1917, the infamous Zimmermann note became public. The note
was actually a diplomatic cable from Germany's foreign minister to the
Mexican embassy, promising that in the event of war with America, a
Mexican-German alliance would be formed, and the incentive for Mexico
was implicit guarantees for return of territories (Texas, Arizona, and New
Mexico) seized by the United States. Intercepted by British intelligence,
the code was broken by the famous Room 40 and passed on to the Americans, where it created a firestorm.

The stage was set for U.S. entry into the war. Ultimately, unrestricted
submarine warfare and German ruthlessness in conducting the war on
the ground and at sea, distorted and publicized by a very successful
propaganda "spin" campaign by the British, turned American opinion
and finally persuaded the United States to enter the war. The relevance
of that propaganda campaign should not be lost today on America's

failing public and preventive diplomacy. In April 1917, the United States went to war on the side of the Allies.

Wilson's moral leadership was critical to making the war acceptable for Americans and for reinforcing the flagging Allies, who had been bleeding themselves white on the Western Front for three long years. From the bully pulpit, Wilson injected his idealism and sense of crusade with passion and conviction in his speeches. This was a "war to end war." And most famous, this was a war to make the world "safe for democracy." The yellow press was not quite as influential as it had been in 1898, but the crusading aspects of American idealism were just as powerful in its engagement and war aims.

On January 8, 1918, Wilson summarized his idealist approach in a statement of war aims known as his famous Fourteen Points.[15] While these points sincerely reflected Wilson's passion and intellect, the propaganda value was immense. The Fourteen Points came at a crucial time to offset the leaked reports by Lenin's Bolsheviks of the Tsar's secret treaties with the Allies that confirmed Russian imperialist interests in remaining in the war. With the Fourteen Points and, more importantly, the might of fresh American soldiers and an ally undamaged by war, the Central Powers would be defeated by this giant swing in the balance of military power. As American forces deployed to Europe, even with Russia's leaving the war because of the Bolshevik Revolution, Germany was facing exhaustion. In October 1918, Germany called for a peace conference. On the eleventh hour of the eleventh day of the eleventh month of 1918, the guns fell silent. Armistice had been declared. The war was over.

War had not adjourned politics in America. In November 1918, Americans went to the polls and returned a Republican majority to both houses of Congress. The campaign had been heated, with ex-president Teddy Roosevelt strongly attacking Wilson. Unlike Churchill, who, twenty-seven years later, would lose his prime ministership after winning the next war, Wilson was still president. However, Wilson faced strong opposition from a Republican and increasingly isolationist Congress. Despite that opposition, in January 1919, Wilson startled the nation by announcing that he was going to Paris as part of the Peace Delegation, the first sitting president to visit Europe.

Eleven days later, Wilson further shocked the nation and Congress. In naming the peace commission, he placed on it not a single Republican member of Congress. The only Republican was Henry White, a career diplomat. The political response was predictable. Roundly criticized for his "messiah complex," Wilson had inexplicably not conferred with the Senate—who, after all had to ratify any peace treaty—and had purposely not selected even one of their ranks to sit on the commission. The snub was politically fatal. Having been repudiated by the November election results and therefore weakened at home, Wilson still chose this independent course of action.

Upon his return home in February 1919, Wilson met with Senate and House committees to discuss the League of Nations. After a week of discussion, the redoubtable Senator Henry Cabot Lodge introduced the so-called Republican Round Robin that was signed by thirty-nine senators or senators-elect who would serve in the next Congress, more than the one-third-plus-one total needed to defeat any treaty. The letter objected to accepting the League of Nations until after a peace treaty had been made and approved by the Senate.

A year later, the Versailles Peace Treaty was concluded in Europe. But American ratification of the treaty would be defeated through an excruciating parliamentary process that included the attachment of dozens of reservations by the Republicans that Lodge knew the Democrats could not support. With Wilson falling horribly ill, the Senate declined to ratify the amended treaty. The Republican tactic succeeded: The Democrats voted the treaty down, finding the Republican amendments unacceptable. Hence, as politics often works, Wilson and the Democrats were cynically accused of defeating the very treaty they sought to have approved.

In place of idealistic Wilsonianism, isolationism was becoming resurgent. America saw itself as strong and self-sufficient. The traditional nonentanglement and self-interest–driven policies of Washington, Jefferson, and Monroe had served the nation well. Questions and concerns about the League and loss of sovereignty to international institutions rankled then, as they do today over the United Nations. Republicans asked questions of why the stars and stripes should fly below the flag of a super-state (the League); questions of why American soldiers should go "to Hejaz in Mesopotamia to protect King Hussein against the Bedouin" filled the press. Hearst was a leading anti-Leaguer, and his slogan "one hundred percent Americanism" became a rallying cry for opponents to the League. So the League went its own way and America, preoccupied with its own prosperity and indifferent to asserting its strength abroad beyond trade and economic interests, unwittingly helped pave the way for the fascist and communist revolutions and the inevitability of a second world war.

The fault lines were significant. Both Roosevelt and Wilson had been reformers. Both had sought to right social evils and flaws in the Constitution by making election of senators subject to popular vote. Many of those reforms were beneficial and addressed public concerns as well as public interest. The decade after the Civil War was a permanent blemish on American history, in failing to turn former slaves into functioning members of society. The first decade and a half of the twentieth century made important inroads in reforming political, economic, and social injustices. Entry into World War I cost the nation 116,000 dead, far fewer than the European states who lost the flower of their manhood in the millions. The lists of war dead on statues and memorials in any English village or public school make the point about the costs of that war.

The biggest fault lines, though, lay in the failure to plan for the peace and for economic sustainment of victors and losers. The roots of World War I were sown at the end of the Napoleonic Wars. After a hundred years of mostly peace, the political system in Europe became unbalanced and destabilized. After World War I, the seeds for the next conflict were taking hold. Lenin had seized power in Russia, turning it into the Soviet Union. Hitler was a little over a decade away from making Germany into the Third Reich. Japan was on its way toward a militarist and territorially ambitious government that would conquer much of East Asia as a way of guaranteeing access to precious resources it did not possess.

Similarly, despite the economic boom after World War I and because of the absence of international trade, economic, and banking mechanisms to balance out flows of goods and money, there were no means in place to prevent a systemic failure. The upshot, including a series of protective trade tariffs, and the issue of post-war debt and reparations, led to a condition of enormous economic and financial instability in Europe. The Allies, much like the Republican radicals in Congress after the Civil War, were out for revenge and reparations. Germany was burdened with debt it could never possibly pay off.

Economies in Europe teetered. Life was difficult, and the death and destruction of the war were crippling. Then, in October 1929, stock crashes collapsed the American stock market, ushering in the Great Depression, a depression that would only worsen until it was finally overcome when the World War II turned America into the arsenal of democracy and revitalized the U.S. economy. The American Dream went bankrupt. Banks failed. Farms failed, and agriculture was coincidentally hit by one of the worst droughts in history (aided and abetted by poor "scientific" farming practices) that turned the Midwest into the "Dust Bowl." About half of Americans lived at or below the poverty line.

Franklin Delano Roosevelt was swept into office with heavy Democratic majorities in March 1933, a strong reaction to the hapless Herbert Hoover and the Great Depression. Roosevelt had campaigned on a balanced budget and traditional palliatives to correct the suffering economy. But the Depression would grow still worse.

Despite an alphabet-soup list of programs that were part of FDR's New Deal and the famous first hundred days of his first term, the nation was mired in economic malaise. Pessimism was rampant. The culture was reacting to the shock and despair of the Depression, and the hard times and economic desperation turned the nation inward. Wilsonian idealism and the sense of crusade had passed as if fads. Partisanship was present, and anti-Rooseveltism among the Republican party bordered on hatred for what were seen as FDR's anti-business and liberal views. And even with large majorities in Congress, FDR could not always bend Democrats to his will. His failed attempt to pack the Supreme Court was a major setback for FDR administered by his own party.

1935, the Great Depression, and the Rise of Fascism and Communism

As the Civil War was a period of extraordinary crisis for the United States, arguably the nation's worst, the Great Depression was the economic equivalent. The nation was preoccupied with an unparalleled domestic crisis. Millions were out of work and faced daily despair in the search for jobs.

Resisting the preference to avoid foreign entanglements, the United States had played an active role internationally in the 1920s. But by the mid-1930s, neutrality was reshaping the American public mood. Having led the Washington Arms Conferences and participated in other international agreements to outlaw war a decade earlier, Americans now had little interest abroad. The post-war disillusionment over the failed League of Nations and the associated World Court, the negative effects of war debts and reparations, and, most of all, the Depression were reinforced by reaction against the so-called and grossly mischaracterized "merchants of death," the arms merchants who conspired to start wars in order to sell arms.

A Senate committee chaired by Gerald P. Nye of North Dakota held lurid hearings on munitions and their trafficking during the neutrality period, 1914–17, before American entry into World War I. Bankers and munitions manufacturers, contrary to the facts, were seen as the "blood-suckers" who dragged America into war to protect their loans and profits. Of course, the epithet "merchants of death" persists today. Yet the impact of these hearings and public reactions impelled the nation toward a mentality of neutrality.

The Italian–Ethiopian crisis of 1935, the beginning of the Spanish Civil War in 1936, and Japan's assault into China in 1937 were all reasons for foreign involvement and interest. Hitler's rise and German rearmament were further grounds for involvement. But America persisted in looking inward, and the Neutrality Act of 1937 made it illegal for Americans to enter into overseas conflicts.

Culture had been very much affected by the "Roaring Twenties" and the backlash against Prohibition, which banned consumption of alcohol. FDR oversaw the ratification of the 21st Amendment on December 5, 1933 that ended Prohibition. But the excesses and attitudes of the twenties were very much dampened by economic hard times. Crusade was restrained. The enthusiasm of 1898 and 1917 for making the world safe for democracy had gone dormant. America had little appetite for foreign adventures, even if U.S. Marines were seeing active service abroad.

Fault lines were widening, though. The Soviet Union had begun to internationalize the spread of communism and sided with the Loyalists in Spain, defending the government against the rebels, who were led by Franco and supported by Germany and Italy. Rejecting the strictures of the Neutrality Act, a number of Americans fought on each side; among the intellectual elite, the Spanish Civil War became the battleground in the contest between ideas of the left and the right. It was clear to some—Churchill and Roosevelt in particular—that the Third Reich was developing an unhealthy appetite for power and territory. Churchill was in the political wilderness and out of office; and Roosevelt, to run for an unprecedented third term in 1940, very much had to navigate around public attitudes opposed to joining in what would become, in 1939, World War II.

A parallel with today concerns common threats. By 1938, Hitler and the Third Reich were a clear and present danger to the West. In large part due to the revulsion against war, understandably a legacy of 1914–18, public attitudes in Europe refused to accept the danger of Hitler then, much as the public today sees the "war on terror" in narrow terms unconnected to the dual revolutions in the Arab and Muslim worlds. Even with the Hitler–Stalin Non-Aggression Pact signed on August 23, 1939 and the invasion of Poland a week later, Americans clung to isolation—although there were a few important exceptions.

Congress would pass three naval shipbuilding bills beginning in 1934, named for their sponsors in both houses, Vinson–Trammell (for Congressman Carl Vinson and Senator Park Trammell), to deal initially with reducing unemployment. As the Nazi and Japanese threats grew, these bills authorized laying the keels for the battle fleet that would win the next war. One wonders where the equivalent of a Vinson–Trammell bill for national security is to be found today.

Second, in 1940 and against the strong opposition of the isolationists, FDR initiated Lend-Lease and the transfer of fifty old destroyers to Britain in exchange for rent-free bases in Newfoundland, the Caribbean, and Bermuda for ninety-nine years. Lend-Lease touched off a furious debate, not over whether the transfer would help Britain and would obligate the United States to further assistance, but because the pact was made by executive agreement and not treaty subject to confirmation by a Democratic Congress. After winning his unprecedented third term, FDR submitted to Congress a further Lend-Lease bill called HR-1776, "An Act Further to Promote the Defense of the United States."

"America-Firsters," as the isolationists called themselves, ranted against what they saw as a legislative blank check with the war cry "Kill Bill 1776, not our boys." Lend-Lease carried in the Democratic Congress by a bulletproof margin—60–31 in the Senate and 317–71 in the House. But that November, when the draft came up for extension, it carried by a single vote in the House. After the surprise attack on Pearl Harbor intervened, debate over supporting the Allies, along with the "America-Firsters," disappeared.

Interestingly, the fault lines at home had a common solution. Divided by a sick and sputtering economy and between isolationism and interventionism, December 7 united the nation in ways that are unlikely ever to recur. The Japanese had made a supreme miscalculation in believing that America would never fight. While Americans were polarized over

FDR, the sneak attack effectively made patriotism mandatory. The Arsenal of Democracy was created not in seven days but in an hour and a half on that Sunday morning in Hawaii. The centrifugal forces of government were contained, and the political differences were put aside as America joined the Allies to wage the greatest crusade in history. This was truly seen by most Americans as the ultimate struggle between good and evil.

1945 and the End of World War II

Japan's formal surrender on the teak decks of the battleship USS *Missouri* on September 2, 1945 in Tokyo Bay marked the magnificent performance of what has been called "the greatest generation." Three enemies had been unconditionally defeated and evil incarnate in Adolf Hitler destroyed. The United States had much to celebrate.

First, the United States was the sole remaining—if not the only—superpower of its day. Its economy had not only been unscathed by the war; it had been supercharged and superheated. The war would turn the United States into the dominant economic power of its—and probably *any*—era in history.

The United States possessed a military of over 12 million men and women, who literally were stationed around the world and who were occupying the defeated enemy powers. It possessed the technology for, and had used, two atomic weapons. It had invented or developed the most modern technology, from jet propulsion to radar to computers to plastics and medicines. And it mustered a people who shared a largely common vision of the American Dream.

Unlike the Civil War, when no thought had been given to what to do about the freed slaves and reconstructing the South, a great deal of thought had been given to what to do about the post-war challenges of demobilizing the large armed forces and occupying Germany, Japan, and Italy. FDR and his successor Harry S. Truman and their advisers created the GI Bill that paid returning servicemen enough money to complete college educations. Second, relatively cheap mortgages became available to GI's that would extend home ownership massively and stimulate a housing boom. It is from these two acts of brilliant foresight that much of the post-war economic and social success rested.

Regarding the occupation of the Axis enemies, the lessons of World War I had not been forgotten. Nor had Lincoln's Second Inaugural—"with malice towards none and charity towards all." In 1943, following Secretary of State Cordell Hull's creation of a bipartisan Advisory Commission on Post War Foreign Policy, Congress passed legislation on post-war reconstruction and on supporting an international organization for peace. Germany, Japan, and Italy would be rebuilt and made democracies.

There was fierce debate on how far rebuilding would go. As happened after the Civil War, there was a move in 1944 to turn Germany into a "potato patch" and eliminate heavy industrial capacity to foreclose the possibility of a Fourth Reich. Fortunately, the so-called Morgenthau Plan, named for Secretary of the Treasury Henry J. Morgenthau, to make Germany wholly agrarian was dropped, but not before the Nazi propaganda machine picked it up; harsh speculation lingered in post-war Germany about how the Allies would treat the defeated enemy.

The Conference at Bretton Woods, which would create the World Bank and the International Monetary Fund, and the Dumbarton Oaks Conference, which drafted a charter for what would become the United Nations, were two actions that sought to make the post-war world a safer and more stable place. To reiterate, the lessons of World War I had been taken in. While negotiations among the Allies and particularly with the Russians were filled with uncertainties, great care was given to ensuring that World War II would not become the grounds for World War III.

The time was filled with optimism. The facts that the war was over and that America was greater and stronger were not lost on the public. That Americans had done their duty against an evil foe and then returned home to pick up their pre-war lives was an indication of the selfless and virtuous service that had been rendered. The crusade had ended and was now part of history and lore. There were no new crusades on the horizon.

All was far from perfect, though. In any war, as Iraq later demonstrated, corruption and profiteering are impossible to eliminate. Senator Harry Truman, a first-termer from Missouri, made his mark in the Senate by investigating procurement abuses and cleaning many of them up. That a junior senator could do that—and not always to the benefit of his fellow Democrats who controlled power or of the president who was responsible for overseeing the judicious use of the nation's money—is an interesting comment on the times. It is hard to envisage a crusading junior member of Congress today taking on a sitting president of his or her party by investigation of allegations of wrongdoing. Indeed, the great difficulty that was experienced in merely establishing commissions to investigate September 11 and the intelligence failures associated with Iraqi weapons of mass destruction is a very good indicator of how different politics today is from Truman's time.

But where did the fault lines lie? In the United States, the combination of a booming war economy and ambitious plans for educating and re-integrating service personnel into society had hugely beneficial effects. To some degree, the fault lines were narrowed or even healed by this demobilization. That did not mean that the end of politics and partisanship had arrived. There would always be political differences over key issues. But unlike the end of earlier wars, with the exceptions of the Mexican and Spanish–American wars, which were tiny by comparison, the experience would lead to a stronger nation. Problems of race and other social issues would assert themselves. Truman's decision to integrate blacks into the military was a partial solution to one problem that, however, persists today. However, in perspective, the American Dream, culture, crusade, and partisanship were in balance—and perhaps one of the best balances in our history.

The real fault lines were abroad. Fortunately, they would not run through the defeated powers. However, relations with the Soviet Union would fracture, and the civil war in China would make that country communist and "Red." The result was the disintegration of the friendship and partnership of World War II into the Cold War. The Soviet Union, secretive and paranoid about its security, would erect and retreat behind what Churchill first called an "iron curtain," seizing control of East Europe as a buffer against possible future encroachment by the West. In 1947, a communist revolution spread to Greece. It was at that point that the United States responded forcefully—first with the Marshall Plan and then, along with its former European allies, creating the North Atlantic Treaty Organization (NATO) in 1949 as a counter to the Soviet Union and its encroachment.

The year 1949 was also the year when Chiang Kai-shek and the Nationalists were thrown out of China and retreated to Taiwan as Mao Zedong and the communists won the civil war. In America, the first question raised by pro-Chiang supporters was "Who lost China?" And as China and the Soviet Union were "communist" states, alliance between the two and fear of a communist world conspiracy began shaping American political culture and fashioning a new sense of crusade.

That same year, the Soviet Union exploded its first nuclear bomb, heightening fears about Russian intentions and capabilities. In June 1950, encouraged or provoked by Stalin, North Korea attacked southward, beginning the Korean War. All in all, the post-war world had taken all of five years to move from peace and alliance to cold and hot war, an indicator of how quickly international politics can shift.

Conclusions and Concerns

This abbreviated historical survey of the American Dream, culture, crusade, and partisanship has been conducted wearing seven-league boots and with the broadest granularity of strategic and historical analysis. A great deal of it is germane today. Regarding the dream, leaders and events hold powerful influence. However, innovative and bold ideas that come from leaders are the keys to making this dream credible and real. The Homestead Act of 1862, the GI bill, and GI low-cost mortgages following World War II are among the more important examples of how legislation and bold thinking can empower the dream. The question is whether there are any equivalent and imaginative programs extant today.

Culture too remains a product of politics and events. We have seen how the United States has been powerfully affected by its capacity for crusade. The roots go back to the colonists. During the heady 1840s and the expansion west, the first expression of crusade emerged— "Remember the Alamo" and do battle to expand the United States. The Civil War had elements of crusade offset by the destruction caused by that war and the battlefields that killed and maimed so many soldiers on both sides. Religious and missionary zeal were often present and active forces that impelled action.

The Spanish–American War was the first major American military crusade and was aimed at lifting the yoke of Spain from what America believed to be oppressed and maltreated Cubans and Filipinos. World War I surely was a crusade to make the world safe for democracy, a cry heard today in a different context. World War II was perhaps our finest hour.

Partisanship led to dysfunctional government. The post–Civil War period is the most relevant example of the evils of dysfunctionality as well as the failure to plan for Reconstruction. Perhaps if Lincoln had not been assassinated, the world might have been different. But that was not to happen. Lasting enmity between North and South and black and white was created. The corruption of the latter 1870s and beyond was not noted here in detail. However, in those days, the role of government was much smaller and less intrusive. Given the abundance of resources, the absence of government obligations for social and welfare programs, and the safety afforded by two oceans, there was a great deal of slack in what damage government could do. Competence in the face of complex and irreconcilable issues was less vital then.

In subsequent chapters, strategic analysis will focus on current issues. But first it is important to assess how government has become increasingly unbalanced and dysfunctional, and how vulnerability to all forms of disruption has become irreversible and—if America's enemies choose to target these weaknesses and fault lines—frightening and possibly debilitating.

Unchecked and Unbalanced—
The Enemy from Within:
Dysfunctional Government and
an Exposed Nation

READERS SHOULD ASK IF AMERICAN government is as dysfunctional and incapable of dealing with the major issues of the day as it appears. If the answer is yes, how has this happened and what can be done to correct this imbalance? If the answer is no, why does government give that appearance?

Regarding vulnerability, do America's adversaries understand what leverage this ability to disrupt can yield? And, if so, what must be done to reduce this vulnerability and counter any leverage? Or is vulnerability now part of life, given these threats, and do Americans need to take on a stiff-upper-lip attitude and simply get on with their lives, muddling through as always, without further angst?

Two seemingly minor anecdotes shed a startling light on the state of government and the vulnerability of any society. The first example concerns the irrationality of the appointment and confirmation process that takes literally months to get new people into office. Not only does the clearance process of FBI background checks require huge amounts of time; but in the poisonous politics of Washington, the need to avoid even the hint of a potential problem of conflict of interest because of financial holdings, business interests, and the requirement for complete disclosure

makes that process so distasteful and expensive that many serious candidates for high office simply refuse to endure it.

Not long ago, to obtain one particular very senior White House position not confirmed by the Senate, the nominee spent well over a million
dollars of his own money in legal fees to cover the costs of lawyers vetting personal finances, a necessity since even small accounting errors
and mistakes in filing the forms can lead to criminal charges and many
times that figure in monetary losses taken in selling off various holdings
to conform with the ethical standards. That is unacceptable to many. But
the anecdote remains real and incredible.

To avoid even a possible hint of a conflict of interest on the part of
senior executive branch officials with major acquisition responsibilities,
in the 1980s, the Senate Armed Services Committee levied special
requirements on Defense Department appointees who were receiving
retirement benefits from defense contractors. Once confirmed,
appointees had to take out a surety bond insuring pensions against their
former employer corporation declaring bankruptcy. The argument went
that if a defense official was receiving a pension from a defense company
in financial trouble or headed toward bankruptcy, that official might
steer contracts to the former employer to keep it in business, protecting
his or her pension.

Defense Department officials did not object, as the policy provided
them a certain immunity to criticism. Before United Airlines ditched its
pension plan in the spring of 2005, that insurance was relatively modest
in cost. After United's action, the cost of the insurance, if it could be
gotten at all, skyrocketed to about $150,000, approximately the annual
salary of the deputy secretary of defense. Indeed, Gordon England, who
was nominated for that post, had his appointment put on hold for a considerable time on this issue. It was finally settled. But England was still
on hold because Republican senators Trent Lott of Mississippi and
Olympia Snowe of Maine objected to the Navy's shipbuilding plan (discussed below) on the grounds that the program slighted their constituents. The surety bond requirement has since been sensibly altered.

England was granted a recess appointment by the president. But the
entire appointment and clearance process still reeks with these extraordinary and often ludicrous rules that are symptom and cause of larger
dysfunctionalities. The disincentives for service in these bizarre and
counterproductive rules are matched and trumped by the appalling

length of time it takes to fill important offices. However, in this era of intense partisanship and scandals that beset all administrations, the difficulty of making rational changes defies the process and contributes mightily to its dysfunctionality.

In 1988, on a midweek summer afternoon, along the Beltway that circles Washington, D.C., two cars heading north between the Connecticut and Wisconsin Avenue exits touched. Minor damage was done. But as the cars pulled off the beltway to report the incident, traffic stalled and was backed up for nearly ten hours. The gridlock on Texas roads in September 2005 caused by the massive evacuation over Hurricane Rita was understandable. However, this pileup on the Beltway was not. Suppose, at some future date, terrorists had planted mines or bombs to explode on major highways at rush hour, killing, wounding, and scaring millions of motorists and travelers. Based on how airport security reacted to September 11, what would these acts of terror create in response? It is difficult to picture the consequences. Nearly twenty years after the Beltway incident, as will be shown, national vulnerability to all manner of events has grown worse.

Vulnerability is not only limited to industrially advanced states. Iraq, devastated by three wars (one against Iran and two against us) and Saddam's dictatorial rule, suffers on a daily basis. The flows of power, oil, water, and food are regularly interrupted. In Baghdad in September 2005, electricity was available around eight hours a day. And the news is filled with reports of oil pipelines being sabotaged and power lines routinely cut.

A Dysfunctional Political Process

In early 2001, the Commission on National Security Strategy/21st Century (known as the Hart–Rudman Commission for its two chairmen, former senators Gary Hart and Warren Rudman) released its findings. One of the most striking concluded that the organization for national security was "dysfunctional." Had the commission been given a wider charter, that finding would have better described the performance of the entire government. The commission also predicted that a WMD (weapons of mass destruction) terrorist attack would hit the United States within twenty-five years. The estimate was conservative, by twenty-four years and seven months, when anthrax attacks struck that fall.

A large part of this dysfunctionality resides in the core of our political system—the Constitution, and the philosophy and practicality that created it. As we saw in the tension and ambiguity over states' rights and central authority that led to civil war, contradictions are inherent in any constitution. The passage of time, technology, and events creates situations unanticipated by any constitution.

Further, governments in open societies that respect the rule of law freely trade off efficiency and effectiveness in favor of civil liberties. In their wisdom, the Founding Fathers no doubt silently believed that the best means to preserve individual freedom was to maximize the inefficiency of government. As a consequence, the Constitution and the system of checks and balances purposely divided power among three branches of government, guaranteeing permanent inefficiency as the ultimate protector of liberty and freedom.

The test is whether this system designed by the best minds of the eighteenth century, in which divided power meant a permanently inefficient government, can cope with the radically different challenges and crises of the twenty-first century, distorted and buffeted by the alchemy of culture, crusade, and partisanship.

It was not by accident that Article I of the Constitution was titled "Legislative Powers" and Article II "The President." The hierarchical meaning was clear. Congress was to be the principal arm of government. The president, as the chief executive, was to be the implementer of the law as set down by Congress, not the center of government. That is one reason why a powerful White House staff and cabinet are not specifically noted in the Constitution. The veto, of course, gave the president a powerful tool to check Congress, one only President George W. Bush (since Millard Fillmore[16]) has failed to exercise so far.

Within Congress, the House of Representatives was to be the people's chamber, with direct elections. The Senate was to be the more deliberative and mature body, whose wisdom and six-year terms would compensate for the "vulgar" in the other chamber. Senators would not be elected by popular vote; they were picked by the state legislatures. And as the Constitution had nothing to say about political parties, it was assumed that their role would be minor.

The first fault line in the Constitution was the Founding Fathers' belief in the primacy of the legislature and the broader reality and impact that politics and international affairs would end up having in making the president the *primus inter pares* in government in those matters. Congress simply lacked the organization and authority to dominate in those matters. Hence, the Constitution offered no solution to the persistent debate over presidential power and prerogatives and possible excesses or limits for obvious reconciliation without consensus or dominance of a single party or ideology across these two branches of government.

In times when the significance of the issues was low, when the United States could literally spend its way clear of danger, or when the peril was so great as to contain these inherently centrifugal forces, accommodation and compromise could be reached. That did not prevent error or mistake. History is ripe with "bipartisan" foul-ups and miscalculations. But lacking the above moderating forces and left to its own devices, this Constitutional contradiction has rarely led to successful outcomes.

Second, the Constitution retained huge ambiguities between Congress and the presidency over the power to make war; the extent of the powers of the commander-in-chief to bypass the law in time of crisis or war and to conduct foreign policy; as well as the authority to control how money that only Congress has the power to appropriate will be spent in practice. These contradictions and tensions are well known and have been exhaustively treated elsewhere; as a result, they are merely noted here and are not analyzed, except to the degree that each has contributed to the dysfunctionality of government. Culture, crusade, and partisanship have tended to exacerbate these gray areas, particularly when there is little common agreement between the political parties on the nature of the dangers and policies to counter and contain them.

Third, there were good reasons why many intelligent Americans urged George Washington to become king, not president. That the president was both head of state and head of government had a sense of neatness, combining both duties under one hat. The danger was that, unlike prime ministers or chancellors who were heads of government alone, dismissing or criticizing a leader who was both was made more difficult. Presidents, of course, have been and are roundly and nastily criticized, often with the foulest language and intent. But there are times, especially in war, where dissent is unfortunately curbed in part because of this dual-hatting and respect for the office, even when fair and objective criticism is vital.

Fourth, the role of the president as commander-in-chief took on different meaning during the Cold War and the nuclear standoff with the

Soviet Union. In the past, surprise attacks such as Pearl Harbor or Hitler's invasion into Poland and later France could be reversed. But a first strike with hundreds of thermonuclear and/or nuclear weapons would be catastrophic and the damage very likely irreversible. A thermonuclear weapon (hydrogen bomb) has a yield measured in megatons (millions of tons) of TNT-equivalent destructive power, about a thousand times greater than a nuclear weapon (uranium or plutonium bomb), whose power is denominated in kilotons (thousands of tons).

The commander-in-chief, with his finger close to the "button" or "football," as the black valise with the nuclear firing codes was called, had the ability to declare, wage, and win or lose a war without having time to consult with Congress, the only body with the power to declare or authorize the use of force in war. Hence, psychologically and emotionally, the presidency inherited a certain authority during the Cold War. Indeed, in October 1973 when Richard Nixon was in the throes of Congress's investigation of Watergate and Egypt and Syria launched a surprise attack against Israel, Nixon's mental state raised great concerns over his ability to deal with the Yom Kippur War crisis.

Soviet leader Leonid Brezhnev threatened, at one stage of that war, to intervene with Russian troops to prevent the Israeli army from completing the destruction of the Egyptian army. Nixon upped the nuclear alert status. Many thought nuclear war was imminent. All the while, in Washington, the crucial question was whether or not Nixon was in full control of his faculties, a chilling reminder of his role as commander-in-chief.

Too often, however, Americans forget what the phrase "commander-in-chief" really means. The president is not the commander-in-chief of the government. Nor is he the commander-in-chief of Congress. He is not the commander-in-chief of the people. He is commander-in-chief only of the military. But all presidents like to exploit that title as much as they can. When President George W. Bush landed aboard a Navy aircraft carrier after Operation Iraqi Freedom had toppled Saddam in 2003 to declare (prematurely) "mission accomplished," he was dressed out as commander-in-chief in a flight suit and helmet and used that title in the most public way to enhance his image, an image the media was delighted to spread with both favorable and unfavorable commentary. The White House has used the title of "commander-in-chief" freely in waging the "Global War on Terror," a war that has still not been declared by Congress and authorized in practice by budgets to pay for it. And the controversy over domestic surveillance and whether the president has the authority to bypass the law brings home how Constitutional ambiguities can have profound political impact. Appendix III covers these arguments and consequences.

As we have seen from the brief historical excursion in Chapter Two, dysfunctionality in government is not new. Yet, these Constitutional contradictions have been put in starker contrast by other factors and realities in how we govern and conduct politics and how the world has changed. FDR could run World War II with a handful of generals, admirals, advisers, and members of Congress. Committee chairmen in Congress (no women then) had great power through the seniority system. While Truman had difficulties with Congress, the same model applied through the Nixon era.

Consensus over the threat of the Soviet Union and Red China meant that politics could stop at the "water's edge"; that Republicans and Democrats, with few exceptions, could agree on foreign policy—a nice legacy from World War II. That was changed by a number of explosive events. The war in Vietnam, the Watergate stupidity, and the emergence of divisive and incendiary social and political issues were principal among them. Lyndon Johnson quit over Vietnam and refused to seek the second term he probably would have won. When faced with impeachment and near-certain conviction over Watergate, Richard Nixon was forced to resign. "The pill," women's liberation and feminism, civil rights, the drug and antiwar culture, along with gay rights and many of the social issues of the 1960s and 1970s, were reflected in—and affected—how the government would respond.

There were other immutable forces that would change the fabric of government. Roosevelt had embedded in the New Deal the legacy of social security that has become part of public expectations and virtually an inalienable right. Lyndon Johnson's Great Society brought Medicare and Medicaid to the dream, and social responsibility was reinforced by Nixonian legislation, including the establishment of the Environmental Protection Agency. All these programs created hugely expensive demands requiring progressively larger funding to meet future obligations. The consequence would be huge liabilities—that is, promises and obligations of government to provide services to their constituencies that someday would come due. The dilemma was providing monies to pay for these liabilities and obligations.

The clash between "guns and butter" was a byproduct of the Vietnam War. But more importantly, the collision led to the creation of what would become huge numbers of interest groups and powerful constituencies who became fierce claimants for a goodly slice of the federal budget. These trends continue. So, on top of the other fault lines in government, the disparities between obligations and liabilities and moneys to pay for them are another; and, as we will see, the gaps are growing quickly.

Discussion of domestic financial, fiscal, and liability fault lines follows in a later chapter. However, the intrusion of the federal government into the lives of Americans in so many vital areas, initiated by FDR, has understandably produced many, many constituents and advocates for each of these programs, normally on a single-issue basis. At a minimum, this intrusion has complicated the political process immensely and has added huge measures of bureaucratic cholesterol and regulation to a system of government that was already purposely inefficient, making adjudication of competing priorities in a disciplined and rational way virtually impossible. The net result has been a super accumulation of issues and problems to which no single policy choice can rally sufficient popular support to ensure a final resolution.

The recent spending frenzy by a supposedly fiscally "conservative" Republican government for crises over Iraq (approaching $500 billion and rising), Homeland Security (approaching $100 billion), and relief for the victims of hurricanes Katrina and Rita (many, many billions) shows how easy it is to lose any measure of discipline. Twenty years ago, whether for reasons of courage or bravado, Congress passed the largely symbolic Gramm–Rudman–Hollings deficit reduction act to force a balanced budget. In the current environment, re-passing that act stands little serious chance of happening. It is easier to spend than to cut, especially when these powerful constituencies are reminiscent of the orphans in Dickens's *Oliver Twist* crying, "More, more."

One consequence of Vietnam and the Watergate scandal was that they caused Congress to revamp the seniority system, in which longevity determined committee assignments and chairmanships. The power of the "Imperial Presidency" was curtailed by legislation such as the War Powers Act, which directed the president to notify Congress before sending U.S. forces into specific actions for periods greater than sixty days. Controls were placed on arms transfers and the authority of presi-

dents to make them without Congressional consent. These all had profound effects on trying to right the balance back toward the Congress
after Vietnam and Watergate.

During this period, an upsurge of social issues and ultimately the dominance of constituency politics would hold great sway over politics. Following debate over the birth-control pill, the right-to-life and abortion
issues were moved to the center of American politics. In 1973, in the
famous *Roe v. Wade* ruling, the Supreme Court held that based on the
narrow right to privacy, abortions were Constitutional. The court had
ruled on many important cases, beginning with *Marbury v. Madison* in
1803, in which Chief Justice John Marshall changed the complexion of
government forever by asserting the court's right to declare laws unconstitutional, something unmentioned in that document.

Over time, because of intense debate on issues ranging from crime
and civil rights to legalizing drugs and gun ownership, not only did many
of these social issues result in serious legal proceedings to adjudicate settlement; they also polarized and, in some cases, demonized politics by
setting up diametrically opposed advocates and petitioners who were
rarely amenable to resolution. Take the "right to life"—how opponents
of abortions put it—and those who advocate a "woman's right to
choose"—supporters of abortion.

From an entirely rational view, outside religious beliefs, it is difficult
to find fault with the argument that in certain cases when the life of the
mother is at risk, abortion should be legal and available. At the other
extreme, it is abhorrent that abortion should be sought as a routine and
reasonable alternative to birth control. While most Americans would
accept these points of view, the fact is that for Republicans and Democrats
alike, this is a "third rail" of American politics. Bill Clinton got it right
when he declared that abortions should be "safe, legal, and rare." But
that view does not square with many powerful interest groups for
which the right to life or the right to choose is the single issue of most
importance.

Hence, because this polarization is now a permanent part of American
culture, the matter of choice or right to life has probably become as
adversarial as any issue in our history since slavery. On the extreme
right, hatred of abortion and the taking of an unborn and unprotected
life has led to bombings of abortion clinics and killings of those who perform these procedures. (So much for the sanctity-of-life argument.) And

this controversy has been extended to stem-cell life research and even to what should be taught in science at public schools concerning Darwinism and creationism, with the notion of "intelligent creation" serving as a surrogate for the latter.

Gun control is another example of how American culture reacts. The Second Amendment specifically states that "a well regulated militia, being necessary to the security of a free State, the right of the people to keep and bear and Arms, shall not be infringed." With the emergence over the past decades of the National Rifle Association, the Constitution withstanding, gun ownership has been a polarizing issue and one that candidates from both parties routinely support. Gun-control advocates in Congress are not only chastised by the NRA and its supporters; they are targeted for electoral defeat.

Any interest group has a right to support any candidate. However, the number of extreme organizations of the left and right has metastasized into the thousands, many well financed, entirely partisanized, each keen to win its particular battle. It is this mixture of culture, crusade, and partisanship that plays very heavily on the process and in many ways leads to dysfunctionality.

The phenomena that polarize these many social issues in America are not common in democracies in Europe or north of the border. There, little to no controversy exists on abortion, guns, religion, and even drugs. The reason is not that Europeans are disinterested. But the political processes there are not as vested in the need for constituencies and interest groups to provide funds for campaigning. What has happened in America is that these highly politicized social issues have opened a huge fault line. On the one hand, many Americans are not swayed by these politicized issues. On the other, single issue groups have become far more active and influential in helping to both select and elect candidates. The result has been to distort and subordinate broader matters of general national importance to more politically charged single issues. To repeat, before the NRA committed the unbelievable blunder of accusing federal law enforcement of Nazi-like tendencies, causing President George H. W. Bush to resign his NRA life membership, what president ever stood up to that organization in an aggressive fashion? Gun-owning and hunting have become presidential pastimes, reflecting the current trend of politics rather than a return to the days when trapping and killing dinner was a part of everyday survival.

Few phenomena have had the impact on politics that television has had. The famous Kennedy–Nixon presidential debates of 1960 were the precursors of this transformation in politics and the effect on campaigning made by television. Television had covered earlier presidential races as well as Congressional hearings, notably the Army–McCarthy hearings in 1954. But with access to countless living rooms and a medium that surely favored certain politicians, the symbiotic relationship was assured. As Americans became increasingly glued to their TV screens, and those screens became color and then successively larger, the symbiotic relationship became addictive. Nationally prominent politicians needed airtime. And it became clear that candidates who mastered this medium had far greater chances of being elected.

Television airtime is rarely free and usually expensive, particularly at prime time and on the major networks. Hence, fund-raising was crucial in attracting the mother's milk of politics—money. This circular need and cycle between money and campaigning flourished—if that is the right word. Today, while there are no exact figures on how much money is poured into television, not merely by candidates but by constituencies and interest groups for or against specific issues and candidates, the amount is in the many-billion range. A double danger is related.

First, candidates and sitting elected officials, especially those not in assured or safe seats and those who are running for the top office (president), are preoccupied with raising money. This is time-consuming and often demeaning. To attract funding often means pulling punches on issues or reluctantly agreeing to expedient compromises that would not have been necessary if financing were not needed.

Second, the impression is created that politics is about being elected more than governing. And surely the time consumed at fundraisers and the like is time away from the duty of governing. For those who follow Congress, the workweek is often only a day long as members race off late Thursday to constituencies at home and return late Monday or early Tuesday to the Capitol.

Third, as will be discussed later, attack ads and negative advertising often work and have contributed mightily to a far greater harshness and adversarial character to politics. Politics now extends to dueling advertising campaigns for and against not only candidates for elected office, but specific pieces of legislation and nominees for senior appointments such as current UN Ambassador John Bolton and recent judgeships on the Supreme Court.

The explosion in political action committees and other organizations with huge electoral war chests would have been less dramatic if they had managed to cancel each other out. Instead, competition has become fiercer between and among these groups. Many use the most outrageous and inflammatory rhetoric to make their points or attack their opponents, all protected by free speech and the First Amendment. That in the 2004 election George W. Bush could have been attacked for flying jet fighters in the Air National Guard or that John Kerry's courage and patriotism could have been smeared on specious grounds demonstrated the adversarial tone of government. One recommendation that follows is a requirement for fact and truth in advertising in political campaigns to eliminate at least some of the fabrications, distortions, and mendacities that corrupt and demean the political process.

So how did all these factors and forces come together to make government dysfunctional? What is the evidence of this dysfunctionality? How deep are the fault lines, and how exposed are they to shattering? Enter culture, crusade, and partisanship and their impact on the political process.

The tensions and contradictions inherent in the Constitution are neither surprising nor unknown. No political system is without some— or many—points of conflict. But when major fault lines stemming from these contradictions give way, society and systems can crack. This is exactly what happened to the Soviet Union. The profound irrationality of the Soviet system could not tolerate Gorbachev's *glasnost* and *perestroika*. The pressures from introducing even a modicum of openness to a hitherto closed and secret society, and restructuring to a socio-economic system so corrupt and antithetical to reform, were irreversible and irresistible with, in retrospect, predictable consequences. The Soviet Union shattered and disappeared.

The growth of government and its associated budget, and the growth in the influence of government on fiscal and monetary policy through tax laws, spending and borrowing, and a mass of regulatory agencies including the Federal Reserve, Security and Exchange Commission, and many others, have made Washington ground zero for corporations, businesses, interest groups, professional and trade associations, unions, teachers, not-for-profit institutions, retirees, veterans, and virtually any other organization with reasons for protecting and advancing its agenda and particular interests. The sheer size of this universe at last count is some 30,000 lobbyists to promote clients' needs. By accurate count, in 2000, the federal budget listed 1,400 new programs that were the type of pure patronage known as "pork." Five short years later, in 2005, "pork" accounted for 15,000! The consequence has been not quite gridlock, but standoff. And the lobbyist scandal set off by Jack Abramoff brought "earmarks" into public view.

The general description is a political system in which literally thousands of individual constituencies and claimants for resources, power, influence, or access jealously guard their turf to the point where it is in no one's interest to attempt a fundamental reform or redistribution of those elements. At the same time, powerful interest groups and many single-issue or ideologically driven constituencies, from the Christian Right to the NRA to NARAL, hold great influence on members of Congress, where polarization tends to be greatest and the famous Bush 43-ism applied to the war on terror surely applies more strongly here—"you are either with us or against us." Hence, there is not only a muzzle on dissent and debate; far worse, debate descends into ad hominem fist-fights of attacking and humiliating the opponent rather than serious pursuit of issues and solutions. The confirmation hearings on Supreme Court nominees—Robert Bork in 1985 and Clarence Thomas in 1991—demonstrated the passion, the venom, and in general the squalor of how major decisions and votes are made—a disgrace for anyone interested in an exchange of ideas and making a fair and objective evaluation of a dedicated and able judge.

The result has polarized the two political parties in two ways. Both the Republican and Democratic parties have become far more polarized against each other. And both are polarized around the ends of the political spectrum that defines the two parties. The Republicans have become more rightist, and the Democrats have divided between left and center. An incisive paper prepared for the Third Way Middle Class Project makes those cases.[17]

One conclusion is that the "red" (Republican) and "blue" (Democratic) states have become "redder" and "bluer," meaning party affiliation has become far stronger. The great "center," the moderate majority of Americans, has nowhere to go. As a result, "today's crisis of confidence in political leaders is in large part a crisis of competence at home and abroad. The American people are learning the hard way that visions are not plans and hope is not a strategy."[18]

Best of Breed—If We Can't Get Defense Right, Then What?
Beyond this level of political gridlock and dysfunctionality, the prepon-
derance of huge numbers of constituencies unwilling to shuck power or
funding leads to paralysis. The Department of Defense (DoD) is surely
one of the most efficient and well-run departments in government, with
a strong reputation built on the performance of its military and civilian
personnel and an undeniably critical role in the fight against terror and
jihad. Sadly, the DoD offers many case studies on the dysfunctionality of
the process and how rational decision is often unobtainable. If Defense
cannot get it right, then neither can the rest of government.

The Department of Defense employs about 1.4 million uniformed
military, a million civilians, and a National Guard and Reserve component of about another million. Its budget for 2005 was over $420 billion.
Given the wars in Iraq and on terror and supplemental bills to cover the
added fiscal demands, it is difficult to calculate exactly how much the
Department is actually spending, an extraordinary observation brought
home by a recent General Accounting Office study that showed that
DoD did not have control or detailed knowledge of its accounting of a
large part of its publicly appropriated funds.

For that sum, the department purchases everything from F-22 Raptor
aircraft which can cruise supersonically without using afterburner (a
remarkable technological achievement) and invisibly, at about $300 mil-
lion a copy, to radar, to day-care centers to look after dependents of military parents, to health care for life for its retirees. By every measure,
men and women in uniform are serving with courage and distinction in
extremely difficult assignments in Iraq and Afghanistan. Unlike Vietnam,
where discipline had disappeared, drug use was common, and "fragging"
(killing of officers and senior non-commissioned officers) was a preferred
way of avoiding dangerous missions, the exact opposite is true in Iraq.
Had the morale and attitude of service personnel in Iraq and Afghanistan
not been so visibly positive, public opinion certainly would have turned
against that war long ago.

The five sides of the Pentagon are illustrative of the complexity of its
organization, and the politics of its budget process demonstrate how the
government functions—or, in this case, does so on at least a rational basis.
By law, the Pentagon's absolute boss is the secretary of defense. He issues
the orders (approved by the president) that direct the military commanders. The secretary is responsible for the decisions over which hun-

dreds of billions of dollars worth of procurement programs will be funded, cut, or amended. He, of course, is assisted and advised by a large personal staff in his office (the Office of the Secretary of Defense or OSD) and by the chairman and vice chairman of the Joint Chiefs of Staff, along with the Army, Navy, Air Force, and Marine service chiefs and the Joint Staff. The secretary is also responsible for spending about 85 percent of the total national intelligence budget, which is estimated at $50 billion a year.

The three service secretaries of the Army, Navy (and Marine Corps), and Air Force report to the secretary of defense as well. But, despite the appearance of a monolithic and centralized command and control structure embodied in one person, the Pentagon is fragmented across many offices, agencies, and fiefdoms. The procurement process by which the goods, services, and systems that underwrite the department's military, logistic, support, infrastructure, research and development, and personnel needs are acquired is a graphic illustration of how far dysfunctionality reaches in this, the most efficient and well run of government departments. That there are literally hundreds of thousands of pages of rules and regulations governing procurement is the first sign that something is amiss.

The services are entrusted with procuring the sinews of war—called under the law as authority to "train, maintain, and equip." The services have direct pipelines to Congress. And the services are fragmented, with many different offices and officers responsible for parts or all of thousands of programs totaling hundreds of billions of dollars.

All procurement and acquisition is legally under the jurisdiction of the Undersecretary of Defense for Acquisition, Technology, and Logistics—a separate chain of command established to make procurement more efficient. The responsible program executive in each service reports to this individual. Congress is the dispenser of the coin of the realm and intimately involved in keeping with its Article I responsibilities by appropriating the requested funding. Yet, because of years of experience in which trust and confidence between the department and Congress has oscillated from some to none and because moving money between programs and spending lines has been extremely restricted, huge fault lines exist within this highly complicated and arcane process.

How does this process operate in practice? Navy shipbuilding provides a marvelous insight, replicable across much of government, that shows how offices, agencies, and departments go about funding programs amidst this ménage of budget cycles, interactions with Congress, competition for dollars, and the overtly political character of the process. Today, few doubt the need for a strong military and a strong navy. Twenty years ago, in 1986, the Navy numbered nearly 600 warships. In 2006, with the Soviet Union gone, the number is 281 men-of-war. Whether that is the right number or not is not the issue. Here is the heart of the dysfunctionality problem.

For the past several years, Congress appropriated about $10 billion a year, on average, to buy warships. There are six major shipyards, all owned either by Northrop Grumman or General Dynamics,[19] and are represented by members of Congress who passionately support maintaining those yards to assure constituent employment, irrespective of party affiliation. Senator John Warner of Virginia, Republican chairman of the Senate Armed Services Committee, is rightfully protective of the Newport News Shipyard. And Democratic Senator Joe Lieberman of Connecticut fought successfully to keep the New London submarine base open after the Base Realignment and Closure Commission had recommended it for closure. Here is what the Navy faces.

The cost of the newest nuclear aircraft carrier for construction alone is currently estimated at about $10 billion, probably a low figure. The latest destroyer, DDX, will cost about $3.3 billion for the first ship and just over $2 billion for follow-ons. The *Virginia*-class nuclear submarines cost about $2.5 billion each, increasing to $3 billion in later years. Those estimates, if history is any judge, will also prove low.

Assuming a ship has a 35-year life expectancy, to sustain a Navy of 280 ships would require, on average, buying eight ships a year. Even if warship costs averaged out at $2 billion each, and that too is a conservative figure, then buying eight per year will require some $6 billion more than will be approved. The costs of the new aircraft carrier are spread out over nine years. However, the Navy simply cannot maintain anything close to its recommended ship levels. Indeed, at current prices, the Navy is facing a future of as few as 125 to 150 ships. That shortfall between needs (or obligations) and budgets is broadly representative of most programs across government. The Navy is in trouble unless one of three things happens.

First, Congress can appropriate more money. The shortfall each year to maintain a fleet of 280 ships is $5 to 7 billion. Given the budget pressures, absent an event such as a war in Korea or the Taiwan Straits, Congress is simply not going to authorize funding to that level.

Second, the Navy can redesign itself in one of two ways. To fit future budgets, the Navy will be forced to buy far fewer aircraft carriers and the latest destroyers and submarines and more less-expensive ships such as Littoral Combat Ship (LCS) currently at a bargain price of about $220 million each. But reductions in buying the larger warships will not support the current shipbuilding base. Hence, an understandable battle will be fought by the shipbuilding corporations and their Congressional supporters to buy the more expensive warships, even if they appear unaffordable to the Navy.

Or the Navy could attempt a radical transformation of its forces by modernizing its still relatively young fleet, extending service life expectancies of ships to forty years or more (HMS *Victory* was 46 at the Battle of Trafalgar in 1805, and wasn't retired from active service until 1812; and the USS *Wisconsin* was 47 when she was last in combat in the Persian Gulf in 1991), transferring still-capable ships to a cadre or reduced-deployment status to save money, and buying fewer new ships. It could also move beyond the LCS to even more radical designs for warships.

But the response outside the Navy would be predictable. Shipbuilders and Congress would object, and Congress would almost certainly reject such plans, to preserve constituent and shipyard interests. Retired admirals and officers who grew up with these marvelous men-of-war would express strong reservations about such a radical shift. And within the service, persuading advocates of naval aviation, surface ships, and submarines to accept this transformation would be difficult for even a John Paul Jones.

A third outcome is most likely, and it appears that this will be what occurs. The Navy has set a tentative goal of 313 ships as the needed number. Under this plan (which still defers the tough choices into the future), Congress will need to spend an additional $2 to 3 billion a year on shipbuilding. The Navy will opt for buying fewer new ships, say a handful of DDX's rather than the twenty or thirty that were once in the proposed program. Since the fleet does not need one-for-one replacement immediately, this is the path of least resistance. Congress might also choose to take the path of "partial funding"; that is, authorize construction of a warship in one year and pay for it over time. The problem is obvious: At some time, the bill will still come due. At that stage, the Navy will be closer to the decision point when it will need one-for-one replacement and can least afford it.

Therein rests the crisis. To repeat, it is not only the Department of Defense and the Navy, Army, Air Force, and Marine Corps that face similar funding crises; the symptom extends throughout all of government, as newspaper stories on future crises over social security, Medicare, and Medicaid programs remind us.

The debate over "how much defense is enough?" is as old as the nation. In the Cold War, the presence of the Soviet Union helped answer that question. For the first few years after the Cold War ended, the United States did not move aggressively enough to exploit that opportunity with major force structure changes. Then, since September 11 and the subsequent wars on terror and in Afghanistan and Iraq and the Bush 43 administration's focus on transformation of the Department of Defense, dealing with these force-level and dollar problems became far more complex and the choices more difficult.

Without an enemy today that possesses a conventional army, navy, or air force (putting the future of China aside), there is no righting function and no clear answer as to how the future Navy—or, for that matter, the Army, Air Force, and Marine Corps—will fare. Government is simply not capable of taking tough choices and making tradeoffs—and not merely among and between the military services. One clear outcome suggests a much smaller future Navy, possibly numbering 150 ships, roughly half of what it possesses today.

The case of the Navy and the Department of Defense is not isolated. Every program, from Medicare to Homeland Defense to Social Security to "No Child Left Behind," is encumbered with similar fault lines in terms of insufficient long-term funding and the iron grip of constituency politics. The *Washington Post* editorial quoted in the frontispiece singling out our "inability to grapple seriously with public policy" was titled "Government's Disgrace" and underscores the depth of this dysfunctionality. Without some means to adjudicate beyond horse-trading and compromise in Congress, which just defer taking tough solutions, this dysfunctionality will continue.

The explosion in federal spending and associated deficits and debt and the magnitude of future obligations cannot be supported by the finite amount of money that is available. If the nation continues borrowing at a similar pace, interest rates eventually will soar and foreign creditors will look elsewhere to invest the dollars they hold from the huge trade surpluses accumulating overseas. At some stage, the market and financial reality will dictate that tough choices must be made. Because of the dysfunctionality of government, when those times arrive—and if nothing changes—those choices will almost certainly be made in the most ham-fisted ways. The image of the Navy of 300 ships today being cut in half will not be atypical of many government social, health-care, and retirement programs if action is deferred or does not fully address the heart of each problem. Then, the American Dream and promise will surely be at risk of shattering.

A *Totally Vulnerable Society*

One of the ironies and fault lines of modern society is the magnitude of its vulnerability to disruption, whether by man or nature. The fragility of states to the forces of nature could not have been brought home any more vividly than by the tsunami of December 2004 and Hurricane Katrina eight months later. The former killed about 300,000 people and destroyed hundreds of thousands of homes, offices, buildings, schools, temples, bridges, and structures. Katrina wrecked New Orleans, along with a goodly part of the Gulf Coast.

Preparations and responses can always be better. The response to Katrina was a disgrace. With all the resources, energy, and effort poured into homeland defense, four years after September 11, the nation learned that it was still not ready to cope with a disaster of that magnitude. While the response to the more subdued Hurricane Rita, which followed shortly thereafter, was better, Katrina was a shock to the system. But the fact was that, as King Canute could not turn back the tides, some natural disasters are unavoidable. And each reminds us of how vulnerable mankind is to the force of nature.

One way to drive this point home is to ask the reader to take a short walk around the neighborhood in which he or she lives and take the perspective of a terrorist planning an attack to kill, harm, and disrupt the community. The possibilities would only be limited by the imagination of the individual. Then consider how disruption of vital services such as water, electricity, food distribution, medical treatment, mail, banking, garbage collection, and transportation would affect the local area and the city, state, and region as well.

As president, Bill Clinton established The Presidential Commission on Critical Infrastructure Protection. The commission identified eight national infrastructures "so vital that their incapacity or destruction would have a debilitating effect on our defense and economic security." The eight areas identified were transportation; oil and gas production and storage; water supply; emergency services; government services; banking and finance; electric power; and telecommunications. These big eight covered information and communications, physical distribution, energy, banking and finance, and vital human services.

The information and communications sector involves the public telephone networks and the Internet. Telecommunications and computers are part of this sector. Obviously, nature can disrupt these through electromagnetic disturbances and storms that down power lines, or lightning strikes that take out power-box junctions. But deliberate physical and electronic attacks are real. Hackers around the world consistently try to break into or destroy computer systems and programs with "worms" and other rogue viruses. In 1999, two colonels in the Chinese Army wrote an interesting book called *Unrestricted Warfare*, which analyzed how the vulnerability of these systems could be exploited in war.

In a visit to Beijing in September 2004 to lecture at the People's Liberation Army's (PLA) National Defense University, this writer had many exchanges on information warfare and Chinese notions of how to employ it against American information systems. While Chinese understanding of these systems was excellent, along with understanding American military doctrine, the PLA did not appear to have any actual systems or capabilities to turn theory into practice. But clever terrorists and hackers do. Newspapers have reported hundreds of incidents of real and attempted acts of information warfare directed at computer and electronic systems.

The physical distribution sector within the United States covers 4 million miles of public roads, 25 million trucks operated by nearly a half million trucking companies, and 200 million motor vehicles. The nation has over 400 major airports, 6,000 transit entities, 1,900 seaports of all sizes (many on lakes and rivers), and 1,700 inland river terminals. Page 29 of the report graphically lists the possible threat of downing bridges over the Mississippi River, and the consequences. With 90 road and rail bridges spanning the huge river, downing a handful would disrupt cross-country transport for an indefinite period. And if such a contingency was spelled out in an official report mindful of security, imagine what professional terrorists must be thinking.[20]

The energy sector covers power generation and distribution as well as storage and exploration for energy. Al Qaeda has listed the power grid as a priority target. And, as U.S., Mexican, and Canadian grids are interconnected, the clever terrorist could operate north or south of the border with effect.

Banking and finance are the nation's lifeblood. Here, disruption can also be clever. With some trillion dollars invested in largely unregulated "hedge funds" (a hedge fund bets on the value of some commodity or investment either rising or declining, and wins or loses on the outcome), there is much mischief to be made. In 1998, a little-known hedge fund in Connecticut called Long-Term Capital Management bet about a billion dollars on Russian debt, and lost. Given that it was leveraged by at least 100 to one—meaning that every dollar invested obligated an additional hundred dollars—and probably a great deal more, the impact of its collapse threatened the entire international financial system to cover its losses. Seventeen large and powerful banks were investors. Each had to pay billions to cover the losses. The point is that to a sophisticated person, this form of warfare (that is, manipulating the outcomes of these bets) offers a huge opportunity for disruption.[21]

The last sector in the study was vital human services. Water supplies, emergency and health services, post and mail, and routine government services such as social security and unemployment checks are all part of this group. Al Qaeda has listed water supplies as a priority target. Introducing poisons and viruses or diseases is difficult to do effectively. But polluting water with chemicals and other dangerous materials would be hugely disruptive, not only because of public health but also due to cleanup and remediation.

Three other areas of vulnerability are noteworthy: food (including milk); paper; and GPS (global positioning system). Poisoning or attacking food supplies is not new: The Germans tried to infect U.S. cattle with anthrax during World War I. Milk would be an ideal candidate for attack. If toxic materials could be placed on paper supplies, then newspapers, money, mail, and even toilet paper would become possible carriers. The effect on any society of contaminated paper would be profound. Finally, while it is probably years before terrorists will have the ability to jam or affect GPS, such an attack would have enormous disruptive influence.

The Shift in Strategic Damage Paradigms

There is a critical point to consider: the shift in damage paradigms, a further conclusion from the discipline of strategic analysis. Natural disasters have always occurred. However, the prospect of nuclear war is only six decades old.

During the Cold War, East and West maintained tens of thousands of nuclear and thermonuclear warheads. The strategy to prevent nuclear war was deterrence; and deterrence meant that even if one side would strike the other first, sufficient nuclear forces were available for a retaliatory strike that would destroy the enemy. Assured destruction meant that in a nuclear war there were not going to be winners and losers, just losers; and that both sides, if there were to be any survivors at all, would at best lose substantial percentages of the population and huge slices of industry and the means of production. Worse, given that plutonium has a half-life of some 24,000 years and was one of the key nuclear explosive elements, death and damage wrought by long-term radiation could have kept civilization from returning to normality for centuries.

Fortunately, only two nuclear weapons have ever been used in anger: on Hiroshima and Nagasaki. During the Cold War, deterrence and the calculus of assured destruction were powerful ingredients to prevent a nuclear war from starting. While metaphors of two scorpions in a bottle were fashionable in the 1960s to describe the standoff in which both adversaries would fatally poison the other in a fight, it turned out that neither superpower had either a mind or a cause to challenge the other to mortal combat. In fact, in retrospect (as will be shown later), the cultural and ideological differences between the United States and the Soviet Union probably extended the Cold War by years.

With the Cold War long over, a different paradigm has replaced assured destruction in the minds of our adversaries. The enemy will be assessed in the next chapter. However, it is clear that al Qaeda and the jihadists understand the power of leverage. Their ideas, ideology, and terror are aimed at disrupting societies and causing as much pain as possible. The costs to the adversary are not high. But the effects on society are huge.

The threat or use of terrorism targets the vast vulnerability of our societies, in order to disrupt and damage our way of life. The prospect of eternally removing shoes and jackets in airports is a small indicator of how effective these disruptive tactics are in generating long-term or permanent effects. As these groups metastasize into truly capable organizations, they will adopt more sophisticated methods of maximizing disruption and pain.

Osama bin Laden did not appreciate the extent of the West's vulnerability to disruption prior to September 11. The assumption was that the Twin Towers in New York and the Pentagon and presumably Congress and the White House in Washington, D.C. were the most symbolic of targets. Attacking and hitting them was the strongest political signal al Qaeda could send. It is probable that bin Laden did not think the towers would collapse. Standing as burned-out hulks would be constant reminders of al Qaeda's reach. Nor did al Qaeda appreciate how much economic damage would be achieved by those attacks and the subsequent disruption each caused. Finally, just as Japan was shocked by America's reaction to Pearl Harbor, bin Laden probably assumed that the U.S. response to September 11 would have been a continuation of the Clinton administration's "tit for tat" policy and not an outright assault on Afghanistan and the overthrow of the Taliban. Al Qaeda learned its lessons quickly.

The Internet has become the ubiquitous command, control, and information system for the jihadists. Although an exact figure is difficult to compile, there are probably some 4,000 different Web sites that claim to be, or are, al Qaeda–related. On them are posted vast amounts of information and instruction. The March 11, 2004 and July 7, 2005 attacks in Madrid and London were planned using instructions on the Internet. The current priorities listed for attack on these Internet Web sites are transportation (and Madrid and London were cases in point), electric power distribution and grids, and water supplies and related infrastructure. More on how jihadists employ the Internet follows in the next chapter. The point is that manuals, plans, maps, and other essential material for organizing and conducting all manner of attacks is readily available. In some cases, the means of transmitting this material is more effective and efficient than how the United States military organizes its war and operational planning, and surely more accessible.

How Vulnerable Is Vulnerable?

The attacks of September 11 did not reveal the full extent of the nation's vulnerability. A well-planned, well-executed surprise attack is virtually impossible to stop. The Washington/Baltimore snipers who terrorized the capital region with random shootings around Christmas 2003 demonstrated how easily it was for two men to induce panic, and raised the specter of what teams of trained snipers could achieve if they were dispersed to dozens of locales such as malls and shopping centers.

Over the past decade there have been literally hundreds of commissions and associated vulnerability assessments of America's infrastructure. The most effective—if not the only—example of how vulnerability assessment led to effective response was the so-called "Y2K" (Year 2000) problem. Many have forgotten the damage that was about to be caused at midnight January 1, 2000 by computers not programmed to shift from 1999 to 2000. Every conceivable system and piece of infrastructure dependent on computers was susceptible to failure, from traffic lights and railroad signals to the international banking and financial system.

The global response was serious and well coordinated. As far as anyone knows, no major damage related to Y2K computer problems was reported. Either the extraordinary action or a greatly exaggerated problem was the reason for this success. But the formation of the Department of Homeland Security, the reorganization of the intelligence community, and hundreds of billions of dollars spent withstanding, there has been nothing else in any of these other fields approaching the Y2K response. It is not difficult to understand why. Y2K was a global threat engaging government, civilian, business, and industrial sectors. Each had to work. The private sector understood.

The Global War on Terror is very much still undeclared by Congress, although purists will observe that funding approval is itself tacit endorsement, along with the resolution authorizing force passed by Congress. However, the public has not been called to arms. There is, and will be, no draft, and no "Rosie the Riveters" are replacing men on assembly lines so they can go off to fight the war.

Nor has the private sector been asked to do anything out of the ordinary. At the state, local, and corporate levels, security is a much higher priority, judging from how buildings now require identification, and police as well as the public are far more observant of out-of-the-ordinary events. Yet, there has not been a well-coordinated, orchestrated response by government similar to that in Y2K. One wonders whether that was a failure of leadership, or a danger so massive that, absent an overt declaration of war and mobilization of the public, it was not conducive to lesser solutions.

The Magnitude of the Problem

Before returning to the real and perceived vulnerabilities of the United States, understanding a few of the foundations of any effective remedial and preventive solutions is important. In 2003, a major study was launched on the vulnerability of the Port of New York and New Jersey. The aim was to assess the strengths and weaknesses of the current and planned organization to cope with disaster and disruption and to make appropriate corrective recommendations.[22]

Three observations led to the recommendations, and were dramatically and tragically underscored by the response to Hurricane Katrina. First, three years after September 11, the Department of Homeland Security had failed to issue a national architecture for homeland security, including an emergency response-and-action plan to deal with a broad number of contingencies and crises. Such a plan would have contained standardized rules of engagement and operational doctrine so the federal, state, and local first-responders and emergency response personnel would have a common framework for coordination. Armed with that plan, DHS would then have coordinated with the fifty states and major cities to tailor specific plans unique to each area. No doubt New Orleans would have had the flooding contingency carefully considered.

Second, the absence of coordination between federal, state, and local officials was glaring. In the case of New York and New Jersey, while there were many competent professionals at every level, bureaucratic politics; fights over turf, money, power, and authority; and the lack of any single chain of command and assignment of authority, responsibility, and most importantly accountability severely limited effective and coordinated responses. This is something that the DHS and federal government were derelict in failing to accomplish.

Finally and inconceivably, there is still no electronic or fiber backbone and emergency communications system to link local first-responders with city, state, and federal assets. This is not a matter of technology or bandwidth. Most youngsters are connected by Blackberry and E-mail with dozens of friends and routinely communicate that way (rather than in face-to-face communications, a new social phenomenon with interesting and still-unpredictable consequences). And the existence of long-life batteries and hand-powered electrical generators (not dissimilar to the ones we took on patrol in Vietnam forty years ago, for exactly the same reasons) belies the excuse that in a crisis, electrical power almost certainly would be lost.

In the face of real dangers and threats to the nation, September 11 should have shocked the United States out of its complacency and false sense of security. Since then, hundreds of billions, if not trillions, of dollars were spent to ostensibly protect the nation against terror. The Department of Homeland Security was created. Intelligence was supposedly reformed. Americans were assured that better means were in place to deal with disasters, whether imposed by terrorists or nature.

Then came Katrina. The response of government at all levels was not merely "unacceptable," in President Bush 43's words: It was *derelict*. The reflexive question was: How did this happen? But the more important question is whether this failure unmasks a political system that is no longer capable of its most sacred obligation, that of protecting its citizens. No one is asking this question. And if the answer was yes, would anyone pay attention?

A few observations are important. Even if the nation was perfectly organized, the catastrophic consequences and full destructive might of a Category 4 or 5 hurricane can never be contained. The legions of individual acts of compassion, charity, and courage that occurred reflected our better angels. And, in crisis, many things simply go wrong. But these are not excuses for a system of government that failed in coping with Katrina.

When Katrina hit, as mentioned, four years had elapsed since the Twin Towers were struck. Four years after Pearl Harbor, the United States was preparing to celebrate Christmas 1945. The war in Europe had been over for seven months; the war in the Pacific for three. From a standing start, America had mobilized a military of twelve million and defeated enemies who had conquered a substantial portion of the globe. So, how does America's post–September 11 performance compare with that war?

After three years of life, the Department of Homeland Security had only just completed a national response-and-preparation plan to deal with terrorist attack and—one presumes—natural disasters such as Katrina. But coordination and communications between and among first-responders and local, state, and federal officials and offices are missing in action. Indeed, it appeared that the department's leadership ignored that plan as well as the National Incident Management System that had been put in place to deal with disasters. And no electronic or fiber backbone has yet been put in place to link officials at all levels with the capacity to talk and exchange information on a rapid and reliable basis.

Homeland Security Secretary Michael Chertoff claimed that as late as Thursday of that horrible week after Katrina hit, Louisiana officials had not informed him of the use of the Superdome as a refugee center. Part of the problem was confusing the Superdome and the Convention Center and not appreciating both were being used for emergency shelters. Perhaps the department ought to be provided with a few more television sets, as virtually no one in America watching this crisis unfold was unaware of the hopeless conditions at the Superdome or the Convention Center.

Frustration on the part of the Army and National Guard units over the absence of local leadership and anyone in charge was palpable and often turned into fury, as frequently reported by the media. Tensions between local, state, and federal officials were understandable but should have been anticipated long in advance. And where was local and state government in taking preventive steps years earlier, from asserting more forcefully the need to strengthen the levees and flood-protection capabilities guarding New Orleans, to understanding that over a hundred thousand of its residents lacked cars in which to flee an impending disaster? The Louisiana Congressional delegation may have a great deal to answer for. And if it turns out that those members of Congress did their jobs and Congress would or could not act in advance to fund protective measures, then that body must be held accountable.

The remedial actions are obvious:

- First, the president must order the Department of Homeland Security to broaden its focus, from merely battling terrorism to coping with disruption and disaster irrespective of cause.
- Second, DHS must be given a specified time, say sixty days, to coordinate disaster planning at the state level and at least with the largest 25 cities in the country.
- Third, the White House adviser for homeland security must be directed to develop a plan within, say, sixty days to eliminate the lack of coordination and communication among all levels of government, and be given a year to implement it with exercises and tests to ensure compliance.
- Fourth, an electronic and fiber backbone to link first-responders with

state and federal agencies through an emergency communications system must be created and installed within a year.

Interestingly, none of these steps has been taken to date. In the 9/11 Commission's final report, issued on December 5, 2005, the blunt conclusion was that the United States was still not sufficiently prepared to deal with disaster. The Commission specifically noted the failure to share information across agencies and the lack of interoperable communications among first-responders as problem areas requiring immediate action. The fault line returns to the dysfunctional nature of government. Surely no public official wishes future failure. But the lack of accountability and the absence of authority still have not been corrected. Americans should be outraged. Yet, what has happened? The answer is not enough.

America the Exposed and the Psychology of Vulnerability

All societies are vulnerable to disruption, whether by man or by nature. Nor is terror a new weapon and danger. The Indian Wars of the eighteenth and nineteenth centuries saw plenty of terror on both sides. And terrorist attacks are not a post–September 11 phenomenon.

At the end of the nineteenth century, world leaders were at great risk of assassination. William McKinley and Teddy Roosevelt were both shot, the former fatally. The killing of Archduke Ferdinand of Austria–Hungary in July 1914 lit the fuse that exploded in World War I. During that war, as stated earlier, German agents tried (and failed) to infect American cattle with anthrax.

In 1919–20, a rash of bombings aimed at judges and captains of industry, including J. P. Morgan and Henry Ford, injured no one and induced a national panic. The attorney general of the day, Mitchell Palmer, had about five hundred Americans taken into custody without charge. All were released, and the perpetrators were never found. To deal with this wave of terror, Palmer assigned a young Justice official named J. Edgar Hoover to form a bureau of investigation, the precursor to the FBI, to hunt down the bombers. Hoover failed in his charge, but the FBI flourished.

Homegrown American terrorists are not unique. For decades, the KKK was a terrorist organization operating against blacks, Jews, and other minorities. Snipers have held out in bell towers. In 1982, someone still unknown placed cyanide in Tylenol bottles that were sold over the counter throughout much of the nation; several died as a result. In 1995, Timothy McVeigh blew up the Alfred P. Murrah Building in Oklahoma City, killing 168 innocent civilians. The self-styled "unabomber," Ted Kaczynski, sent his letter bombs through the post until he was apprehended. So there has been plenty of experience with homegrown terrorists.

With the experience of the Cold War and the natural safety of two ocean barriers, Americans could believe that terror was "over there." Nightly television images of the latest horrific terrorist episode, from car bombings in Israel and Israeli Defense Force–targeted assassinations of suspected Palestinian terrorist leaders, to the Chechen assaults on Russians, to many other outrages, were viewed by Americans without much fear and trepidation of that happening here, no matter what our history should have told us. September 11 profoundly changed that emotional and psychological calculus.

Intuitively—and no matter how bizarre the Homeland Security Department's threat-level condition at home was judged, or its directions for Americans to buy enough duct tape and plastic to cordon off an airtight room just in case a WMD attack were announced—Americans did not take the danger seriously. Little was really done, and relatively few households have emergency evacuation plans or supplies as occasionally happened in the 1950s and 1960s when Civil Defense was created to contend with a Soviet nuclear strike. Even then, bomb shelters and the mantra taught in every grade and high school of "duck and cover" were not taken all that seriously except by a few.

Americans have an almost schizophrenic reaction to terror. On the one hand, there is very real concern about terrorist attacks, made more so by constant government and daily news reminders of the dangers, from security screening in airports to office buildings. On the other hand, there is a sense of complacency. Unfortunately, government, irrespective of the party in control, will attempt to override complacency by often exaggerating the threat.

The London transport bombings of July 7, 2005 provide an interesting insight into public psychology. The scrappy British, in the tradition of the Blitz, turned their stiffest upper lips to the bombings and went about their business undaunted. Then, only days later, a second wave of bombings hit. No civilians were killed, other than a hapless Brazilian civilian brutally gunned down in error by the Special Police, who must have panicked or were so untrained as to be incompetent. That a second attack could happen so quickly was a massive shock to the system, in many ways more so than the first. In the first attack, that three of the suicide bombers were British-born Muslim citizens, the fourth naturalized, seemed inconceivable. These two points went a long way toward making the average Briton a great deal more worried about the proximity of terror, and made government passage of the Anti-Terror Bill easier despite a revolt by Labor backbenchers against the Prime Minister's recommendation for a ninety-day period of detention without recourse to judicial review.

What Americans must understand is that the United States will exist in a near-permanent state of vulnerability until such a time that terror is no longer a threat. This is not a new condition. From the first colonists to the pioneers who moved west, life was filled with danger. Disease, famine, droughts, floods, storms, hot and cold weather, wild animals, Indians, and dozens of other life-threatening forces had to be overcome. That was one reason for people to have large families, so that some children would survive.

Unless and until Americans recognize that complete and total security are no longer possible, we can never be secure. A major psychological shift in thinking must take place, and it must start with education and understanding. More will be said about education and understanding later, in the conclusions and recommendations.

But Let's Not Overreact

Two directly opposed conclusions define future direction for shaping policy and attitudes. First, Americans must face up to an inescapable fact: Society is entirely vulnerable to massive disruption if the attacker is clever, capable, ruthless, and lucky enough. Such disruption need not entail the use of WMD; taking out part of the power grid for a considerable length of time; shutting down bridges or major transportation routes; and infusing major viruses that incapacitate computers and information systems on a massive basis will do tremendous damage. Even anonymous threats are sufficient to disrupt. In the current environment, few officials would dismiss a warning phone call, E-mail, or message that a bridge was mined or viruses had been planted in information systems.

Second, in contrast, Americans must get over the fear of vulnerability. FDR said that the only thing we have to fear is fear itself. We need a hard-headed understanding of the dangers, not to overreact to them. Take WMD. Here strategic analysis applies.

The prospect of a nuclear weapon detonating in an American city is a national nightmare. The prospect of anthrax or smallpox or some other outbreak of a possibly incurable disease is just as chilling. And chemical or radiological attack is the third leg of WMD.

But the simple fact that these prospects are frightening and are the stuff of movies and novels is no reason to overreact. Terrorists could conceivably obtain a nuclear weapon, although from whom is unclear. It is exceedingly unlikely that these groups will have the technical capacity to build a bomb for a long time to come, if ever.

As far as is known, none of the other nuclear powers (Britain, France, India, Pakistan, Russia, China, and Israel) has any reason to provide terrorists with a weapon. North Korea and Iran may or may not have nuclear weapons. Why either would wish to provide a weapon to a terrorist group is not clear either, as most weapons can be traced to owners; if a North Korean or Iranian bomb were used by al Qaeda or a similar group, Pyongyang and Tehran would be ground zero for a response. Surely that is the view from Ankara to Tel Aviv and beyond.

While designing a nuclear weapon can be done following instructions downloaded from the Internet, engineering a working weapon requires incredible sophistication. Terrorists beyond jihadists possess neither the skill nor the technical tools. Building a dirty bomb is easier, as it merely has to spread the contaminated material. But highly enriched uranium and especially plutonium, the explosive sources for a nuclear bomb, are incredibly dangerous and require precise handling. Terrorist organizations, despite what you see in the movies, do not possess these skills and are unlikely to find them for some time to come.[23]

Weaponizing chemical and biological agents likewise requires technical skills. It is true that if one can make beer, one can make biological weapons. But putting those in an effective and usable form, as Saddam learned, is not easy. The point is that what we need here and now is a rigorous examination of the real dangers and likelihood of danger.

Having suggested a practical assessment of vulnerability, the magnitude of a nuclear calamity requires careful vigilance and preventive action, irrespective of the likelihood of attack. As the military plans for a major conventional war, the United States must prepare for this form of attack. By implementing a national response plan, ensuring coordination among federal, state, and local responders and creating an emergency communications system, much of the foundation will be put in place for dealing with future disaster. Of course, there will be no easy or simple solutions to the balance between investing for public health and natural disease and for biological attack. Preparing for the latter clearly reduces resources for the former. The public must be kept informed of the realities and likelihoods of these kinds of attack and not led to panic or undue alarm by the threat of the unknown.

Finally, who is in charge? That is the scariest question of all and gets to the heart of the dysfunctionality of government. The answer is: no one.

The problem, however, with crying "wolf" is that, at some stage, a wolf must be produced. Along with other security checks such as Project VISIT, a photographing and fingerprinting of foreign visitors arriving at air and sea ports, the United States created the image abroad of becoming, if not an armed camp, then one preoccupied with stopping terrorists. The general criticism was that these measures were incomplete. There was no way to continue delaying or canceling air flights indefinitely without paying a huge price in lost tourism and business or through retaliation by other countries. Indeed, VISIT did not check foreign visitors from over two dozen friendly states and would not have caught shoe-bomber Richard Reeves.

The impact of these security actions on protecting America will become clearer only over time. However, if the object of America's adversaries is to terrorize, they did so merely by threat. In cost-exchange terms, for the equivalent of a few intercepted e-mails and phone conversations that cost at best a few dollars, the United States incurred, and incurred on others, millions if not hundreds of millions of dollars of expense. Those expenses are only likely to grow, and the cost-exchange ratio is not in our favor.

The Global War on Terror provides to the terrorists a huge advantage in imposing costs, if they are clever enough to exploit that leverage. If it cannot be proven that attacks were prevented and at least a few terrorists apprehended, the psychological and political backlash will also be costly. Indeed, America's credibility is at stake. Prudence and caution are understandable and justifiable. When used to excess or wrongly exercised for purposes of political expediency, public sentiment will grow negative. Instead of advancing the war on terror, improperly applied precautions will have the opposite effect, making the United States leadership look feeble, worried, and uncertain of how to deal with the danger in effective ways. That possibility too must be eliminated.

The Enemy from Without

WHEN THE SOVIET UNION IMPLODED, Georgi Arbatov, the peripatetic director of the USA–Canada Institute in Moscow and one of the USSR's true *cognoscenti* regarding relations with America, quipped: "What will you do, now that we have taken the enemy away from you?" In those days, even if the USSR had been an enigma wrapped in a riddle, as Churchill put it (and Russia certainly was not), gaining a good understanding of the Soviet Union and the nature of that enemy could be accomplished. Why relatively few Americans succeeded in this endeavor is covered in a later chapter. Hence, there are two sets of questions that must be answered.

First, does the United States, driven by its culture and penchant for crusade and often contaminated by the damaging forms of political partisanship, really need a permanent enemy around which to rally the nation? Or is the United States now mature enough to face the world without requiring the presence of an evil foe to contain its passion for crusade and the centrifugal properties of government? If the answer to the first question is yes, must that enemy be characterized as evil, and demonized accordingly to make the danger sufficiently clear-and-present, so as to persuade a skeptical public to rally 'round the flag and the banner of patriotism?

Second, irrespective of whether or not America needs a permanent enemy, do we as a nation have the collective capacity to understand the nature and intent of the current foe? Or have culture, crusade, and partisanship become impenetrable barriers and obstacles to that end? If the answer to understanding is no, what can be done to reverse that fault?

Regarding long-term evil enemies, the Nazis and the Soviets nicely filled the bill. And, after September 11, Osama bin Laden and Islamic terrorists more than adequately became the current embodiments of evil incarnate. Using terms like "axis of evil" and "evil ones," the Bush 43 administration rammed home the idea of doing battle against what was not merely wrong, but also morally repugnant, made so by taking the lives of innocent civilians. The misjudgment is that this simplistic demonization completely missed the reasons and motives that caused individuals to take up terror and suicide as the means of achieving political ends. Hence, irrespective of the need for a permanent enemy, understanding the adversary is made far more difficult. Many of the reasons why the United States failed to get the WMD issue right in Iraq apply to deficiencies in understanding the real nature of the threat and thus the ability to take appropriate action.

This failure to understand may indeed be an inseparable part of our culture. We tend to be so conditioned by such a uniquely American perspective that, as foreign objects are rejected by the body, attitudes and realities that do not conform with our general thinking and perceptions are treated in a similar fashion. The reaction to September 11 demonstrates this argument. Americans find it impossible to understand who would carry out such a heinous attack against innocents and who would be prepared to die in the process. Such actions are not within our intellectual universe to understand, let alone share.

There are plausible and probably accurate explanations that offer insight into what motivated al Qaeda and the perpetrators to undertake those acts, with nineteen men committing suicide in the process. These are discussed below. However, even in discussions with serious and informed people about suicide and martyrdom, a combination of incredulity and reluctance to accept these explanations usually keeps those conversations brief. As a result, Americans dismiss or do not understand the basic reasons that explain why our adversaries are prepared to commit suicide in the taking of what we see as innocent lives and what their aims are. Hence, formulating an effective counterstrategy is rendered more difficult by this absence of understanding, which is therefore a huge fault line in our strategic thinking processes.

An overwhelming sense of humiliation and desperation, and a cultural and religious bias to regard jihad and martyrdom as the noblest of acts, form the root causes for these individuals. The sources of humiliation have other grounds that are explained below. Martyrdom parallels Japanese conduct during World War II, when suicidal banzai and kamikaze attacks were relatively common tactics. Fleet Admiral Chester Nimitz, who commanded U.S. naval forces in the Pacific during that war, emphasized this point obliquely when, in looking back at all the battles, he observed that the only thing Americans did not anticipate in advance was the kamikazes. The notion was too foreign to be accepted. Yet the danger was clear, present, and deadly.

Who Is the Enemy, and Is "Enemy" Even the Right Term?

The word "enemy" usually connotes someone with whom differences and grievances are so great and passionate that war, whether hot or cold, is a distinct possibility. "Enemy" often implies hatred and a condition of intense mutual hostility that often leads to visceral and emotional, rather than rational and dispassionate, responses.

It is vital to understand what motivates enemies (as well as friends and uncommitted states) in order to derive effective means of response and determine whether or not war and force of arms are the only—or best—alternative. Given the association of "enemy" with what Americans see as truly evil, as opposed to those who merely disagree or dissent with our policies or are prepared to use violence to achieve their ends, perhaps in today's world the United States should drop the use of the word "enemy." After all, with whom is war very likely? "Adversary," "rival," or even "unfriendly" are better terms. And to the degree that dispassionate and highly rational thinking are essential to achieving one's aims, removing the sense of hatred and other equally charged emotions is important.

The phrase "Global War on Terror" should be considered in a similar light. The fact is that this is not a war on terror. Terror, like disease, poverty, drugs, and injustice—against which other "wars" were waged, with marginal success—is a tool and a tactic. Regarding our adversaries who are engaged in a battle of ideas and ideologies, we face a struggle far broader in scope and width.

During the long Vietnam War, North Vietnam was the prime "enemy," and "evil" at that. The ruthless tactics of its principal ally in the south, the Vietcong, employed terror and torture to intimidate and coerce many innocent civilians. The 400-some American pilots shot down and captured over the North were treated brutally. And, from the ideological perspective, the "evil" was communism, which, if not stopped at the Mekong, would spread to the Mississippi.

The truth was far different. The war was about nationalism and unification of two halves of the same state, not the triumph of communism. It took too long for most Americans to understand the truth, a truth that was far from invisible.

Today, North Korea and Iran are not necessarily enemies, even though both were consigned to the "axis of evil" by President Bush 43 and are now the only surviving members. Yes, there could be war on the Korean peninsula. And if Iran pursues a nuclear-weapons program, no doubt the prospect of sanctions and more than a hint of military action will follow. However, the notion of "enemy," reminiscent of the Cold War and possibly the lesson of the 1938 Munich agreement (i.e., that appeasement never works), restricts or prevents the use of diplomatic and political solutions. It also is too closely associated with hatred and hence risks a bias toward emotionally driven responses.

Cuba and Venezuela are not enemies in the true sense of the word, even though we have profound differences and difficulties with both. Aside from an oil embargo, neither is in much of a position to do much real harm to the United States (although some would argue that President Hugo Chavez might see it in his interest to destabilize the region). The argument that the best way to depose Castro is to recognize Cuba is unfortunately rendered impossible by Cuban–American political clout in Florida and by the refusal by Republicans and Democrats to strike a bolder stance for fear of offending voters in what was and is a critical swing state in national elections, 2000 in particular. Nations normally associated with us such as France and Germany, who disagree with American policies particularly regarding Iraq, should be not be regarded as enemies nor consigned to ignominy on the basis of those differences when both are hugely important allies. And China is not an enemy, at least not yet.

Unsurprisingly, jihadist extremists are declared our avowed enemies, and we are obviously engaged in a fierce battle with them. Yet the term "enemy" is used too promiscuously, along with the slogan "Global War on Terror." But consider one glaring contradiction that alone repudiates the notion of a "Global War on Terror": Who is the terrorist?

In fighting this global war on terror, there are very real distinctions between and among "terrorists." Members of the IRA, Red Brigades, Basques, Chechens, and Tamil Tigers, to name a few, are terrorists. But the United States had not declared war against all of them. The reason was that these groups were not "international" terrorists; their terror was confined to a specific state and its citizens. Rarely did it cross borders, and these groups were not directing violence at the United States. Some would argue that this definition is a distinction without a difference. The significant difference was simply that none of these organizations had directly targeted America.[24] So what is this "Global War on Terror" really about, and why should its name not reflect that purpose?

The battle against the jihadists is a war of ideas, ideologies, and ambitions. So why are these so-called terrorists the "enemy"? What makes them that? And what motivates them? Strategic analysis is crucial here, to understand why individuals and groups oppose the United States to the point where terror and suicide bombing are the *modus operandi* and, from our perspective, the taking of life is done indiscriminately and without any regard of harming "innocent" men, women, and children.

To most Americans, and reflecting our culture, the jihadists are enemies because they attacked first, well before September 11, and because they lack any kind of moral compass in using indiscriminate terror to kill and maim. The October 1983 bombing of the Marine (and later French) barracks in Beirut was the work of Hezbollah, a terrorist organization with deep roots in Iraq. The first attempt at the World Trade Center in 1993, followed by the wave of bombing attacks against Khobar Towers in Saudi Arabia in 1996, U.S. embassies in Africa in 1998, and the USS *Cole* in 2000—these were all the work of Islamic terrorists. The culminating event was September 11.

As President Bush 43 originally made his case, "the terrorists hate us and our democratic values." They were out to harm and kill as many Americans as possible. And note the emphasis on hate. What better definition of "enemy" than those intent on destroying America and the American Dream? But as with many simple definitions, the problem is more complex.

For the moment, then, from a strategic, political, and ideological view, the enemy is Islamic extremism and extremists, those who use religion as the means for demagogues to rally converts and zealots to wield bombs and weapons against all infidels, on the grounds of establishing some form of caliphate or fundamentalist Islamic order as Iran has done. But this is a very incomplete analysis. And it neglects other potential enemies, from organized crime, drug cartels, and freelance homegrown terrorists such as Timothy McVeigh to the still-unknown perpetrators of the anthrax letters in the fall of 2001.

Tectonic changes are sweeping across the globe, changing the old order and more than occasionally creating violence and chaos. Beyond these realities, the United States must recognize that when adversaries or friends oppose us, there may be good reasons that explain why. Understanding those reasons is essential in creating an effective strategy to compensate for, or overcome, those differences. As we will see, al Qaeda and the jihadists have reasons and grievances that gave rise to their call to arms. We may be in no position to rectify any of those grievances, nor might we have any cause to do so. However, as Sun Tzu opined thousands of years ago, a commander's first duty is to know the enemy. We do not.

What Motivates "Terrorists" and Revolutionaries?

This strategic analysis begins by answering the question: What motivates terrorists and revolutionaries? Many reasons and explanations emerge. In some cases, the nihilism of destroying the existing order is sufficient. This was the case that drove many anarchists to arms and suicide in the latter part of the nineteenth century.

But political motivations are more powerful forces. In most revolutions and insurgencies, political forces are the root cause of the movements. The American Revolution is a case in point. Americans first rebelled over excessive, unjust, and arbitrary tariffs and taxes imposed on the colonies by London without any recourse, rebuttal, or indeed opportunity to exercise political rights as Englishmen, which the colonists still were then. Grievances were over sovereignty, self-government, and political disfranchisement, exacerbated by the economic and psychological costs of a long series of progressively harsher restrictive, expensive, and punitive laws and taxes imposed by London without consultation.[25] And, of course, power and control, as well as oppression and harsh inequality, are highly motivating forces for revolution and political change.

Lenin and the Bolsheviks were similarly motivated by the injustices of the Tsar and the ambition to impose a new, more equitable, and ideally better political order for mankind, based on communism and a classless society. Ideology and idealism offered the hope of a better world, a dream common to many if not all political visions and promises. Lacking, in its early stages, an army with which to battle the existing regime, revolutionaries used the most obvious and available weapon: terror.

Lenin expressed the resort to terror vividly and simply. The purpose of terror, he opined, was to terrify. Through terror and disruption come the means for exerting sufficient leverage to crack the fault lines of any political order. And once that order is destroyed, perhaps a new one will emerge.

Hitler based much of the National Socialist vision on the humiliation and despair of losing World War I and on the painful reparations that crippled German economic recovery. Desperation and hopelessness are key ingredients for revolutions and terror and for using grievances as the argument for redefining the nature of power and politics and who is in charge. And, of course, the evil genius in Hitler's scheme was to seize power legally through the existing political structure and the ballot box.

While motivations vary and nationalism and a sense of patriotism are powerful, terrorists and revolutionaries usually have some broader political purposes. These purposes are usually derived from perceived inequality, humiliation, and isolation from the decisions and policies that will have profound effect on their lives.

Reading the Web sites of many Islamic groups, the grievances that are cited to motivate and rationalize jihad are easy to identify. In general, these grievances contain most or all of the following causes that, in the Muslim world, explain why American policy is disliked and opposed, even by so-called moderates. From them arise major demands, including the end of U.S. aid to Israel; the elimination of the Jewish state and replacement with an Islamic Palestinian one; withdrawal of Western forces from Muslim territory; restoration of Muslim control over energy; replacement of U.S.-protected Muslim regimes that do not govern according to Islam; and the end of U.S. support in the oppression of Muslims by Russian, Chinese, Indian, and other governments in conducting the so-called global war on terror. For others, such as the Jordanian-born and leading Sunni insurgent in Iraq, Abu Mus'ab al-Zarqawi, infidels include Shia Muslims. Hence, war against infidels is legitimate under this bizarre interpretation of Islam.

Too often, Americans reject or ignore the notion of grievances and humiliation as key motivational factors, choosing to allow a messianic and crusading view of the enemy to dominate judgment. Furthermore, most Americans do not have even a general understanding of Islam or any comprehension of why individuals become suicide bombers. The cultural gaps are simply too wide.

At the top of the extremist hierarchy, Osama bin Laden and his number two, Ayman al-Zawahiri, are driven and probably obsessed by the burning ambition to change society. In that sense, bin Laden and al-Zawahiri may differ little from Lenin and Hitler in their revolutionary intent. Afghanistan, under Soviet control, was the test bed for waging a war to defeat the infidel, in this case a full-fledged superpower. Fighting alongside the Mujahadeen, bin Laden saw how effective the jihadist strategy, driven by Salafist ideology and ideas, expelled the oppressor and put in its place a fundamentalist Islamic regime in the form of perhaps the even more oppressive Taliban. Of course, the Mujahadeen were amply aided by the United States, principally with the Stinger missile that inflicted enormous pain on the Soviets.

Although from a family of enormous wealth, the tall and thinly built bin Laden was not a favored son. His early years were spent with his mother in a sheltered upbringing. Returning to Saudi Arabia flush with a success in Afghanistan that exceeded any logical expectation of forcing the Soviets to fail, bin Laden found himself ignored, excluded, and disfranchised by the Saudi princes. Reportedly, bin Laden petitioned the ruling family for permission to move to Iraq and topple Saddam. Whether he had a real plan or not, the idea was summarily rejected. However, for reasons of frustration or revenge, bin Laden concluded that the conservative and Wahabi Saudi leadership was the enemy and had to be replaced.

The motivating forces for the subsequent leaders and elite of al Qaeda and other extremist groups reflected similar passion. Political ambitions and the aim of establishing some form of a fundamentalist regime loyal to a strict and extreme interpretation of Islam dominated the thinking of these individuals. For some, restoration of the caliphate of the eighth century was the goal. For others, the aim was global: radicalizing into a worldwide Islamist state the 1.3 billion Muslims who were spread from the west coast of Africa to the eastern tip of Indonesia. But the diversity of Islam, both regionally and in actual practice of the faith, made this global vision unachievable, much as Soviet communism completely failed in turning its international ambitions into reality.

For the foot soldiers of jihadism, the motivations are more mundane. Desperation, humiliation, and hopelessness are principal reasons. Grievances date back two centuries to Napoleon's conquest of Egypt and the ensuing decades when European colonialism subjugated many Muslim lands. The Salafist movement was created and motivated by these external crusaders and infidel occupiers. Today, "enemy" occupation of Arab and Islamic homelands, from Gaza and the West Bank to Iraq, are prominent sources of humiliation and desperation.

There is no "average" jihadist. But there is a general profile. Within Arab and Islamic states, the jihadist is usually from a relatively good family, at least middle class. Educated, the individual has probably been recruited by friends and less so by family ties. Rare is the free agent who is a walk-in recruit. Security is too important, and vetting, such as it exists, probably goes back to the recruit's early adulthood. The United States and much of the West tend to ignore the compelling power of humiliation, desperation, and hopelessness in inspiring and motivating adherents of jihad.

Consider a young male in the Arab world or in an Islamic state. Probably unemployed (Egypt, Iraq, and the Maghreb) and certainly underemployed, well educated, humiliated, and disfranchised from obtaining a good job or access to the political system (Saudi Arabia and Egypt) and the prospect of joining a more elite level of society, changing the political order ultimately through revolution is a seductive siren's call. The call preaches that there is no higher duty to Islam than serving in a jihad to establish a state faithful to the teachings of the Koran; and that in that struggle, martyrdom is a privilege irrespective of the offer of seventy-two virgins in heaven, given the number of female suicide bombers.

The West simply does not, will not, or cannot grasp the power and the attraction of this message and the appeal it has for many Muslims. In a perverse way, this is an Islamic variant of "ask not what your country can do for you, but what you can do for Islam." While there are no estimates of how many jihadists have taken up the cause, in 2004 the CIA estimated that between 50 and 70 million were likely candidates and—at least—fellow travelers. Given the soaring anti-Americanism in many Islamic states, it would be hard to believe that that number is declining.

Jihadist Extremists

What is in a word? "A great deal," is the answer. Today, terrorists are often called Islamic radicals, Islamic extremists, and even Islamo-fascists. In the summer of 2005, concerned that the phrase "Global War on Terror" was inappropriate to the dangers emanating from radical Islam, the Pentagon trotted out an alternative: the global struggle against violent extremism. Within that same week, President Bush 43 delivered an address in which he specifically mentioned "the Global War on Terror" eleven times. So much for a name change, or at least for coordination between the commander-in-chief and his military establishment. And in the Quadrennial Defense Review (QDR) released in February 2006, the Pentagon continued to classify the enemy as "violent extremists."

Applying any form of the word "Islam" to extremism and radicalism creates an unwanted and unfortunate perception of associating an entire religion with terror, violence, or—as in the phrase "Islamo-fascism"—Nazism. Using the word "jihad" has the downside of its specific reference to "holy war," imputing an unintended legitimacy. My alternative is to call the adversary "jihadist extremists"—that is, those who are perverting Islam with ideologies, ideals, and ideas that are inimical to the teachings of that religion, that are therefore illegitimate, and whose purpose is revolution and overthrow of the existing order.

By the standards of other religions, particularly Judeo-Christian ones, non-extremist practices in Islam regarding the role of women, polygamy, sharia (the religious law) and associated issues fall outside mainstream Western values and accepted social norms. This inherent conflict between forms of conservative and fundamental (but not radical) Islam and Western values will not disappear. As Islam continues to spread, profound and possibly irreconcilable social and legal problems could arise. However, it is religious extremes that are the immediate danger.

Unlike the Nazis, who were always a homogeneous party, because there are many disparate radical groups with competing interests and supporters, no single statement covers the aims, aspirations, and intentions of jihadist extremists. Over time, three conditions can change. First, a great leader or overriding ideology emerges that disciplines the jihadist extremists. Second, as with al Qaeda, loose association of these groups under a general rubric that allows considerable leeway is encouraged or occurs. Third, extremist views are increasingly rejected by the larger Islamic community or, because of failure or internecine conflict, the force behind these groups sputters and dissipates.

The evolution of the Communist Party after World War I is partially suggestive of how jihadist extremism might progress. Russia abounded with revolutionary and extremist parties and splinter groups across many political persuasions. Having seized power, Lenin and then Stalin consolidated control and systematically liquidated the opposition both against and within the CPSU (Communist Party of the Soviet Union). The last great debate turned out to be between socialism in one country (Stalin) and permanent revolution (Trotsky). Stalin, of course, won, and Trotsky's assassination by ax in Mexico in 1940 was the final chapter. Similar homicidal consolidation occurred during World War II during the Warsaw uprising, when Stalin let thousands of Polish communists perish, using the Nazis as the means for liquidating potential opposition. During the Tet Offensive in Vietnam in 1968, Hanoi similarly permitted the Vietcong to be killed by the U.S. military to eliminate potential opposition.

The general vision of jihadists is for a traditional and fundamentalist Islamic regime in the greater Middle East with access to, or control of, Saudi (and Iraqi) oil and Pakistani nuclear weapons. But extremist movements are not yet sufficiently robust or mature to succeed as the Taliban did in Afghanistan. However, these movements possess great patience, a virtue not necessarily shared with the United States. Should a coup or revolution end the Saudi regime in the near term, bin Laden probably presumes that the West would establish some form of protectorate for the oil fields in the eastern provinces, most likely with a local puppet regime in charge. Nuclear weapons in the hands of jihadists would make such an option for the West very dangerous, possibly too much so to undertake.

What happens if—or after—such a jihadist regime forms is an interesting question to examine. At one end of the possibilities, such a regime could be introspective and seek a live-and-let-live arrangement with the West. On the other, ambitions for a true Islamic, global caliphate could produce an activist and aggressive set of expansionist policies that would lead to greater conflict regionally and globally.

Given the revolutionary ambitions of most of the groups, the outcome is likely to favor the latter and not the former. However, from a non-jihadist perspective, a radically driven fundamentalist regime sitting astride the bulk of the world's oil reserves and possibly armed with nuclear weapons in the midst of perhaps the most volatile and potentially explosive region on earth is as close to strategic catastrophe as anyone would wish. And preventing that doomsday scenario from happening must be among the highest priorities of the West, no matter the view on the necessity for invading Iraq.

The mother of all nightmares, of course, is the nuclear question. As this book goes to press, Iran's ambitions for building nuclear weapons could lead to a real crisis. Clearly, the vulnerability of any target to attack—but particularly ones with huge political significance such as Jerusalem, Baghdad, Riyadh, Karachi, and Tehran—clears one's mind. Over time and with the spread of delivery technologies, the target set would stretch to Europe, America, and Southeast Asia. A second frightening scenario outside jihadist threats is whether a confrontation between India and Pakistan could be precipitated in which the Indians saw no other alternative except to pre-empt Islamabad's nuclear capability.

How serious is the potential magnitude of the danger from jihadist extremism? A century ago, as Lenin's communists were one of many radical parties and ideologies trying to remake the map of Europe, no one predicted that the Bolsheviks would be able to seize power in Russia, overthrow the Tsar, and create the Soviet Union. At the end of World War I, Hitler and his nascent National Socialist movement were dismissed. Yet Hitler won through the ballot box and turned Germany into the Third Reich that, at least in his mind, promised to live for a thousand years.

Osama bin Laden is neither Lenin nor Hitler. However, his ideology and vision are, to the properly motivated (and humiliated or desperate) people, not substantially different from Leninism and Nazism. Given that the leaders of the Islamic radical movements are well educated and bright, and with 1.3 billion Muslims to draw from, it is not inconceivable that an able, charismatic leader will emerge. To assume otherwise is to place our fate and future in the laps of the gods.

The Salafi-Wahabi Jumble

Part of the failure to understand what drives jihadist extremism is mirrored by a failure to appreciate the divides among various factions in Sunni Islam, the largest branch of that religion. Ayman al-Zawahiri drove this point home in 2001, proclaiming "Victory for the Islamic movements . . . cannot be attained unless these movements possess an Islamic base in the heart of the Arab region."[26] While calls for reformation of Islam as the means to overcome al Qaeda are fairly common in the West, interestingly, Sunni reformation movements have been active for more than a century. The irony is that these movements, known as Salafist, are antithetical to Western security.

There is a further misperception that the traditional Sunni Wahabi clergy, particularly in Saudi Arabia, is supportive of al Qaeda and provides the ideological basis for the movement. Indeed, the bulk of the Sunni clergy are very much opposed to revolution as defined by the Salafists. And even in Saudi Arabia, with both Wahabis and Salafists, there is a huge split between pro-establishment clerics and the revolutionary groups.

History and contemporary politics are at work. Still unnoticed in the West are the two revolutions sweeping through the Arab and Islamic worlds. Both revolutions are a clash between old and new and between those who wish to impose fundamental change and those who oppose it, favoring the status quo. Politically, within the Arab worlds, democracy is not the driving force. Enfranchisement and access to power are.

In an age of instant communications and few barriers to dissemination of information, within the Arab world increasing numbers of people wish, expect, or demand a stronger say in determining their futures. From the Emirates to Saudi Arabia to Egypt, increasing pressure is being applied to the political leaderships and elites for change. Elections, new to Saudi Arabia and allowing a broader slate of candidates to run for office in Egypt, may or may not reflect these pressures and may simply prove cosmetic. However, in Egypt, the big winner was the Muslim Brotherhood, a onetime radical group that had been outlawed. Should the Brotherhood win power, that by no means would be a step forward for democracy. Whether or not slow progress to greater political involvement will diffuse these forces is the question. However, potentially profound political shifts are in play between those seeking to keep power—the House of Saud and the Mubarak dynasty, to name two—and an increasingly active public.

The second revolution is taking place in Islam. It is complex and diverse. But part of the revolution and those who would impose profound change do not stem from modernists wishing to become latter-day Martin Luthers. Instead, Salafists and radicals are anxious to return

Islam to earlier and more fundamentalist eras. The debate goes back to medieval times.

The Sunni scholar Taqi ad-Din Ahmed ibn Taymiyya (1263–1328) is a starting point for contemporary understanding of revolutionary Salafism. The enemy then was the advancing Mongols, who threatened Egypt. Because the Mongol king had embraced Islam, rallying Muslims behind the Mamluke rulers of Egypt abutted against the strictures preventing waging jihad against fellow Muslims. Ibn Taymiyya reasoned that because Mongol tribal law could persist alongside the sharia, the Koran was disrespected and Mongols were apostates. Today's radical Salafists use that precedent for waging jihad against Muslim rulers who do not impose sharia exclusively and permit other legal codes to persist. Iraq raises an interesting case for the revolutionary Salafists today.

The medieval debate is prologue to the current discussion. The real Salafist movement originated in the late nineteenth and early twentieth centuries. The reform movement, largely Egyptian-based, sprang from the excesses of the Ottoman Empire in repressing the Arabs it controlled and the domination of the West, not only politically but in terms of cultural, trade, and intellectual advances. In fact, British domination of Muslim populations in India and elsewhere, magnified by the superiority of the West to things Islamic, all were profound shocks and distresses to a culture that prior to the eighteenth century regarded itself superior. Interestingly, one of the Ottoman Empire's most stupendous mistakes was to ban the printing press in 1485, on the grounds that mechanical treatment of the language was sacrilegious. Hence, when Napoleon arrived in Egypt in 1798, there were no printing presses, a further factor that enabled the West to establish its superiority.

Jamal as-Din Al-Afghani (1839–97) is considered the father of the modernizing movement in Islam. An Egyptian, Al-Afghani believed that the defeats of Islam and the caliphate by the West were due to the corruption of the Muslim religion, not the more conventional view that Western science and technology simply provided better and more powerful tools that vanquished the Ottomans and others. Al-Afghani's conclusion was that the Muslim problem was theological: corruption had to be replaced with religious revival. In this revival, revolution and revolt were justified.

From Al-Afghani's rationalism, other scholars took note. Muhammed 'Abduh (1849–1905) was one of Al-Afghani's best students and later became the Grand Mufti of Egypt, the first well-known Salafist to make his way into the highest ranks of the clergy. 'Abduh believed that understanding how religion was practiced during the first generations of Islam was the key to revival. He coined the term "salafiah" to cover his teachings.

'Abduh's followers took two different paths. The first applied rationalism to advocate secularism in the Muslim world. These ideas blunted resistance against Arab nationalism and socialism. The other stressed the purity of religion and became the precursors to al Qaeda and the jihadist extremists, who had profoundly different views of Islam and would become violently anti-secular.

Wahabism, a strict Sunni sect, appeared in the 1700s and remained confined to the Arabian Peninsula. In South Asia, the Deobandi and Barelvi movements evolved separately from the Egyptian model. The issue there was quite different. The minority Sunnis had ruled the Mogul Empire (a familiar ring to Saddam and Iraq) until the British imposed direct rule in 1857 following the Sepoy Mutiny, at which time they had to live under the majority Hindi population. These movements espoused building purely Islamic institutions and living wholly Islamic lives, excluding non-Muslim influences. Not until the 1960s did the revolutionary tendencies in South Asia provide the tinder for the incendiary thinking of these Salafist revolutionaries.

Perhaps the most famous of the revolutionary Salafists was Sayyid Qutb (1906–66), an educator and member of the Muslim Brotherhood. Expanding on the notion of jihad against apostate rulers, Qutb called for armed struggle against secular regimes of the Muslim even if the consequence was to kill other Muslims. Qutb was hanged by Nasser in 1966. And the Muslim Brotherhood parted with the Salafist Revolutionaries over the issue of deposing secular Islamic regimes.

Anwar Sadat, who replaced Nasser in 1970, was assassinated by Salafist revolutionaries in 1981. A further crackdown on both the Muslim Brotherhood and the Salafi Revolutionaries followed. In 1979, the Soviet occupation of Afghanistan provided the proving grounds for testing revolutionary Salafist doctrine and strategy, as Spain had been prior to World War II. From the mountains of Afghanistan and Pakistan, bin Laden and al-Zawahiri would make their mark and turn the Salafi creed into a virulent and effective arm of jihadist extremism.

Wahabism followed a different path. Born in the desert, a marriage was forged in 1744 (the Saudi government says 1747) between

Muhammed Bin Saud and Bin Abdul Wahabi, who articulated a strict view of Islam that has carried forward. The common thought today is that Wahabis are responsible for the bulk of terror and the ideological basis for jihadist extremism.

There is little doubt that the Saudis have supported strict views of Islam, in part as a weapon against Israel. Some Wahabis were encouraged to move out of Saudi Arabia so as to reduce the number of potential troublemakers. And Saudis have funded madrassas—religious schools that teach only the Koran and espouse radical and extremist practices within Islam.

A profound difference separates Revolutionary Salafists and Wahabis and the survival needs of the Saudis. The Salafists are out to overthrow the Saudis and what they view as other illegitimate, apostate Islamic regimes. Prior to September 11, the Saudis chose to keep many of the Salafists, as well as more radical Wahabis, outside the kingdom. Since then, there has been a crackdown.

In addition to the various Sunni radical groups, Shia revolutionaries also are powerful and indeed control the Iranian Islamic Republic. Within Iraq, there are divergent groups of Shia. The Badr Brigades, tightly linked with Iran, and local militias such as those loyal to Moqtada al Sadr are competing for power in the south. And the connection with Shia extremists and Hezbollah, a creation of Iran, with the Arab–Israeli–Palestinian conflict shows the complicated interrelationships that exist.

Very few Americans understand, or are even interested in, this history or these relationships and distinctions. As a result, headlines and sound bites often create skewed attitudes and erroneous perceptions. Terror and extremism become lumped together. Distinctions between and within Sunni and Shia groups and relationships vis-à-vis Israel are ignored or entirely missed. The upshot is that the public is largely uninformed of fact and reality. When government does not provide sufficient information and education or enough depth in its statements, intelligent public input is lost. The results are obvious in how policy unfolds; and many crises are made worse or addressed with such half-hearted measures.

Some Frightening Evidence

On November 24, 2002, the full text of what was reported as Osama bin Laden's "letter to America" was published in the *London Observer*. While the authenticity of authorship cannot be verified, the letter conveyed a chilling philosophy, a scathing list of grievances, and a plan of action for the West to respond to the assault on Islam.

The letter asks and answers two fundamental questions. "Why are we [the fundamentalists] fighting and opposing you? What are we calling you to do and what do we want from you?'

The letter asserts that "you attacked us and continue to attack us . . . [and] . . . you attacked Palestine," and claims that the West attacked "us in Somalia; supported the Russian atrocities against us in Chechnya; the Indian oppression against Kashmir and the Jewish aggression against us in Lebanon." "Us" presumably is the world of Islam, not the radical fringes.

The letter then accuses the West and non-believers of specific acts to "steal our oil wealth at paltry prices . . . planning to destroy the Al-Aqsa mosque [in Jerusalem] . . . occupy our countries . . . starved the Muslims of Iraq . . . and are only a few examples . . . of your oppression and aggression."

America comes under specific attack. "You [America] may then dispute that all of the above [i.e., the grievances] does not justify aggression against civilians, for crimes they did not commit and offenses in which they did not partake.

"This argument contradicts your continuous repetition that America is the land of freedom, and its leaders in this world. Therefore the American people are the ones who choose their government of their own free will; a choice that stems from their agreement to its policies. Thus, the American people have chosen, consented to, and affirmed their support for the Israeli oppression of the Palestinians, the occupation and usurpation of their land, and its continuous killing, torture, punishment, and expulsion of the Palestinians. The American people have the ability and choice to refuse the policies of their government and even to change it if they want.

"The American people are the ones who pay the taxes which fund the planes that bomb us in Afghanistan, the tanks that strike and destroy our homes in Palestine, the armies which occupy our lands in the Arabian Gulf and the fleets that ensure the blockade of Iraq. These tax dollars are given to Israel for it to continue to attack us and penetrate our lands. So the American people are the ones who lead the attacks against us, and they are the ones who oversee the expenditure of these monies the way they wish through their elected candidates.

"The American army is part of the American people. It is helping the very same people who are shamelessly helping the Jews fight against us. The American people are the ones who employ both their men and women in the American forces that attack us.

"That is why the American people cannot be innocent of the crimes committed by the Americans and Jews against us" [italics added].

The letter then offers the United States a plan of action to redress these grievances. From an American perspective, the plan is entirely unworkable. However, it does provide good insight into the grievances.

The first step is for America to embrace Islam and benefit from the sereneness and goodness of the "seal of all the previous religions" that guarantees, by the way, "total equality between all people without regard to color, sex, or language." The second is "to stop your oppression, lies, immorality, and debauchery that has spread among you. We call you to be a people of manners, principles, honor, and purity and to reject the immoral acts of fornication, homosexuality, intoxicants, gambling, and trading with interest [i.e., usury]."

Following a blistering critique of America's immoral behavior, the letter continues: "You are a nation that exploits women like consumer products or advertising tools calling customers to purchase them. You use women to serve passengers, visitors, and strangers to increase your profit margins. You then rant and rave that you support the liberation of women. You are a nation that practices the sex trade in all its forms, directly and indirectly. Giant corporations are established under the name of art, entertainment, tourism, and freedom and other deceptive names you attribute to it."

Regarding human rights, the letter notes: "You captured thousands of Muslims and Arabs, took them into custody with neither reason, court trial, nor even disclosing their names. You issued newer, harsher laws.

"What happens in Guantánamo is a historical embarrassment to America and its values, and it screams in your faces—you hypocrites, 'what is the value of your signature on any agreement or treaty'?"

This type of argument is found in most of the writings of contemporary Salafists. In *Knights*, al-Zawahiri made similar arguments. His strategy was not to defeat the United States in direct conflict, which would be impossible. Instead, the tactic was to use spectacular terror attacks to change the conflict by enlisting the support of the Muslim world into a "clear-cut jihad against infidels."

The letter is eerily reminiscent of left-wing rhetorical attacks against the United States. It can be dismissed as no more than that, if one wishes. However, taken in context with the foundations of jihadist extremism and the revolutionary movements within Islam that are Salafist or radical, the language and arguments are important in better understanding the grievances and motivations that are driving these jihadists. From Britain's experience in the American Revolution, one can see that ignoring or downplaying this line of argument comes with considerable risk.

On July 9, 2005, al-Zawahiri sent a letter to Abu Musab al-Zarqawi, who was leading the insurgency in Iraq. Because the Director of National Intelligence (DNI) made the letter public, there is sound reason to respect its authenticity. A Web site used by al-Zarqawi repudiated the letter, and critics cast further doubt on its credibility by citing a possible disinformation tactic by U.S. intelligence or by using the letter as a means of informing the political leadership of the nature of the danger.

Regardless of authenticity, the letter is remarkable for several reasons. First, it argues for a political strategy to shape the outcome. Second, it calls for maintaining popular support, the Shia, until jihadist rule has been achieved. Third, it lays out the steps to be taken "if our goal in this age is the establishment of a caliphate in the manner of the prophet . . . in the heart of the Islamic world."[27]

Quoting directly from the letter, al-Zawahiri notes explicitly:

- The first stage: Expel the Americans.
- The second stage: Establish an Islamic authority or emirate, then develop it, and support it until it achieves the level of a caliphate over as much territory as you can spread its power in Iraq, i.e., in Sunni area, is in order to fill the void stemming from the departure of the Americans. . . . There is no doubt that this emirate will enter into a fierce struggle with the foreign infidel forces and those supporting them among the local forces . . . to make it impossible for it to establish a stable state which could proclaim a caliphate, and to keep the jihadist groups in a constant state of war, until these forces find a chance to annihilate them.
- The third stage: Extend the jihad wave to the secular countries neighboring Iraq.
- The fourth stage: It may coincide with what came before: the clash with Israel, because Israel was established only to challenge any new Islamic entity.[28]

As alarming as the above are the attitudes toward suicide and jihad. In a remarkable interview conducted in August 2005, Abu Bakar Ba'asyir, alleged Indonesian terrorist leader and purported to be chief of the al Qaeda linked Jemaah Islamiyah organization in Southeast Asia, provided important insights into the thinking of these radical groups.[29]

Living quite comfortably in a large jail cell, Ba'asyir was described as being surrounded by visiting family and students, who keep him well supplied with news, magazines, and food. Fasting twice a week, he is visited monthly by his wife and exudes "politeness and is all smiles."[30] On the subject of martyrdom and suicide bombing, the cleric responded:

"There are two types of infidel [non-Muslim] terms for suicide: first, those who commit suicide out of hopelessness; second, those who commit suicide in order to be remembered as a hero. Both are types of suicide and there is no value in it.

"In Islam, there are also people who commit suicide out of hopelessness and we call this killing oneself. But if a person defends Islam and according to his calculations must die in doing so, he will still go and die for Islam. . . . The consideration is this . . . If I must die and without my dying Islam will not win, then dying is allowed. . . . *Because to die in jihad is noble* [italics added]. . . . And the best way to die is as a martyr (*shaheed*)."

To finish this point, the cleric noted: "There is no better deed than jihad. None. The highest deed in Islam is jihad. If we commit to jihad, we can neglect other deeds."

When asked about nuclear weapons and whether their use was justified, Ba'asyir answered: "Yes, if necessary. But the Islamic Ummah [body] should seek to minimize the intensity of fighting . . . Allah has said in verse 8 chapter 60 that we should equip ourselves with weapon power . . . but preferably to scare and not to kill our enemy. The main goal is to scare them. If they are scared, they won't bother us, and then we won't bother them as well. But if they persist, we have to kill them. In this way, the Prophet Muhammed sought to minimize the fighting" (by deterring first).

The bottom line is clear.

Other Villains?

In a search for enemies, the United States government currently has three and a half. The first is al Qaeda and like-minded terrorist organizations. Numbers two and three are Iran and North Korea. The half-enemy is Castro and Cuba. So far, Venezuela and its president Hugo Chavez are covered by the case against Cuba. Lurking in the wings is China, about which much more will be said.

Understanding of the enemy—as evidenced by the senior levels of government, at least through public statements—seems incomplete at best, or driven by ideology or emotion. President Bush 43 has explicitly said that he "loathes" Kim Jung Il, who has allowed or caused the deaths of hundreds of thousands of his countrymen through famine and disease. As a result of Kim's "loathsome" behavior, the United States under Bush 43 has refused to strike up a direct dialogue with North Korea, using instead the Six-Power Talks with Japan, China, Russia, and South Korea.

Iran and the United States have had a stormy relationship. The provenance was U.S. involvement in the overthrow of the Massadegh government in 1954 and its continuing support of the Shah until revolution ended his rule in 1979. America's de facto alliance with Iraq in the Iran–Iraq war was not helpful. And while the United States apologized and made compensation for its derelict shoot-down of a civilian Iranian airliner in 1986, that act continued to poison relations.

Iran is a proud nation of some seventy million intelligent, well-educated, resourceful people. If it decides to acquire nuclear weapons, it will. The United States has no effective means of preventing that. Still, Iran need not be an enemy. Its close Shia links with Iraq and its geography and energy reserves make it a key regional actor. However, given this history and images of the so-called student assault on the U.S. embassy in Tehran that kept diplomatic personnel captive for 444 days, American emotions are still raw. And President Mahmoud Ahmadinejad's call to "wipe Israel off the map" was an outrage that did not inspire confidence in his mental capacity.

Other enemies might emerge. Drug cartels are candidates. With huge war chests, obtaining not merely advanced weapons but elaborate computer and information systems hardware that could be used to disrupt the United States, in part to avoid prosecution and capture, is a possibility. Should Iran and North Korea obtain nuclear weapons, the prospect of further proliferation cannot be ignored. Under the wrong circumstances, Japan could take that route, with enormous consequences. And, while Argentina and Brazil ended their nuclear ambitions, an emerging and assertive oil-rich Venezuela could energize the proliferation problem in

Latin America. The election of Evo Morales in Bolivia with his socialist platform and anti-American bias is a further sign of trouble for the United States in Latin America.

In these circumstances, if there is to be victory in the administration's war on terror, the root causes of jihadist extremism must be mitigated. Elsewhere, possible solutions, beginning with a plan to mitigate the Arab-Israeli-Palestinian conflict and creating a new Marshall Plan for the Greater Middle East, have been proposed.[31] These are raised again in a different context in the conclusions. However, a broad strategic assessment is essential, one that relates adversaries and dangers to solutions, an important policy conclusion.

The difficulty is inducing a government to develop and implement such a comprehensive plan. The next chapter goes into great detail about why these seemingly straightforward and simple actions, as Clausewitz observed in war, have proven close to impossible to implement in practice. The reasons for this failure return to the key themes: a dysfunctional and unbalanced political system made so by culture, crusade, and partisanship.

A Nightmarish Scenario

The nightmare of nightmares is al Qaeda, another jihadist group, or, for that matter, any radical/criminal organization obtaining nuclear or biological weapons. Weaponized biological agents such as smallpox or other ferociously contagious and deadly diseases can conceivably kill as many as, or even more than, an atomic attack. As we have seen, the literature is divided on the intent of the jihadists to obtain and use nuclear weapons.

Consider this hypothetical scenario. An al Qaeda–like group, led by a charismatic character called "the Madhi," has been freely operating in Afghanistan and Western Pakistan. The Madhi has declared a new caliphate state and suddenly announced that his regime has come into possession of several nuclear weapons. The source for the weapons was almost certainly radical elements of the Pakistani Inter-Services-Intelligence agency (ISI), who were supporters of the Salafist ideology and clearly had to have had approval of leading radical mullahs. The Pakistani government denied the Madhi's claim. However, subsequent U.S. and British electronic intercepts uncovered "chatter" on highly classified Pakistani communications channels that seemed to confirm the theft of at least three nuclear bombs. Still, no hard evidence was found.

The United States was in the vulnerable position of not wanting to reveal the source of its information, and an official Pakistani statement on the weapons was critical for further action in the crisis. Meanwhile, the crisis was fired by the increasing likelihood that terrorists had finally achieved the ultimate nightmare and now possessed nuclear weapons.

A Web site in South Africa posted photographs of the purportedly missing weapons, complete with serial numbers. Under great pressure by the release of the serial numbers, the Pakistani government finally admitted that four weapons could not be found, but refused to confirm that a theft had taken place. Two more days elapsed before the Pakistani government finally publicly confirmed the theft. The United States, Britain, France, and Russia announced that each had been providing surveillance and reconnaissance teams to help Pakistan find the weapons. However, there was no confidence that the weapons would be located and every reason to fear that one or more might be used if detected.

Publics panicked. And how did the regional states react? Take India first. Neuralgic about Pakistan's nuclear weapons and with a substantial Muslim population of its own, the Indian high command had been reviewing various military options to deal with the crisis, from the alternative of blackmail to leverage Pakistani interests in Kashmir, to a possible preemptive strike by the Madhi to start a war between the two neighbors and thus allow the caliphate to break away from Pakistani control.

Jihadists, of course, could threaten nuclear blackmail against major cities in the expectation of successfully forcing international recognition of the caliphate. The Pakistani government could easily fall. Still the crisis would not end.

Jihadists are largely Sunni. A confrontation between the Madhi and the Shia of Iran is a second possibility. While Iran does not yet possess nuclear weapons and may never obtain them, such a crisis would certainly give impetus, if not a complete reason, for the ayatollahs to build a nuclear deterrent as quickly as possible.

Third, a Muslim state by geography and interest, Turkey would be involved and possibly engaged. As the likelihood of actual nuclear use grew and Turkey could not be assured it was not on a target list or that radioactive fallout from an attack in the region would bypass it, invoking Article V of the NATO treaty would be a real option. Hence, NATO could find itself directly involved.

Fourth, Israel was already an undeclared nuclear power. As a potential target for a nuclear attack, Israel's most vital interests were at stake. Whether or not Israel would consider preemption of Pakistani- or insurgent-held nuclear weapons and where and how it would obtain targeting data are two of many unanswerable questions.

Fifth, the United States would, of necessity, play the key leadership role. Its technological assets would be requested to locate the missing weapons. In preparation for employing the military option or conse- quence management to cope with the aftermath of a nuclear catastrophe should the rebels use a weapon, U.S. forces would be forward-deployed. That presence would be concurrently a deterrent, a provocation, and a temptation. The deterrent could prevent an Indo–Pakistani escalation or Israeli strike. But the presence would provoke, should regional powers believe that the United States was also a lightning rod. And, with forces in the region, rebels might find them a more tempting target for using a weapon if they had the means of employment.

Sixth, Russia has major interests not merely in preventing nuclear catastrophe but with possible linkages between the rebels and Chechen and other Islamic jihadists. Russia also has proximity, and presumably could deploy air and ground forces if requested.

China would probably sit on the sidelines, preferring to follow the Sun Tzu example of letting the enemy destroy themselves. Still, China might decide that, through the United Nations, it had a role to play in miti- gating the crisis.

The last major nuclear crisis was the 1973 Arab-Israeli War. President Nixon ordered the United States to assume a higher posture of defense, from the peacetime level of DefCon 4 to DefCon 3. (DefCon was short- hand for defense condition.) Fortunately, the Soviets had neither the intent nor the means to intervene with military forces to assist Egypt who, after all, had started the war, and the crisis receded.

This scenario would not recede easily, if at all. It would involve global actors and a potentially unresolvable catastrophic crisis. The dilemma between locating the weapons and forcing their use, added to the presence of other nuclear states, is agonizing with no good answer. A jihadist state with nuclear weapons and uncertainty as to intentions would have pro- found affect in every major capital and market around the world. The point is that such a crisis could be more serious, complicated, and possibly uncontrollable than any since Hitler invaded Western Europe in Sep- tember 1939. That is the danger that is posed by jihadist extremism—and this is by no means the worst case. Iran poses equally vexing questions, as its nuclear ambitions have led to action by the Security Council and the IAEA to consider what actions, if any, may be taken to prevent the further proliferation of these weapons by Tehran.

Some Conclusions

Unless the United States and China allow themselves to become adversaries, or war erupts over Taiwan or on the Korean peninsula, the principal external threat to the West is jihadist extremism. The strategy of defeating these extremists simply by killing or capturing them will not succeed by itself. In Iraq, more revolutionaries and insurgents are being recruited than are being eliminated, and by a large margin. The cost-exchange ratio favors the extremists. To succeed in this conflict, a broad geopolitical–economic–ideological approach is critical. Causes that motivate the jihadists, not only symptoms, must be addressed. For the moment, there is no single jihadist group in charge, calling the shots.

The jihadists have been likened to franchise operations rather than control from the center. The analogy is McDonald's, not General Motors. jihadist groups are therefore often disparate actors, with some common interests and the broad goal of changing the political order. The notion of a clear hierarchy and unity of command was negated almost a decade ago when the term "al Qaeda" apparently was first made public. That occurred in 1998, not in an announcement made by bin Laden or one of his henchmen, but in an indictment filed by the assistant attorney general in New York City against the perpetrators of the 1993 bombing of the World Trade Center. The jihadist groups are working, if not in parallel, surely with some common aims. This absence of control can and most likely will change if a charismatic or gifted leader emerges.

The thrust of the jihadists is Salafist in nature and therefore Sunni in character. Humiliation is a driving force. The mantra is to return to a spiritually purer form of Islam. Ironically, then, the adversary is the reforming element. The intent is to rally the bulk of Islamic people in support. Jihad, the waging of holy war, is authorized, and fatwas—the declarations by clerics with the force of law—have been issued to that effect. (Ironically, bin Laden is not a cleric, and therefore his fatwas should have no standing.) The ambition or aspiration is to form some sort of an Islamic fundamentalist state, with or without borders, in the Greater Middle East. This virtual state would seek to morph into a more traditional one. For the moment, Iraq may be the petri dish, as some jihadists view the opportunity presented by the ending of Saddam and the ungovernability of Iraq too valuable and tempting a target to ignore.

Such a state would maneuver to gain access to Saudi oil and dollars and Pakistani nuclear weapons. For the moment, a revolution in Saudi Arabia is probably a low priority. Bin Laden and al-Zawahiri probably believe that if a coup succeeded, the United States, in conjunction with other oil-dependent powers, would occupy the oil wells in the eastern provinces and attempt to roll back the insurgency, much as it forced Saddam out of Kuwait in 1991.

Regarding Iraq, jihadists should not be confused with the majority of the insurgents fighting coalition and government security forces. The number of foreign jihadists fighting in Iraq probably ranges at no more that 5 to 10 percent, quite likely less. So even if the foreign jihadists were eliminated, the insurgency would continue.

To establish some form of Fundamentalist regime, the strategy is opportunistic and one of divide and conquer. Provoking conflict and dissent within the coalition engaged in Iraq and between regional powers and the United States is part of this plan.

Jihadists understand that defeating the United States militarily is impossible and unnecessary in Iraq. The tactic is to force America out of the region, as the Soviets were driven from Afghanistan in 1989. In these calculations, Vietnam, Beirut in 1983 and Somalia in 1993, the Khobar Towers in 1996, and the USS *Cole* in 2000 loom large. The logic is that if enough Americans are killed or hurt, the U.S. will quit, a variant of Japan's logic in planning the attack on Pearl Harbor. Improvised explosive devices (nicknamed IED's), used more perhaps by indigenous insurgents, underscore this tactic. IED's have no impact on tactics or operations. The effect is strategic and political, and the target is the U.S. public. Killing and maiming even a few Americans a week, in this view, will shatter U.S. support for the occupation at home.

Planners operate in secret, are very compartmentalized to ensure security, and draw heavily on very secure use of the Internet. The Internet provides not just requests for proposals regarding potential attacks, but plans for attacks. Nominal plans for the March 11, 2004, Madrid and July 7, 2005, London attacks were posted on the Internet.

For the financing of terror, despite the grade of A– the 9/11 Commission

gave to the money-laundering and preventive activities of law enforcement, jihadists exploit *hawala*, the principal means of transferring
money in the Arab world. Money exchangers are highly trusted. Money
entrusted to them is not sent directly to the recipient. Instead, another
money exchanger in that city or locale transfers funds from his account.
Based on trust, accounts are balanced, but not with double bookkeeping
or the same timeliness as in the West. Hence, the system is very difficult
to interdict. The conclusion is that money is probably less a worry to al
Qaeda than many in the United States believe.

Fundamentalists, regardless of internecine conflict and different
agendas, have a common target: the United States and its allies. So a
bomb or an attack delivered against any of these targets redounds to the
common advantage. Whether the terrorists who blew up the HSBC bank
and British Consulate's office in Istanbul in November 2003 were with or
against al Qaeda, the net effect surely helped that cause.

The aim of terror is to disrupt, divide, and isolate. In Iraq, for
example, during the first stages of the occupation, targets were UN headquarters, the Italian *carbinieri*, and of course coalition forces. Over
time, as the insurgency grew, contract workers, Shia Iraqis, and even
some Sunnis were targeted. Given the presence of al Qaeda cells
throughout Europe, further attacks must be considered likely.

The enemy from without is formidable, motivated, and patient. With a
potential reservoir of well over a billion Muslims from which to recruit,
and the nearly uniform resentment of American policy throughout the
Greater Middle East, their case is not difficult to make. The cost-exchange
ratio (what it costs us to counter them) is grotesquely weighted in their
favor. As of early 2006, the United States had spent over $500 billion on
Iraq. How much have the jihadists expended? The answer is not even a
small fraction. All of this is what makes them so dangerous.

Taken together, the intention of al Qaeda and the jihadist Extremists is
as ambitious as Lenin, Hitler, and others who would change the world.
Terror is a key tool and an increasingly effective one in disrupting,
dividing, isolating, and, of course, terrorizing. Iraq is a separate case and,
ironically, an unexpected bonus for extremists. If the United States and
the Iraqi government prevail, fundamentalism will not be defeated; it
merely will have to move on to the next battlefield. If the United States falters or fails in Iraq, then the fundamentalists will have achieved a major
victory.

PART II

CRUSADES ABROAD

THE TERM "PERFECT STORM" HAS become the perfect cliché. Given the super accumulation of difficult challenges and problems facing the nation, the failure of government to perform, and the imbalance between government promises and obligations and the wherewithal to pay for them, the image is apt. The storm will not hit tomorrow. However, if ignored, it will strike with a vengeance sooner or later.

After examining how the world continues to change since the end of the Cold War and September 11, Part II shows how culture and crusade have affected, and more than occasionally distorted, U.S. policies, strategies, and perceptions regarding past and current adversaries. Partisanship is covered in Part III.

This excursion defines a view of the world as it is, not as we or the Bush 43 administration would like it to be. The villain and hero, depending on one's perspective, is "globalization," the great paradox that at once advances and retards the betterment of society and mankind. However, the forces, factors, and trends at work are far more complex than can be expressed in a single word, and reasonable people can and do disagree on the speed, extent, and consequences of the way change is taking place.

The impact of culture, crusade, and partisanship coexists with other, often more powerful forces. The broadest and probably most influential is the diffusion of all forms of power and how that diffusion is affecting change. Diffusion is the result of many factors—principally globalization, technology, instant communications, commerce, and the explosion of knowledge empowered by the Internet—that gave rise to an abundance of new actors, power centers, and parties with global interests. One critical effect has been the creation of several paradoxes of power.

The first paradox is the recognition that many problems and dangers—from environment to terror—are global, shared by most states, and need a common solution. However, because many more actors are involved in the global process, and few have the power to impose solutions, reaching an effective agreement is complicated, inhibited, and often prevented by the absence of consensus.

The second paradox concerns how the diffusion of all forms of power has reduced the relative and absolute relevance and influence of any single entity—including the United States, even though its power has never been greater. The tensions in these paradoxes pose a central security dilemma for the United States, irrespective of ideological viewpoint.

For Americans who are realists, working in this context may be frustrating and time-consuming, but it is necessary if policy is to succeed. With more interested parties, unilateral action has become anachronistic and counterproductive, except in narrow situations when vital interests supersede the need for obtaining a measure of consensus. For Americans of a "neo-con" or conservative bent, these paradoxes are what produced the unilateral tendencies in American power, uninhibited by others, and the belief that this power can and must be employed for purpose leading to a safer and more secure world.

The Global War on Terror is a clear reflection of these two paradoxes. Most nations do not share the Bush 43 view of the magnitude of the danger or the level of response needed to defeat the terrorist threats. Nor do most nations support what is perceived as his (largely) unilateral exercise of power in conducting that war. Learning how to work within these paradoxes is crucial for future administrations. Teddy Roosevelt's dictum to "speak softly but carry a big stick" has application here. The framework for peace, partnership in particular and prosperity is based heavily on that model. Recommendations for coordinating and consolidating the plethora of bilateral and multilateral cooperative security arrangements and agreements will offer one means of achieving this end.

Despite the uproar over allegations of "black" detention sites in Eastern Europe and U.S. treatment of enemy combatants that required Secretary of State Condoleezza Rice to make a trip to Europe in December 2005 to explain U.S. policies to critical allies, cooperation between law-enforcement and intelligence agencies against terrorists, by all accounts, has been good. However, no other major leader, with the exception of Tony Blair, has devoted much rhetoric to, or even acknowledged the need for, a global war on terror as opposed to coping with terror. And, within the Greater Middle East, the absence of clear distinctions between "terrorist" and "freedom fighter," depending on the viewing audience, has often compounded the difficulties in waging the war on terror.

The reasons for this divergence of attitudes, particularly in Europe, reflect many of the changes in the international environment. Europe has a Muslim population of about 20 million and an attitude less prone to using force in the first instance. Many in Europe do not support what are seen as one-sided U.S. policies toward Israel and are more pragmatic in dealing with states in that region. A few sold weapons to Saddam, and Russia is supporting Iran's nuclear-reactor program for production of electricity and reportedly is selling air defense systems to Tehran.[32]

More than international politics has been altered. The character of war—armed conflict between two or more states—has profoundly changed. Understanding these changes is critical if jihadist extremism is to be successfully countered. The old rules and principles of war do not fully fit the new environment.

In this era so defined by September 11, the fundamental questions of whether the United States is winning or losing the war on terror and of what is meant by winning and losing raise a further paradox. The questions require objective answers. But administrations are reluctant to respond to bad news, if not even incapable of it. Hence, while an assessment is urgently needed, it is unlikely to be conducted in a rigorous and public way by any administration.

Unconstrained by politics, an assessment of progress in the war on terror follows, based on examination of five pieces of unfinished business, identified in a book of the same name and then expanded in a subsequent work.[33] Hurricane Katrina is part of that assessment to determine how the nation has dealt with homeland security in the nearly five years since the attacks of September 11. Those results as well are—as the 9/11 Commission noted in its final report of December 5, 2005—largely unsatisfactory. But whether anyone is listening, and whether anyone will act, are critical questions on which much of our future security, and our promise, will rest.

The historical and changing impact of culture and crusade on U.S. security choices and decisions comes from an assessment of four case studies. The first two deal with China and Russia. China may be a potential superpower; Russia surely was one. How the United States deals with both in the future will prove critical.

The second set deals with Vietnam and the Greater Middle East. Vietnam fortuitously had no geostrategic consequences of import. Iraq does and will continue to do so. Still, culture, crusade, and surely partisanship have worked their worst in regard to where the United States now stands in its mission to democratize that region and thus transform the geostrategic landscape of the Middle East. The landscape may be redefined, but not as President Bush 43 would like.

A final paradox about the pernicious effects of culture, crusade, and partisanship is important to recognize. Inadvertently, jihadist extremists have exploited the weaknesses created by these factors and ironically have turned the best intentions of our crusade against us. The recent treatment of enemy combatants has become an indelible stain on America's honor and reputation. And the Bush 43 administration's secret program to conduct surveillance and wiretapping has raised potentially profound questions over the respective power of Congress and the presidency that could provoke a Constitutional crisis, even though no one will disagree with the need to use every legitimate means to thwart terror. Should other surveillance programs be uncovered, irrespective of legality, then a collision of these two branches would seem unavoidable.

Eight and a half decades ago, the combination of culture and crusade foolishly led to the ratification of the 18th Amendment, prohibiting consumption of alcohol. That amendment had two profound consequences. First, since most Americans ignored it, breaking the law became acceptable and commonplace. Second, Prohibition organized crime and turned it into a big business. Decisions on the treatment of enemy combatants and authorizing surveillance of American citizens reflected strains of the cultural and crusading instincts that brought the ill-advised 18th Amendment.

Believing that September 11 did in fact change everything, the White House assumed that it alone had the responsibility and authority to protect the nation against what it also believed to be an extraordinary threat. As a result, it would make little difference whether or not Saddam actually had weapons of mass destruction. When it came to defending Americans against terror, tapping phones and surveilling citizens were justified by the danger. And when enemy combatants were captured, they could be treated without regard to U.S. law, due process, and the Geneva Convention protections afforded to prisoners of war.

The tragedy is that these actions have had negative effects for the law similar to those of the 18th Amendment. By ignoring or dismissing law and precedent, huge and unintended damage has been done to the foundations of liberty and justice on which the nation and its promise rest. One of the reasons for these actions of the Bush 43 administration is a direct result of culture, crusade, and partisanship.

The World As It Is, Not As We Wish It

ALL NATIONS HAVE UNIQUE AND different lenses for viewing the world. Lenses also distort. As Harvard Professor Stanley Hoffmann put it years ago, Americans expect others to reason as we do, or to be in need of education to bring them up to our level. Here, culture is extremely important. Issues pertaining to war and peace, often cast in terms of good and evil and fanned by partisan biases, reflect uniquely national characteristics. This is particularly true for the United States. Some of these characteristics and effects have been noted earlier; others follow. How the Bush 43 administration chose to regard Iraq and its policies for both the war and the subsequent peace—if that term can be used—reflects what happens when crusading instincts dominate decision-making.

The international scene is in a state of continuous if not profound flux and realignment. Because of factors and forces including globalization; the end of the bipolar Cold War system; virtually unlimited accessibility into most political and economic markets; the explosion in knowledge; societal vulnerability to disruption; and revolutionary changes to the nature and state of war as we have known it, understanding and assimilating the combined impact of these extraordinary, complex, and often interrelated changes and their consequences is both extremely difficult and exceedingly important.

Globalization is as good an example of these phenomena as there is. Globalization, or, as *New York Times* columnist Thomas L. Friedman calls it, a world made "flat" by the instant interconnectivity of communications, news, media, markets, and finance, has had a fundamental effect on politics, economics, security, and society. Not all of those effects are positive. Many are.

Globalization has erased most or all of the traditional boundaries and barriers that divided foreign and domestic policy. The proverbial farmer in Arkansas who sells to Indonesia is probably at least as aware of events there as are desk officers in government responsible for the entire region. Globalization has also provided instant electronic and visual access that transcends borders and is available literally anywhere and at any time.

News is impossible to censor. Indeed, mini-cameras in cell phones now make any owner a potential television journalist. Images, from showing IED's killing U.S. troops in Baghdad to the destruction wrought by the tsunami in Sumatra, instantly flow around the world, reinforcing the power of virtually unlimited access and often complicating the lives of government officials in responding to instant reporting of the news through these sources.[34] Pity the poor spokesperson asked by an aggressive reporter to respond to some significant event that is flashed instantly across the ether or appears on a "blog" that otherwise may take hours to work its way through the labyrinth of government bureaucracy.

Superpower dominance was a vise that had constrained much of the world from exercising fully independent views and policies during the Cold War. The two rival blocs checked each other. With allies and surrogates, it was difficult for third parties to assert themselves. The non-aligned bloc led by India in the 1950s failed to provide a counterweight. And while East and West may have failed in persuading every potential ally or uncommitted state to support their side, a bipolar world surely strengthened the influence of the superpowers. That world is long gone.

For the Cold War, the pillars of American and Western security were strong, well understood, and shared by many nations. Deterrence and containment were crucial, both for the concepts each represented and for the simplicity of conveying a message in single words. Each proved highly effective against the Soviet Union, even with its tens of thousands of nuclear warheads. But those pillars are eroding. The image of America as Samson in the Philistine temple comes to mind.

What is absent is an appropriate intellectual framework for security. In today's world, beyond Iraq, the main adversary lacks a conventional army or navy. Suicide bombers, cell phones, and the Internet are weapons of choice. Can either deterrence or containment work when the foe employs ideas, ideologies, and terror to advance its cause and has no clear boundaries or lines of demarcation that fix its presence? For all of the effort that has gone into the war on terror, no concept equivalent to deterrence or containment has thus far been created. Instead, slogans such as "you are either with us or against us" and "the best defense is a strong offense" are unsatisfactory substitutes.

The record is rife with many statements and documents on strategy, policy, and national security emanating from the White House, Congress, and think tanks. Within government and those responsible for the nation's security, this ménage is less an intellectual basis and more an ex post facto political rationale that gives credence to decisions and actions taken, rather than—as Clausewitz counseled—guiding both. Obviously, any administration will take issue with this criticism. However, we can examine the president's "strategy for victory" in Iraq enunciated at the Naval Academy in November 2005 for inadvertent landmines it contains, in large measure because of the absence of a more rigorous strategic construct.

The president sensibly announced that the strategy was based on transferring responsibility for security from the United States to Iraq. "As they build up, we draw down" was the operative phrase. The pace of that transfer rested on conditions on the ground being the ultimate arbiter of policy. In operational terms, the Iraqi government elected on December 15, 2005, and its military, police, and security forces, had the responsibility to quell the insurgency. That government is still struggling to claim and control the reins of power from its predecessor. And there is the real possibility that it will never do so. Beyond that, deficiencies in Iraqi security forces regarding training, leadership, and logistical and fire support, even if corrected, have led and will continue to lead to severe unintended consequences.

Training can move only so quickly. Since training began more than two years ago, the progress has been painfully slow. To close the leadership gap, junior officers from Saddam Hussein's old army were recruited and, hopefully, shorn of old bad habits. Training thus required indoctrinating both new and old recruits in the ways of democracy, liberty, and the sanctity of human rights—and took additional time, possibly more than events on the ground will permit. Booster shots to ensure that the training holds will be needed. If allegations of Iraqi security forces' brutal treatment of prisoners are correct, this indoctrination will not be easy.

Logistics support is and was put in place to allow Iraqi forces to operate independently. But the American military did not want to create a future Iraqi army that can threaten its neighbors. So fire support in the form of Iraqi artillery, tactical aircraft, and heavy armor was modest.

Absent the necessary military capacity, or even with it, the new Iraqi government could too easily fall back on the old-fashioned way of doing business: through brutality and torture. Hatred and revenge are slow to cool. And while an insurgent may be prepared to die for the cause, if that person knows that a wide circle of friends and acquaintances beyond his or her immediate family will be killed, tortured, or imprisoned, behavior modification is possible. Iraq's history in this regard is far from reassuring, and the temptation to repeat it will be powerful.

If the president is taken literally and events on the ground determine future American policy, the White House has turned Clausewitz on his head. That reversal could be the grounds for grief or failure. Policy must drive the use of force to achieve required aims. The aim in Iraq must be to assure that events on the ground achieve the goals we set, not random outcomes. Otherwise, security and an effective transfer of responsibility will never occur. This inversion of ends and means is typical of the absence of a rigorous intellectual framework.

Second, America's security alliances are eroding, as could be expected with the change in threats. Both multilateral alliances such as NATO and bilateral agreements with Japan and Korea have been predicated on the necessity for a military coalition to counter a military threat. Outside the Korean peninsula and the Taiwan Straits, the threat is no longer completely or even mostly military in character. Yet, aside from phrases like "coalitions of the willing" and "closer cooperation" between and among law-enforcement and intelligence agencies, no new alliances have been created for the post–9/11 world. A huge network of often disjointed and unconnected bi- and multilateral arrangements instead has sprouted up like weeds in a forest. And transforming alliances, even in NATO, has been difficult.

Third, America's understanding of the world, the limitations on its power and influence, and the opportunities that can be seized upon have not kept pace with the changes. The negative side of culture has tended to insulate America from closely and analytically examining many of these trends and realities. The wrong application of crusade has caused administrations to misjudge and miscalculate the utility of military force and, as most readers appreciate, fail to plan adequately for the post-war period in Iraq. Partisanship and the intense polarization of politics it has caused have resulted in strategy based more on ideological conviction than on objective analysis.

Fourth, trade, economics, and commerce reflect these global transformations and, for better or for worse, are realigning how nations go about providing for their livelihoods. The difficulties that the manufacturing sector in the United States has been and is still experiencing result from these different economic and commercial patterns. General Motors, one of only two corporations still on the Dow-Jones since its inception a century ago (the other is GE), has a credit rating in the category of "junk" bonds, illustrating the power of these economic forces and the tyranny of history. To a large degree, the costs of health care and pensions are making many sectors of the economy noncompetitive, as GM fully understands. The challenge is clear, and the question is whether the market or the government will force the necessary response. If it is the latter, then the outlook is not good, given the generally low level of government performance.

Since the central focus and presumably most lasting legacy of the Bush 43 administration will be the Global War on Terror, appreciating the nature of war and how it has been transformed is an important starting point in making an objective assessment.

The Changing Faces of War

What does the word "war" mean? And whatever that definition might have been in the past, has it changed in the twenty-first century? The answer to the second question is an emphatic "yes." War has been changed dramatically in at least three ways: by nuclear (and possibly biological) weapons; the absence of boundaries to define enemies; and the lethality of modern war.

War, as Clausewitz and Sun Tzu wrote, is a violent clash of wills between sovereign states fought by (more or less organized) armies. The notion of enduring principles of war was established by, and generally reflected the thinking of, the greatest and even lesser philosophers and practitioners of war. Among these general principles were disarming the enemy as a necessary condition for victory; that wars were fought between and among recognized states; that war aims ranged from all-out or unconditional victory to more limited outcomes such as seizing territory or gaining a concession; and that knowledge and intelligence about the adversary were crucial, if not always attainable, commodities.

The principal instrument of war was military force supported by the tools and resources of the state. Because war was waged between well-defined states, it was conducted with a certain amount of international legitimacy and with rules and laws of war to govern (some of) its conduct. The principal object was to defeat the enemy by destroying the will to resist traditionally, by eliminating the means to fight or creating the perception that resistance was useless. And, as Clausewitz most famously advised, war was to be directed by policy, not the converse.

Not all wars were "winnable." Many were fought to a draw. But one fact remained inviolable, at least until 1945: Before the Cold War, the defeated power had no means to destroy the enemy once its army was neutralized and its ability to resist eliminated. True, "pyrrhic" victories such as Carthage's costly assault on Rome that led to its ultimate defeat persisted throughout history. But in 1945, the development of nuclear and later thermonuclear weapons forever altered the conduct of war. No longer did winning and losing have the same traditional meanings if the "defeated" state's nuclear or thermonuclear weapons still destroyed the society of the "victorious" state.

Had there been a war between the Soviet Union and the United States or China, it risked becoming nuclear and thus thermonuclear. A thermonuclear or H-bomb is about a thousand times as powerful as the weapons that destroyed Hiroshima and Nagasaki. In the nuclear age, as Chairman Mao understood, "a few atom bombs were enough," meaning to deter the enemy. But the "defeated" nation still had sufficient nuclear strength to launch an attack on its adversary with enough power to destroy the so-called winner many times over. Hence, the notion of deterrence based on the threat or ability to obliterate society, called mass or assured destruction, fundamentally changed prior enduring notions about winners and losers.

Whether the principles of deterrence that emerged during the nuclear years apply to the twenty-first century, and the threat of stateless groups using terror as a tool and mass disruption rather than destruction of society as the lever to achieve political ends, is a vital question. Should biological agents be developed to the point where they could threaten the existence of societies, that too could have profound effect on the strategic balance and how wars against terror and related political movements will be waged. With the end of the Cold War and the events of September 11, 2001, the question of what constituted war was no longer fully answerable by traditional rules, logic, and experience.

Terror is as old as war. Terrorist organizations threatened many states and political orders. In Europe toward the end of the nineteenth century and the beginning of the twentieth, terrorists and anarchists tried to collapse the political order. Terrorists targeted heads of state. World War I was precipitated by the assassination of the archduke of the Austro–Hungarian Empire. Yet that war and the others of the last century were fought among states. Even Vietnam, which began as an insurgency, ended with the North Vietnamese Army, organized in traditional formations, overrunning the South.

With President Bush 43's declaration of a Global War on Terror against ill-defined "terrorists" and terror networks that lacked borders and boundaries, how "war" is viewed, waged, and defined strategically, politically, and operationally has been profoundly altered—and for a considerable period, too. Adversaries no longer need borders for definition nor states for legitimacy. They can operate anywhere, using the ether. In a sense, the Internet and instant global communications provide a technological alternative for groups seeking to achieve their own political agenda.

Finally, technology has redefined the basic conduct of war. For, at least through the late 1980s, a common characteristic of war was that virtually every rock, arrow, spear, bullet, projectile, and missile thrown, launched, or fired missed its target. Except in close, hand-to-hand combat, precision and accuracy and therefore "lethality" were of exceedingly low orders. In World War II, for example, it took many dozens of rounds to kill a tank and huge numbers of bombs to destroy major industrial complexes. For advanced states, lethality and accuracy have changed "conventional war."

Today, the opposite relationship for lethality is true. Not only do weapons hit on the first shot, but the probability of destroying or neutralizing a target with the first hit is very high. Combined with the notion of "effects-based targeting" or operations in which a target is broken down to the smallest vulnerability to determine the minimum effort required to neutralize it, a real revolution has occurred. The caveat applies to conventional war. What, for example, is occurring in Iraq today—or in many other regions where insurgency or the more violent end of criminal activity constitutes the threat—is not as easily affected by this revolution in accuracy, precision, targeting, and lethality.

As a consequence, the most profound questions about war, its nature, and how it might be fought in the future demand answers. On the one hand, "conventional" war could break out on the Korean peninsula, between India and Pakistan, or, more remotely, in the Taiwan Straits between the People's Republic and Taiwan. War in the Middle East, something that has happened every decade since World War II ended, can never be assumed away. On the other hand, as the political use of terror increases and gains fuller access to technologies that can do great damage, such as those employed in information warfare, traditional notions of war will become less—or even no longer—applicable, creating another paradox.

For the United States and most Western states, the military has the most robust and advanced technological capability. As in the past, it will remain a preferred instrument of response. However, less capable and possibly less technologically advanced law-enforcement, intelligence, and non-military tools are often the more appropriate means to address these challenges. Reconciling this paradox remains a test for all governments.

War, Peace, and the Future

Years ago, American movie mogul Sam Goldwyn was fond of saying "making predictions, especially about the future, ain't easy." So where are war, violence, and conflict headed? Clausewitz asserted that "war was an admixture of policy with other means." But, in an age when terror, surely for the United States, has taken on such a powerful and different political context, should there be different assessments about the nature of war and the role and use of force and violence to achieve political ends? History provides one insight for an answer.

A hundred years ago, the century of relative peace and stability in Europe, following Napoleon's defeat at Waterloo in 1815 and the Congress of Vienna that redefined the political order, was coming to an end. Asia had already erupted in a series of conflicts including the Sino–Japanese War in 1894–95, the Boxer Rebellions in China in 1900, and the 1904–05 Russo–Japanese conflict. In 1914, the era defined by Metternich and the demise of Napoleon exploded into World War I. From World War I came the seeds of World War II and from it, the Cold War. In the aftermath of the Cold War, what will come next?

On the positive side of the ledger, while conventional war has some chance of occurring in Korea, the Taiwan Straits, South Asia, and the Middle East, the probabilities are no greater than in the past. Perhaps the result of the war in Iraq may have the effect of deterring war in other parts of the Gulf, with or without long-term U.S. presence.

On the other side of the ledger, global terror and violence are not waning. Regarding the former, to many states, terror is not new and has been part of the dangers for a long time. It took a September 11 to make the United States as sensitive to the terrorist threat and direct attack as other countries had been for decades. However, future forms of terror could copy the riots that swept through many French cities in November 2005. Started by French citizens of Muslim descent frustrated over second-class treatment, these riots are potential harbingers of trouble and reinforce the preoccupation of Europe with such a large indigenous Islamic population. A future al Qaeda tactic surely will look toward inciting future acts of local violence and unrest by disenfranchised Islamic populations.

What else has changed? Recognizing that the threat has shifted from an adversary with a powerful army to one that uses other means, defining the danger and risks has become far more difficult. Putting the threat in quantitative or even qualitative terms is perhaps impossible and certainly illusive.

It was relatively clear what the military strengths of Nazi Germany and the Soviet Union were. Ambiguities were neatly bypassed by shifting from focus on capabilities to intentions, the latter also being hard to define. However, because of the ideological or political consensus of the time, Soviet intentions as defined by an administration were important for rallying public support. Today, no consensus or understanding exists of what exactly the scope of the threat of terror is, or what the real intentions of terrorists are, beyond hating Americans and wishing to kill them.

Meanwhile, the strategic Cold War paradigm of massive destruction has evaporated. In its place is the danger of mass disruption. Certainly a weapon of mass destruction can still do a great deal of damage. But society is not at risk of total destruction.

Extremists aim to use terror or its threat to disrupt. The intent is to make life as difficult and frightening as possible. Taking Russian school children hostage or threatening attacks merely to alarm and panic are examples. The snipers that terrorized the Washington, D.C.–Baltimore area in late 2003 and the fire in a New York subway that nearly shut down that system for a week a year later are reminders of how potentially vulnerable society is to disruption. Even in war-ravaged Iraq, that infrastructure, from electrical grids to oil production, is regularly subject to disruption by insurgents.

Perhaps the least visible and morally most significant impact of the changes in war is found in the rules and laws about how war is waged and conducted. Dealing with suspects detained in the war on terror raises the most profound dilemma of balancing the need to protect the nation with the rule of law and civil liberty. There are no easy or simple answers. In December 2005, the battle between Congress and the White House over "cruel, inhuman, and degrading" treatment of enemy combatants forced the Bush 43 administration to retreat from opposing such legislation and under duress sign a bill forbidding torture. Along with the issue of terrorist surveillance and the possibility that still undisclosed spy programs may be in place, the stakes of conducting a war against terror could threaten to and actually shift the balance between security and liberty in ways that do real damage to the nation.

An Examination of the War on Terror

Donald Rumsfeld, the charismatic and combative U.S. Secretary of Defense since early 2001, asked in a memo: "Are we winning or losing the global war on terror?" It was a rhetorical question. Clearly, any American administration, and especially one as disciplined and unwilling to acknowledge even the smallest misstep as George W. Bush's, will have a redounding and robust response. "It may be a long, hard slog," to borrow another Rumsfeldian quote, but "we will stay the course" and "we will prevail."

Given the political spin that the Bush 43 administration knows how to apply brilliantly, the message is one of optimism. On October 13, 2005, the president held a nationally televised videoconference with nine U.S. soldiers stationed in Iraq, one of whom was a woman, and an Iraqi sergeant. The news from the front was buoyant. Queried by a hesitant Bush 43, whose breathing bordered on hyperventilation, the sol-

diers presented positive and well-rehearsed answers (caught on video-
tape before the conference) about progress on the ground in defeating the
insurgency and the growing ability of Iraqi security forces to take on
the fight on their own.

At face value, there are strong arguments to make that the United
States is winning the war on terror and is much safer today than it was
on September 11. The first argument is that the nation is now alert to
the danger. Based on this "wakeup" call, the United States has spent
hundreds of billions, if not trillions, of dollars on bolstering its security.
Afghanistan was a success in hurting al Qaeda and removing the Taliban.
Iraq will work out, too.

Second, greater cooperation among intelligence and law-enforcement
agencies has provided the means to arrest, confound, and prevent terrorists from doing their worst. While there is no single number available
of suspects and actual terrorists who have been captured, detained, or
killed, the figure is perhaps in the low tens of thousands. The life's blood
of terror, money, has been severely drained, an argument confirmed by
the 9/11 Commission's grade of A– given to the effort to prevent money
laundering.

Third, as noted, the war has been taken to the enemy abroad. No
known terrorist attacks from jihadists have taken place in the United
States. Along with the defenses put in place by the Homeland Security
Department, the record would indicate that America is safer.

Finally, reforms to intelligence, while imperfect and needful of time to
take root, are working.

The problem is that while those arguments seem convincing, by
focusing on symptoms, they fail to get to the fundamental issues and
causes of jihadist Extremism. If there is life and endurance to these
causes, then a strategy based primarily on eliminating the terrorists by
killing, capturing, or neutralizing them will not work. Consider an
assessment that examines causes and effects rather than symptoms.

Using five pieces of unfinished business, evaluation of the war on terror
leads to conclusions that are not shared by the administration.[35] The first
piece of unfinished business was understanding the nature of the threat.
The second was the organization of government to produce effective policies. The third was reducing national vulnerability. Fourth was using old
alliances and constructing new ones to contain and eliminate the threat.
Finally was dealing with the causes of jihadist extremism.

Understanding the Danger

The Bush 43 administration took office with a narrower view of the world than its predecessor. It attempted to adopt a "no-nonsense" hard-nosed business approach, clearly reflecting the president's MBA and his experience in the private sector. The logic went as follows.

Nation-building was too expensive and did not work. The United Nations was unwieldy, highly inefficient, and probably corrupt, and it offered a platform for many third-world states to launch verbal attacks on the United States. Because of potential threats from Asia, principally China and North Korea, missile defense was essential, and the ABM Treaty stood in its way. Finally, the military had to be transformed for the new century.

For its first seven months in office, the administration was adrift as it pursued those tough-minded yet vague aims. ABM and the Kyoto Global Warming Treaties were scrapped. A mini-crisis over the knockdown of a Navy surveillance aircraft over Taiwan flared with China. For all of the star quality of its cabinet, the administration seemed inept in the conduct of foreign policy.

September 11 changed that and literally transformed the administration. In explaining why the United States had been attacked, the immediate reaction was to argue that the terrorists who had perpetrated these monstrous deeds did so because they hated American freedom and democracy and were out to kill and harm Americans because of that hatred. American values were what the "Islamic radicals" so detested and were reasons for motivating the terror.

Furthermore, the administration was determined to link Iraq and Saddam Hussein with al Qaeda and September 11. The war on terror would be extended to a war on Saddam. After the great success in Operation Enduring Freedom, which ended the Taliban rule, it would be only a matter of time before it was Iraq's turn. While there were many throughout government and elsewhere who disagreed with the White House's understanding of the danger based on the belief of sheer hatred of American values and fear of democracy as the reasons for the attacks, those opinions did not carry much weight with the president.

The administration was also trapped by history. Rightly or wrongly, the most powerful reason why the United States is resented and even hated in the Arab and Muslim worlds rests on what are seen as grossly unfair and one-sided American policies toward Israel and the autocratic regimes in the region that are its allies, namely Saudi Arabia and Egypt. Unless there is a radical shift in U.S. policies that is credibly received in the region, that hostility and animosity against America will persist.

Ironically, no good deed goes unpunished. One of the accomplishments of the Bush 43 administration has been achieving a Palestinian state and building the foundations for a "two-state" solution. However, the war on terror and the war in Iraq have eclipsed that achievement. Perhaps with the breakaway of Israel's two old "warhorses," Shimon Peres from the Labor Party and Ariel Sharon from Likud, to form a new centrist party, the prospect for peace became slightly brighter. But Sharon then suffered a massive stroke and Hamas, labeled a terrorist organization by the U.S. government, was elected to office in a fair and free ballot to lead the Palestinians.

The strongest evidence, aside from the record and continued statements by the administration over misjudging the nature of the terrorist threat, also provides the most powerful critique of the failures thus far in bringing democracy to Iraq: the controversies about ignoring or manipulating pre-war intelligence over WMD; planning for the post-war; the assumption that Americans would be welcomed as liberators, not occupiers; the hope that the turnover to a new Iraqi government would go swiftly; and the plan for the United States seeking an early withdrawal.

It has taken time, but the White House and thus the government finally have recognized that the Global War on Terror is more than simply a war against terrorists, and that there is a political agenda on the part of those who oppose the United States and the West. But the administration has not fully acted on that basis. The forces of culture, crusade, and partisanship have continued to distort the danger. What lies ahead in the war on terror and Iraq is very much undetermined.

The fundamental issue remained understanding the realities in Iraq and the nature of jihadist extremism. There have been few signs that the administration had decided to address the causes of extremism, preferring to continue the war "over there." The chilling thought, expressed by the chairman of the 9/11 Commission, former New Jersey Governor Tom Kean, was not "if" there would be a future terrorist attack in the United States, but "when."

Correcting Dysfunctional Government

Just after George W. Bush assumed office, as noted earlier, the Hart-Rudman report called the nation's security organization "dysfunctional." The characterization "dysfunctional" remains a vast understatement. Despite the "reforms" introduced post–September 11 for intelligence and the creation of a Department of Homeland Security, the nation remains organized under the National Security Act, first passed in 1947. That Act assigned national security responsibilities and authorities on a "vertical" basis to the departments of Defense and State and to the intelligence community. With a threat such as the Soviet Union that allowed a vertical organization, the Act worked.

At a time when the threat is neither a state nor a conventional army, and hence anything but "vertical," the United States is still organized as it was during the Cold War when the Soviet Union was the enemy. In essence, this "vertical" structure must deal with a "horizontal" threat that cuts across most if not all agencies of government. But it cannot, because of the malassignment of responsibility, authority, and accountability.

WMD shows why a "vertical" organization is not capable of dealing with a "horizontal" threat. Homeland Security, Health and Human Services, and Transportation, as well as State, Defense, and the CIA have key responsibilities. Yet who is responsible for what, and who has the authority and spending power, are not clearly defined. This is also confused by Congress, who chooses to fund particular programs to meet constituent needs rather than to ensure competent administration. The Energy bill with some 6,000 "pork projects," up from "only" 1,400 several years ago, demonstrates this reality. And there is no accountability. The final report of the 9/11 Commission made this absence painfully clear.

Beyond this antique structure, law enforcement and intelligence are obviously crucial. However, those organizations have critical flaws as well. The chief law-enforcement agency, the FBI, is charged with counter-terrorism and has become the domestic equivalent of Britain's MI-5, responsible for intelligence at home. But a paradox makes the FBI ill-suited for conducting counter-terrorism.

As a law-enforcement agency, the FBI must provide the evidence and grounds for successful prosecution in a court in which the rights of the accused are protected and the due process of law prevails. In counter-terrorism, preemption and actions that do not necessarily stand up in a court of law are needed. How then does the FBI resolve this contradiction in terms of operations, training, and rules of conduct? It cannot and will not.

Intelligence is divided among several dozen agencies, offices, and departments. The Department of Defense is a major provider, sponsor, and consumer of tactical intelligence gathered by very expensive and advanced surveillance systems, from overhead satellites and eavesdropping devices to local capabilities. Engaged in Iraq and Afghanistan, it has huge tactical requirements to be filled. Balancing military requirements with other competing priorities was never, and will not become, easy.

A director of national intelligence was created by law, along with a counter-intelligence center. These recommendations and many others emerged from the 9/11 and WMD commissions. The latter was impaneled to assess why intelligence failed to predict the September 11 attacks or find WMD in Iraq, and what should be done to correct those deficiencies. As it will turn out, the legislation was too much of a predictable compromise to be effective. By creating another layer in intelligence, the process will be more, not less, constricted.

Senate Intelligence Committee chairman Pat Roberts wanted to disestablish the CIA and start all over again, an eminently sensible and politically unacceptable alternative. Others, particularly in the administration, wanted little or no change. Here was a tough issue. And the way it was resolved demonstrated how and why the process of government was not capable of dealing with an issue of extreme consequence.

There were other flaws. A national intelligence center that would focus on better understanding the threat and proposing appropriate policies was not established. Normally, the National Security Council was the clearinghouse for those assessments. Unfortunately, the NSC and the so-called interagency process that is supposed to cut across this vertical structure have not been utilized or reorganized for those tasks. Hence, the end result was to add only another layer of bureaucracy at the top with the addition of the DNI.

The 9/11 Commission continued to monitor these matters and to report that these changes have not made the progress that is needed to keep the nation safe and secure.[36] At this writing, there is little appetite to make further changes in intelligence or law enforcement, whether by executive order or legislative fiat.

The intelligence failure over whether the administration manipulated or misled the nation in going to war will loom larger and will exacerbate and be exacerbated by the partisanship and polarization of the political process. The furor over Representative John Murtha's call for withdrawal from Iraq "as soon as practicable" continued into 2006 as the nation struggled with Iraq. In that process, almost assuredly, one outcome is predictable: No real reform will be imposed on the agencies of government. That marks the height of dysfunctionality.

Reducing National Vulnerability

All states are vulnerable. Even war-torn Iraq experiences disruption on a daily basis. Before September 11, there were a large number of vulnerability studies, from commissions to examine the national infrastructure to specific assessments on the various specific sectors. Y2K, the crisis that was to occur at midnight of 2000 as many computer systems and programs were not configured to register 2000, surely engaged much of the world on a vulnerability that never materialized. However, vulnerability remains.

Not long ago, Los Angeles airport was shut down because a tiny pocket battery caught fire and the fear was that this had been part of a failed terror attack. The March 11, 2004 bombings in Madrid influenced the election in Spain that threw Prime Minister Aznar out of office. The second attack against the London Underground and transport system in July 2005 was psychologically powerful in reinforcing British vulnerability to terror, even given the experiences of the Blitz (though most British citizens were not alive then) and the IRA. Disruption is the new aim of those seeking to use terror or its threat to achieve political purpose.

The saddest evidence of how well or poorly the nation has done in preventing and responding to vulnerability comes from Hurricane Katrina. The performance was horrible.

In the face of real dangers and threats to the nation, September 11 should have shocked the United States out of its complacency and false sense of security. Since then, vast sums were spent, ostensibly to protect the nation against terror. Americans were assured that better means were in place to deal with disasters, whether those imposed by terrorists or nature.

Final assessments and investigations will show how incompetent and disorganized all levels of government were in responding to Katrina. The testimony by former FEMA director Michael Brown to the Senate Government Committee in February 2006 provided a further and stunning critique of the failure of the Executive to organize the Department of Homeland Security, into which FEMA was folded, and of Congress to provide any oversight reinforcing the inability of government to provide for the common good.

Strengthening Alliances

Arbatov's query about "what will you do now that the enemy is gone" remains important in a second sense. The United States is, by far, the strongest and wealthiest state on the globe and in history. But what is that power worth?

NATO has been the central foundation for U.S. and Western security since 1949. Within NATO, the most effective alliance in history, America is the leader. Throughout NATO's nearly sixty years of life, there have always been issues that divided and nearly split the alliance, from its initial membership of twelve to the current twenty-six. However, through its first four decades of life, NATO remained a military alliance against a real military threat.

The Vietnam War, deployment of cruise and Pershing missiles into Europe to offset Soviet intermediate-range forces against huge opposition in the early 1980s (along with strategic missile defense), reshaping the alliance after the Soviet Union collapsed, and the U.S.-led invasion of Iraq were all potentially destructive forces to NATO. So far, the alliance has survived and succeeded. NATO has made valiant efforts to transform from a military alliance without a direct military threat to an alliance able to deal with the challenges of the new century.

For the past fifteen years, NATO has undergone a series of transformations to cope with the post–Cold War and twenty-first-century demands. In the Clinton administration, the decision was made to expand NATO eastward, admitting former Warsaw Pact members into the alliance once they had passed through the Partnership for Peace (PfP). The PfP was the training ground for membership, and required not merely realignment of the military but, more importantly, the transition to a democratic government and an open-market economy.

In addition, NATO formed the Mediterranean Dialogue to engage littoral nations of North Africa in coping with the challenges of the current era. After the remarkable Prague Summit of November 2002, NATO established the NATO Response Force or NRF, designed to conduct expeditionary operations from humanitarian support to stabilizing and peacekeeping missions to dealing with terrorism and preventing the spread and use of weapons of mass destruction. The NRF was to operate outside traditional NATO guideline areas in Europe. Ultimately, if funded and fully equipped, the NRF will number about 25,000 trained troops, prepared and equipped to operate for a substantial period even in distant regions.

The greatest and most recent division and near-fracture of the alliance was over Iraq. Germany and France strongly opposed the attack. Spain, with the fall of the Aznar government, withdrew its forces from Iraq. And, while those rifts are beginning to heal, the controversy over detention of enemy combatants in "black" sites in Europe has reopened old wounds. Fortunately, the alliance remains united on Afghanistan.

The test for NATO remains the future of the NRF. Member states will have to drastically alter spending priorities and force structure in order to shift from focus on a static European battlefield to dynamic ones further afield. Military–social–industrial complexes in each member state are resistant to making these changes. So, if the NRF cannot be properly manned, trained, and equipped, it will be largely a paper tiger with corresponding impact on future alliance solidarity.

Without a clear and present military threat looming even beyond the distant horizon, and given the huge differences that exist on both sides of the Atlantic over the need for a global war on terror and the extent of the real danger, the already powerful centrifugal forces within the alliance will become greater fault lines. Divided on Iraq, NATO still is moving ahead in Afghanistan. By mid- to late 2006, if all goes well, NATO will take charge throughout all of Afghanistan to assist in bringing stability, good governance, and a way of mitigating the epidemic of drug trafficking that threatens Afghanistan's future as a cohesive state.

Thus, NATO is very much at yet another crossroads. Committed to stabilizing Afghanistan and probably to a limited expansion of the training mission in Iraq, the future of the alliance lacks a secure foundation on which to build, beyond shared values and a legacy of success from the Cold War.

Meanwhile in Asia, the Kabuki dance the Bush 43 administration is doing with North Korea and in a different sense with China is not necessarily improving relations with its Asian allies and friends. North Korea remains a standoff regarding nuclear-weapons ambitions. The Six-Power Talks have made limited progress. The solution is direct bilateral talks between North Korea and the United States, something the Bush 43 administration has been unwilling to consider. Hence, North Korea is an open sore that will not automatically heal and may metastasize into something far worse.

The question is whether China will be a friend and potential partner or a foe. The U.S. Congress sees China's military buildup as both a danger and an opportunity. Congress is worried that China could challenge the United States one day, as well as develop the capacity to invade Taiwan. On the other hand, the buildup can be used to justify more spending on American naval and air forces.

The administration is ambivalent on China. Several studies done by the Department of Defense and the ground rules for the Congress-mandated Quadrennial Defense Review see China as a potential "peer competitor," a term that means "possible adversary." With the emphasis on rebuilding ground forces that are so actively engaged in Iraq and Afghanistan, a Chinese threat is the basis for rationalizing air and naval forces. Australia and its prime minister, John Howard, have given good advice in asking the Americans not to make China an enemy. However, whether Americans will heed that recommendation is by no means clear.

Given these uncertainties, America's allies and alliances are clearly worried. There is far from any agreement on the Global War on Terror. Europe, after all, has nearly 20 million Muslim inhabitants. With the murder of the Dutchman Theo van Gogh, the attacks in July 2005 against London transport, and the riots in France by enraged youth, sensitivity to the indigenous Muslim communities is an understandable reality—and in some cases an obstacle to waging the war on terror, as the terrorists are all Muslim. Hence, social reality tempers strategic choices. On balance, the alliance picture is decaying.

While NATO has always been at one crisis or another, there is little doubt that the alliance is floundering over Iraq and over the future in dealing with the American version of the Global War on Terror. Asia presents other issues. Failure to obtain agreement on North Korea's nuclear programs is a persistent problem, and the prospect of a crisis can never be dismissed. Division of American views toward China is another indicator of uncertainty.

China has also begun to present glimmers of a more hostile and aggressive attitude toward Japan. Rather like Chinese attitudes hardening against Taiwan over the past few years, the same could happen with Japan. The crux there is the future of Japanese military rearmament.

Some in the Bush 43 administration favor such an outcome, on the grounds that a stronger Japanese military would balance China and North Korea and thus be in the U.S. interest. However, taken to the next step, that could mean a nuclear Japan. The experiences of the last century suggest that greater instability and chance for tensions, and not the reverse, would be the more likely outcome.

Rectifying the Causes of Jihadist Extremism

The jihadists have been clear in stating their grievances with the infidels and with the West. The Arab–Israeli–Palestinian conflict; illegitimate Islamic regimes in Saudi Arabia and Egypt, among other countries; control of regional oil; and repression of Islam worldwide are among them. Obviously, neither all nor even a few may be resolvable from the West's perspective. However, the United States has not undertaken in a formal way any strategy or plan akin to the Marshall Program, announced in 1947 to rebuild Europe and Japan and therefore help contain the spread of Soviet communism.

Progress had been made, prior to the October 2005 earthquake in Pakistan and Kashmir, to calm the tensions between India and Pakistan. But the Israeli–Palestinian conflict is not better. Egypt and Saudi Arabia, despite recent elections, remain autocratic societies. The Saudis continue to finance Wahabi madrassas outside their borders. Poverty and despair still persist throughout much of the Muslim and Arab worlds. Focus has been placed on the GWOT—that is, hunting down and capturing or killing the terrorists and breaking up the networks. And within Europe, attempts to assimilate local Islamic populations have not proven successful.

American preventive and public diplomacy continue to lag far behind the need. In 2004, a report done by the Department of Defense Science Board on strategic communication issued a scathing indictment and proclaimed that the United States was losing the war of ideas. The appointment of presidential confidante Karen Hughes as Undersecretary of State for Public Diplomacy was hailed as a great step forward. However, the task is beyond any one person to correct. As a result, the activities to rectify the causes of jihadist extremism are largely unsatisfactory outside the GWOT. And the GWOT can only provide a limited solution to a part of the larger challenge.

What Does This Mean?

In basing one's answer on these five measures and the response to Hurricane Katrina, it is clear that the United States is surely not winning the war on terror and could be losing it. Neither the administration nor Congress seems inclined to demand or impose significant course corrections. And the American public is not interested yet in becoming more vocal and pressuring their elected officials for action.

The bet seems to be that enough is being done and eventually, like the hoola hoop of the 1950s and the leisure suits of the 1970s, the terrorists will gradually disappear. This is a bad bet. Unfortunately, no one seems to be listening and no one seems willing to act. If that is the case and the adversary is as persistent, flexible, and dangerous as it appears, the United States and the rest of the world are in for difficult times. Iraq is the most immediate test case. However, even if Iraq miraculously embraces democracy, that is by no means the stake through the heart of the beast. Far more must be done. But will it?

A Further Reminder

All actions have consequences—some intended, many not. As wars beget wars—from the Napoleonic Wars, the seeds for World War I were planted; from it, World War II; and from the Cold War, today's conflicts against jihadist extremism—policy begets reactions. Noted earlier were the unintended consequences of U.S. support to the Afghan Mujahadeen, which helped empower al Qaeda, and the overthrow of the Taliban more than a decade later, which empowered the warlords to make poppies and the drug trade about half of current-day Afghanistan's gross domestic product (GDP).

In viewing the world as it is, or as we think it is, one huge fault line has been the failure to conduct sophisticated analysis of second-, third-, and subsequent-order consequences. The process simply does not allow it. In this world in which power has diffused and continues to spread, future effects of policy and action can never be perfectly mapped. However, unless or until a better method evolves, the United States will be permanently impaired. The impact of culture, crusade, and partisanship is a further impediment to producing successful—or at least necessary— strategic analysis in order to understand better the consequences of American actions and the need to make appropriate course corrections when needed.

The Chinese Puzzle and the Russian Enigma

PERHAPS NOWHERE IN AMERICAN HISTORY have culture and crusade figured as strongly as in relations with China and Russia, at least prior to September 11 and the subsequent Global War on Terror. Idealism and pragmatism understandably have been in tension in U.S. dealings with China and Russia. Over the past decade, the dark side of partisanship began reasserting a largely negative influence, reinforcing ideological convictions that often distorted and colored American perceptions toward China and Russia. And the reverse was also true. China and Russia had, and continue to have, unique views of the United States that often reflected colossal misunderstandings. All three countries have had intimate relationships shaped and molded since the early nineteenth century.

American culture, in these cases, embodied idealism, pragmatism, and a certain amount of idiosyncratic behavior. The spirit of crusade began with the missionary spirit that Americans pursued in proselytizing China beginning in the 1840s. Partisanship was present; but not until the end of World War II, with the rift and then Cold War with the Soviet Union and the emergence of "Red" China and the debate over who "lost" China, did it become especially bitter. Now that the Soviet Union has turned into Russia and "Red" China is no longer an enemy, at least for the short term, in other contexts, the bad sides of culture, crusade, and partisanship have been twisting and distorting American policies to the point that American security is being damaged, possibly irreversibly.

Russia is no longer a superpower. It is, however, still a very important state. Straddling Eurasia, attempting to maintain a democratic and free market system, rich with oil and other natural resources and still possessing formidable nuclear weapons, Russia represents both an opportunity and a challenge for the United States. Despite the personal bond between presidents Bush 43 and Putin, assuming it still exists, residual distrust from the Cold War has yet to disappear and still motivates some members of Congress and the administration.

While Russia acceded to the expansion of NATO eastward, its borders to the south and east are by no means stable. The Chechen war still smolders as Chechen terror continues. Despite America's own very personal war on terror, Putin's tactics against the Chechens and terror, as well as his perceived clampdown on the media and other forms of free expression, have provoked predictable U.S. criticisms on the grounds of human-rights abuses. Russia is thus not a close friend, and the relationship could deteriorate over these and other differences. That Russia is awash in money largely due to its oil exports makes it more independent and aloof from the United States.

China represents a more complex challenge for the United States. Still a communist state with more or sometimes less tight party control, China practices free enterprise, with some crucial exceptions. There is little visibility into the relationships among state-owned banks and state- and privately held corporations and companies. The accounting system is rudimentary at best. Financial solvency has been maintained through loans and debt offerings made by state-controlled banks without sufficient—or even credible—collateral. While the country's economic growth rate is estimated at 7 to 8 percent per annum, the immutable requirements levied by a population of 1.3 billion people when as many as 300 to 400 million live at or below the poverty line demand continuing economic progress. The bet is that GDP growth will enable Beijing to improve the lot of the majority of the people. But what happens if the economy falters or the financial system crashes? History reminds the ruling elite of many earlier Chinese insurgencies and peasants' revolts.

China's large trade imbalance with the United States due to low

Chinese costs of labor has provided Beijing with billions of dollars. The U.S. side has pressed for devaluation of the yuan, something China has done only on the margin. A more significant matter is China's pirating of intellectual property, which the United States has been forceful about but not fully successful in ending. The absence of full intellectual and property rights protection in China is a major obstacle blocking investment and a cause for concern. Because of these and other points of conflict with the United States and associated bad press, China elected to drop its bids to acquire the U.S. Unocal oil company and the Maytag Corporation, producers of home appliances, so as not to create further friction.

Of greater concern to the United States is Beijing's military buildup. China is modernizing its roughly three-million-strong People's Liberation Army (PLA). Its navy is growing in size and capability. Each of these trends is worrisome to the United States and to regional states as well. On his first trip to China as defense secretary in October 2005, Donald Rumsfeld made the Chinese fully aware of American concerns over China's military modernization. China explained that the West was exaggerating the pace and scale of its military programs. The point is that China is somewhere between friend and foe, and the balance seems moving in the wrong direction.

Some in Congress see the military buildup as an opportunity for a stronger U.S. military. F-22's and carrier strike groups make a great deal more sense against a Chinese enemy than against jihadist extremists without any organized military. Others in Congress see China as a danger. Either way, unhealthy attitudes are likely to emerge, distorted by both sides and by culture, crusade, and partisanship.

A *Thumbnail History*

American involvement with China predated the formation of the United States and was driven by trade and commerce. In 1784, the year after America won its independence, a tiny sailing ship, *Empress of China*, left New York harbor destined for Canton, China, 13,000 miles away. In its cargo were assorted goods including ginseng, then regarded as a cure for impotence. A year and a half later, she returned laden with strange products, including tea. The reported profits for the expedition were about 25 percent, just enough to tempt other merchants to follow suit. Thus, China trade grew. By 1801, nearly three dozen American ships had put into Canton, the only port then open to foreigners.

American interest in China was slow to develop. Little public mention of "China" was made in the press. China's "Middle Kingdom" complex, in which China perceived itself as the only truly great and civilized nation, surrounded by barbarians and "foreign devils," remained a barrier to trade and commerce until 1839. That year, superior Western military technology and the full force of commercial interests in trade led to a one-sided clash between Britain and China in what became known as the Opium War.

To foreigners, the main sticking point in relations with China was the failure to gain equality in treatment from the Chinese mandarins, who refused to abandon the Middle Kingdom complex and the assumed superiority of Chinese culture. To the Chinese, the cause of the dispute was British insistence of forcing the opium trade on China and turning thousands of Chinese into addicts in order to turn huge profits on the drug trade. The "Medellin cartel" of the era was run by John Bull. The result was a brief, lopsided war.

Chinese war canoes, ancient muskets, and spears were impotent against British arms. In 1842, the Treaty of Nanking forced China to cede the island of Hong Kong to the British and open five other ports (Canton, Amoy, Foochowfoo, Ningpo, and Shanghai) to trade. The war evoked American sympathy for the Chinese, in large part because a wave of Anglophobia had been building in the former colonies. Americans also had commercial interests in China that would soon lead to American clergy taking their message (and crusade) to convert these "heathens" to Christianity. As a result, a squadron of naval ships commanded by Lawrence Kearney arrived in Chinese waters that same year and gained a "most favored nation" agreement that opened these five ports to all foreigners. The foundation for the "Open Door" policy was laid.

Two years later, Caleb Cushing, the first American commissioner to China, arrived in Macao. Backed by the power of his small fleet, Cushing admonished the local authorities that to not receive foreign envoys would be considered "an act of national insult and a just case for war" and threatened that he would travel to Beijing (it was called Peking then) and deal directly with the emperor. The bluff worked. Cushing secured a formal most-favored-nation treaty and an explicit recognition of "extraterritoriality," meaning that Americans accused of most crimes in China would face trial before an American consular officer, not a Chinese court.[37]

Following the Opium War, commerce between the United States and China boomed, and by the mid-1850s, trade with China had reached a new high point as the famous and swift "clipper" ships plied the Pacific waters. American missionaries, now assured of access to China, arrived in increasing numbers to embark on a crusade of sorts to proselytize and convert Chinese to Christianity. One of the converts became a leader of the Taiping Rebellion that lasted from 1850 to 1864 and claimed an estimated twenty million lives, the bloodiest civil war in history.

During the ensuing decades, Western states continued to carve China up, imposing new treaty demands for trade and access. After the Crimean War, Britain and France trounced the ill-prepared Chinese and extorted new treaties at Tientsin in June 1858, followed by further hostilities on the Pei-ho River the following year in which the British were forced to retreat. The allies assembled a much stronger force and in 1860 captured Beijing and imposed the Convention of Beijing on China.

America, distracted by crises at home that would lead to the Civil War, demurred joining the allied force. Indeed, the U.S. argued that this was a continuation of its traditional policy of nonentanglement with European states. However, Washington argued that the allies' purposes were "just and expedient," a marvelously cynical policy as America avoided the need to fight while reaping the fruits of war wrested from China by the European states.

China unsuccessfully resisted the assaults and intrusions by the West and later by Japan, which had been "opened" in 1854 by Commodore Matthew C. Perry (the younger brother of Oliver Hazard Perry, the hero of the Battle of Lake Erie in 1813) and his "black ships." Japan, unlike China, recognized the danger posed by the outside world and, with the Meiji Restoration in 1861, embarked on an extraordinary program of modernization, particularly of its military. In 1894, Japan embarked on a short war with China, taking Korea as the prize. Ten years later, Japan would take on Russia. In the space of fifty years, Japan had gone from a feudal state to one that could compete militarily with the West.

External imperialism became more than an open sore for China. It preoccupied and humiliated China for decades to come. Ending imperialism would become a principal political aim and a rationale for both fearing and opposing the West used by Chinese nationalists, including Mao and his communist followers. A loose parallel between the force of imperialism and the grievances of jihadist extremists surely exists today.

American attitudes toward China were reflected in the "Open Door" policy announced by McKinley's secretary of state, John Hay. American trade with China was small, estimated at about 2 percent of its total, and growing. The United States, having acquired the Philippines in the war with Spain in 1898, was a Pacific power and was concerned that intruding powers would establish high tariff barriers and restrict access to spheres of influence wrested from China. The result was a series of open-door notes on China sent to Germany, Britain, and Russia, who had large stakes in China and then to Italy, Japan, and France. The Open Door policy has since been vastly misunderstood to stand for equal commercial opportunity and the integrity of China. In fact, the policy was narrowly defined to apply to small leaseholds and spheres of influence; it did not provide for equal treatment; and there was no insistence of China's maintaining territorial integrity.

In 1900, foreign occupation precipitated the Boxer Rebellion. Rebellion by peasants against imperial rule was endemic in China. Thousands of fanatical Chinese rose up against the "foreign devils" and laid siege to a number of foreign legations in Beijing. Despite its policy of nonentanglement, the United States joined the 18,000-man rescue expedition and, in August 1900, lifted the siege. With the Spanish-American War and the Boxer Rebellion intervention, the United States had shed George Washington's dictum of nonentanglement. And because it returned the bulk of reparations received as compensation for the Boxer Rebellion, much Chinese good will was generated.

In 1911, the Manchu rule ended. The Dowager Princess died in 1908. Revolutionary study societies had sprung up. Partly by accident, in September 1911, a revolutionary plot was uncovered in Wuchang. A few of the soldiers revolted preemptively on October 10 before the government acted to quash the mutiny. But the Manchu governor fled and the rebellion spread. China was on its way to establishing a republic to be headed first by Yuan Shih-k'ai. Under his leadership, parliamentary rule would be eroded and control of China would fall into the hands of local warlords. The warlord period lasted from 1916 to 1928 and led to a period of local conflict, disorder, and a divided country.

The rise of revolutionary movements began the struggle to reestablish central power. The two most powerful factions that emerged were Sun Yat-sen and the Kuomintang (KMT) and Mao and the Communist Party of China (CCP). Until they split in 1927, both parties seemed cut from the same cloth. Both were largely Leninist-styled organizations that had embraced Marxism-Leninism and co-existed within the KMT. The KMT had allied with Stalin's Comintern. With the breakup, the KMT, associated with the Nationalists, eventually turned on the CCP. The Nationalists, under the leadership of Chiang Kai-shek, embarked on five "extermination" campaigns in 1934, forcing some 100,000 CCP members to break through the blockade and begin the "Long March" to Yenan.

Meanwhile, Japanese incursions into China began with the attack on Shanghai in 1932, leading to all-out war in 1937. That war and Japan's aggression forced the KMT and CCP to reach an uneasy truce. In 1936, Chiang had been captured in Sian by Chinese troops from Manchuria more interested in resisting Japanese aggression than fighting the CCP. Chou En-lai, later to become the People's Republic of China long-term prime minister, directed the CCP to mediate Chiang's release to maintain a united front against Japan.

The two parties repeatedly clashed with each other during the war with Japan. After Pearl Harbor, Nationalist China and Chiang became American allies. A ragged truce with the CCP continued. After the war, in late 1945, General of the Army George C. Marshall was dispatched to China on a mediation effort between Chiang and Mao. Over the course of year, the effort failed. Based on that frustrating experience, Marshall would say that communism could no more live with free enterprise than water with fire.

Mao and the CCP, organizing the people to support revolution, grew in strength while the Nationalists' grip on China weakened. The collapse of KMT control of China and the victory of the CCP in 1949 were perceived by the West as a staggering loss. A half billion or so Chinese were now in the communist camp, and communist China had intimately aligned with the Soviet Union, or so conventional thought went. The question was: Who lost China? In reality, it was the Nationalist regime. A State Department White Paper dated August 5, 1949, called the Nationalists inept, selfish, and corrupt.

The Cold War

One of the great tragedies of World War II was the failure of American political leadership to understand the situation in China, the common roots of the KMT and the CCP, and the flaws, fault lines, and corruption of Chiang's rule. The Korean War then ended any chance for a rapprochement between the United States and China.

On June 25, 1950, North Korean forces, egged on by Stalin and without provocation, attacked southward, crossing the 38th Parallel that had divided the two Koreas since the end of World War II. South Korean and U.S. resistance collapsed. The armies retreated to an enclave at the southeastern tip of the peninsula around the port of Pusan. With the Soviets boycotting the UN and therefore unable to exercise their veto, the Security Council approved a UN response to the aggression. Instead of declaring war, a "police action" was authorized to turn back the invading North Korean army.

Three months later, U.S. General of the Army Douglas MacArthur, the supreme commander in Japan and Korea, pulled off a brilliant, audacious amphibious operation at Inchon, Seoul's seaport on Korea's west coast a few dozen miles south of the 38th Parallel. The North Korean army was routed and fled north, with the United Nations forces in hot pursuit. Just before Thanksgiving, with allied forces closing in on Pyongyang, the capital, and the Yalu River separating the north from China, China warned the UN to halt the advance.

MacArthur disbelieved the threat and was convinced that China would not intervene with military force. He was wrong. The PLA crossed the Yalu and launched two separate attacks, withdrawing after each as a signal of its intent. MacArthur ignored the warning attacks and rejected the advice from Washington that China might intervene. Around Thanksgiving, hundreds of thousands of PLA troops charged south. MacArthur would be later relieved for disregarding orders not to speak publicly about using Taiwanese troops to fight in Korea. While President Harry Truman called Korea a police action, the United States was at war with Red China.

Three years later, a truce ended the fighting. But North and South Korea have been arrayed against each other ever since, and the United States still maintains some 25,000 military personnel on the peninsula. It would be twenty years before the hostility between China and the United States would be overcome.

Triangular Politics

In 1958, Walt Rostow wrote *The Prospects for Communist China*. Rostow would become President John F. Kennedy's deputy national security adviser, promoted by Lyndon B. Johnson to the top spot. Rostow argued presciently that permanent schisms over ideology, history, geography, and politics would turn the Soviet Union and Red China against each other. Rostow's recommendation for American policy was to exacerbate these fault lines.

But a series of mini-crises over the tiny Matsu and Quemoy islands controlled by the Nationalists, which China occasionally shelled; and the standoff between Chiang, forced to retreat to Taiwan; and the mainland hardened American attitudes against Beijing. Indeed, even raising the specter of recognizing China, in the era bastardized by "Tail Gunner" Joe McCarthy, the unstable and alcoholic senator from Wisconsin whose anticommunist tirades and crusades did huge damage to the country, was not merely politically incorrect. It was harmful.

I recall a ninth-grade civics teacher who, in 1954, suggested to his students that China be recognized and that failing to acknowledge China's existence was an act of foolishness. Then one day, a substitute took the teacher's place and he never returned. The suspicion was that he lost his job over his stand on China.

Earlier that year, it appeared that China was preparing for a massive invasion of Formosa (Taiwan) to end the unfinished civil war and finally eliminate the Nationalists. In an unprecedented move to prevent the United States from being caught in a second Korean War, this time in the Taiwan Straits, the Eisenhower administration (having negotiated the Korean truce the year before) asked Congress to approve the Formosa Resolution, sent up to Capitol Hill on January 24, 1955. The joint resolution stated, in part: ". . . the President . . . is authorized to employ the Armed Forces . . . as he deems necessary for the specific purpose of securing and defending Formosa and the Pescadores against armed attack. . . ."

From that time on, American views of China became rigid. It became part of the American culture that somehow America had "lost" China and now faced a "monolithic" communist threat. That empire spanned ten time zones, from the Iron Curtain in the west to the extreme end of Eurasia. Because of the Korean War, the political correctness of the day demanded that the Chinese communists were a permanent adversary. The notion of a crusade to defend the "poor" Nationalists evolved and is still in play, now that Taiwan is a real democracy. Chiang Kai-shek and the Nationalists who had escaped to Formosa were, and remain, pro-tected by the U.S. Seventh Fleet standing between the island and China.

This marvelously simple view dominated how the United States viewed China for a quarter of a century. And the purges at the State Department eliminated many experienced "China hands" who knew better.

These attitudes were further hardened by China's catastrophic "great leap forward" in 1958, a ludicrous plan to modernize the country epitomized by individual households smelting cast iron in their back yards. In 1966, the Great Proletarian Cultural Revolution began. From beyond China's borders, the revolution appeared to signal a nation run amok. Any opposition and dissent was crushed, and mandatory "reeducation" took place in what were perceived as slave-labor camps. The border war China fought with India, no friend to the United States either, confirmed the American perception of Chinese aggression.

The Vietnam War, discussed in the next chapter, sharpened the differences and the mutual hostility between China and America. What eluded many Americans was the growing rift between the Soviet Union and China. China exploded its first nuclear weapon on Christmas Day 1964. However, long before then, Soviet First Secretary Nikita Khrushchev had withdrawn Russian military support and nuclear technical assistance from China. The tensions worsened, and there were several clashes between Soviet and PLA forces along the Ussuri River from March until September 1969.

Richard Nixon assumed the presidency on January 20, 1969, claiming that he had a plan to end the war in Vietnam. Nixon also had grander strategic visions that became known as "triangular politics," in which China was played off against the Soviet Union. Nixon recognized the strategic importance of exploiting the largely invisible fault lines that divided Moscow and Beijing. His national security adviser, Henry Kissinger, began a series of secret trips and meetings culminating in Nixon's trip to China in February 1972 and the profound shift in American-Chinese relations that sprang from "ping pong" diplomacy and the first visit of a Chinese team to America later in 1972.

Moscow realized that détente was better than confrontation in large part because of Nixon's triangular politics. The antiballistic missile (ABM) treaty and the Strategic Arms Limitation Talks (SALT) led to agreements to limit strategic nuclear weapons. Progress in U.S.–Chinese relations continued with the Carter administration's recognition of China and the Reagan administration's expansion of trade and commerce. That progress was halted by a student crackdown in Tiananmen

Square June 3–4, 1989, when PLA forces brutally repressed pro-democracy demonstrations.

From Bush to Bush

George H. W. Bush was a friend of China, having served as chief of the U.S. liaison office there under President Gerald Ford. He and his national security adviser, Lt. General Brent Scowcroft, who had served in the Nixon NSC and filled the same post for Ford, understood the need for maintaining balance between the two states despite the harm done by the massacre in Tiananmen Square. However, Bush would become pre-occupied with other crises, beginning with the invasion of Panama to remove Manuel Noriega in late 1989, and then, of course, the two most profound events of his presidency.

The first was the crisis over Saddam's invasion and occupation of Kuwait in the late summer of 1990; the second was the implosion of the Soviet Union. While Bush 41 won a lopsided victory in the first Gulf War, Saddam would be very much unfinished business, casting a long shadow on his successors, Bill Clinton and George W. Bush 43. Accommodating the new Federation of Russian States and creating further opportunities as Moscow began a long process of democratization was a further piece of unfinished business in Russia and in America.

In the presidential campaign, Clinton accused Bush 41 of kowtowing to the "butchers of Beijing." But after the election, the Clinton administration quickly adopted policies very similar to the elder Bush's. Unfortunately, during the 78-day NATO war in Kosovo in 1999, a "smart" bomb hit the Chinese embassy in Belgrade. Few Chinese believed the attack was an accident, given the accuracy of American weapons; most regarded the incident as an anti-Chinese signal by the United States. Fortunately, the incident died down. However, during the second term of the Bush 43 administration, the question of China as friend or foe would play out.

Friend or Foe?

In the 1970s, the phrase "China Syndrome" was invented in the United States to inflame the debate over nuclear power by fringe environmentalists. So opposed to nuclear energy, these environmentalists conjured up an ultimately absurd doomsday scenario: a reactor explosion of such intensity that it penetrated through the earth all the way to China.

"China Syndrome" became the incendiary war cry in the political fight to prevent the building of new nuclear power plants in the United States.

Today, "China Syndrome" may not be the best term of choice for describing either nuclear power or relations with Beijing, but some in the Bush 43 administration see China as an inevitable adversary. The reason is ideological. Communist regimes, even with market economies, still smack of the Cold War and cannot be fully trusted. China's size, economic growth, enhanced influence around the world, and what some predict will be a military that could one day threaten U.S. and regional interests, are grounds for caution. And part of this concern reflects a political reaction by members of Congress who view China negatively because of what is seen as exploitation of cheap labor made worse by an undervalued currency, a willingness to pirate intellectual property, and increasing global presence that masks political intent for influence as China continues its impressive economic growth.

Of late, China has shown increasing hostility toward Japan. If this continues, those who view China as a foe will have further grounds for that case. For Japan, there remain a number of uncomfortable issues with China, residue from World War II over territorial disputes, apologies for Japanese atrocities committed against the Chinese people, as well as potential economic, political, and even military rivalries as China emerges more visibly and forcefully on the world scene.

So, who is right and who is wrong? Is China a friend or foe; a potential partner and ally, or a competitor who yearns to restore its greatness and dominance in the future? How do we answer these questions and what should our policies be to encourage friendly rather than adversarial relations and future outcomes that lead to peace and prosperity rather than tension, rivalry, and conflict?

Washington is awash in speculation over China. The Bush 43 administration has chosen a policy of speaking softly and keeping its policy on China private. Many believe that despite the absence of a clear or even hinted statement of policy, the White House has pretty much made up its mind about China. But with this lack of conclusive evidence, as in the days of the old Soviet Union when Kremlinologists drew conclusions on the most crucial matters of state based on deductions from bits and pieces of often trivial information, Americanologists here and abroad face a similar task with the current White House regarding China.

The Bush 43 administration supported China's entry into the World

Trade Organization and has been open-minded in terms of free enterprise and Chinese investment in the United States, although the failed bids to buy Unocal oil and washing machine manufacturer Maytag suggest that other than financial considerations were at work. The Treasury Department put the squeeze on China to float the yuan and at least got a positive if modest response. And after the mini-crisis following the April 1, 2001 knockdown of a U.S. Navy Orion reconnaissance aircraft in international waters near China's Hainan Island abated, the Bush 43 administration returned to balanced policies toward Beijing, at least for several years.

Since then, several disparate events and activities have occurred that are being used to suggest a negative change in attitudes. The Bush 43 administration leaned on Israel not to sell China its version of the AWACS aircraft airborne warning system and pressured the European Union not to lift its arms embargo on China. In spring 2005, Secretary of Defense Donald Rumsfeld presented a lecture in Singapore that contained at least a caution to China about containing any military ambitions that might destabilize the region. The Department of Defense recently released an undated annual report to Congress on "The Military Power of the People's Republic of China," about which more will be said below.

The Quadrennial Defense Review, mandated by Congress, was completed by the Pentagon in February 2006. One of the terms of reference called for determining how to influence potential competitors in order to keep intentions friendly rather than adversarial. For "competitor," read China. In the National Defense Strategy of the United States dated March 2005 and signed by Secretary of Defense Rumsfeld, the section titled "How We Accomplish Our Objectives" noted that "We will work to dissuade potential adversaries from adopting threatening capabilities, methods, ambitions, particularly by sustaining and developing our own key military advantages." Again, read China as the potential adversary. The view of the Department of Defense is important. The document on China's military power, to the untrained eye, was a balanced and objective statement of what appeared to be Chinese intentions to enhance its military forces, especially in light of the superior nature of American military weapons and technologies, as demonstrated in both the first Gulf War in 1991 and Operation Iraqi Freedom in 2003.

China was described as a regional power with "global aspirations." While welcoming the rise of a peaceful and prosperous China, the document saw

China "facing a strategic crossroads" and asked which "basic choices China's leaders will make as China's power and influence grow, particularly its military power." The report concluded that over the long term, if current trends continue, China's military capabilities "could pose a credible threat to other modern militaries operating in the region." Clearly, "other militaries" are meant to include the United States and Japan.

Finally, the report acknowledged that the world has little knowledge of China's military motivations and where it is headed. It credited the PLA (People's Liberation Army) with publishing a biannual Defense White Paper and correctly noted that China's leaders continued to guard information about China's armed forces closely. More transparency and better insights into China's defense structure and future direction were needed, a recommendation that few in the West would deny.

Complementing this report were other publications on China by the National Defense University in Washington, D.C., and the RAND Corporation, a well-known think tank that expressed greater concern with China's future direction than the Defense Department account delivered to Congress yielded.

The view from official and un-official Beijing goes along these lines: Chinese military "scholars" read the Defense report with some alarm, arguing that the United States is exaggerating the extent and growth in China's military capabilities. Chinese officials deny that China is moving to establish regional and broader hegemony. But China's preoccupation with Taiwanese declarations of independence is cited as a powerful justification for fielding sufficient military power to annex the island by military means, should such a crisis be provoked by Taiwan. While there is no move to alter the 1979 agreement in which the United States recognized China and which called for peaceful resolution of the conflict based on a "one-China policy," the Chinese Central Committee passed a resolution authorizing a non-peaceful unification should Taiwan unilaterally declare independence.

Unofficially, senior members of the PLA admit that one reason why the PLA is tight-lipped over its plans is that it understands how weak its power is when posed against the United States in other than a direct invasion of the mainland—in which geographic size and numbers of Chinese would overwhelm any aggressor. But China is clearly modernizing its military forces and will continue to do so.

In September 2004, this writer was in China as a guest of the Chinese National Defense University and had the opportunity to meet with, and lecture before, many very senior Chinese military officers. Taiwan was a white-hot issue. In trips that go back nearly twenty years to China, a visitor routinely gets the standard Taiwan lecture. However, during this last trip, there was a particular edge to the intensity with which the Taiwan message was delivered. No doubt, much of this stronger rhetorical response was due to concern in Beijing over Taiwan's President Chen Shui-Bien's threat to declare independence. Yet there was also a certain gravity that had not been so visibly present before.

At the same time, the PLA held a major exercise called "Iron Fist," a division-sized maneuver that was reported on Chinese television and observed by foreign defense attachés. The Chinese troops were well equipped and well turned out in camouflaged uniforms and modern equipment. As a ground force, they looked good. But an experienced eye could not help but notice that the exercise was not organized and conducted in accordance with how a modern force would fight in what the United States calls a "joint and integrated" way, with airpower and other capabilities sewn together in common pursuit of defeating an adversary. In other words, the PLA had a very long way to go before it could obtain the standards common in some Western armies and especially the United States.

This is not a criticism of the PLA. It is a recognition that while Beijing modernizes its forces, this will not occur overnight and probably not for years, maybe even decades. China still has not deployed a solid-fuel intercontinental ballistic missile. Solid fuels are more stable than liquid fuels, can be stored for long periods inside the missiles, and require a greater level of technological sophistication to manufacture. Liquid rockets usually are not fueled until just before firing, meaning that it takes longer from the time the firing order is given until the missiles can actually be fired. China will deploy the DF-31 solid-fuel missile in due course, in limited numbers. However, all Western states have had solid fuels in service for decades. This is one example of how far China must come to match the United States.

There are a few obvious conclusions. Better and more objective insight into China's overall diplomatic and military strategies is needed. More Chinese transparency is in the interest of all. Neither the United States nor Japan should make any assumptions, explicitly or otherwise, about the inevitability of China becoming an adversary or strategic competitor. That could become a tragic self-fulfilling prophecy. Instead, there need to be far more military-to-military and political exchanges. Openness is a reality of Western systems that can be transplanted elsewhere if done with sophistication and care. Getting the Chinese to follow suit, at least gradually, is a sensible policy. To do otherwise would be a blunder.

Not a Puzzle if We Are Smart

China need not be either an enemy or a puzzle. One reason for the above historical perspective was to demonstrate how foreign occupation and imperialism have shaped Chinese attitudes and actions. Nor has the Middle Kingdom psychology been entirely lost. However, American culture has never been all that good at understanding other cultures. In an administration such as Bush 43's, with its preference for seeing the world as it should be, not as it is, and unilateral action perhaps cloaked in a "coalition of the willing," future Chinese–U.S. relations should not automatically be assumed healthy. China is under a degree of suspicion, although the administration refuses to admit that publicly. The emphasis on proceeding with ballistic missile defense and the abrogation of the ABM Treaty, while fiercely denied as being aimed at China, will not be ignored in Beijing no matter how much the administration claims otherwise, nor what North Korea may or may not do with its nuclear and missile ambitions.

The Bush 43 administration very much maintained the spirit of crusade in the Greater Middle East—although the situation in Iraq has dampened, not ended, that tendency. And in Congress, many members view Chinese military "rearmament" as either an opportunity on which to support modernizing our military or a threat that requires a strong reaction. Partisanship meanwhile has restricted having an open debate over China to reach a better understanding of whether the outcome will be friend or foe. Fortunately there are no more Joe McCarthys. But that does not mean that there is better debate.

The Russian Enigma

Churchill first compared the Soviet Union with enigmas and riddles. But actually, while the ruling Politburo (or Presidium, as it was also called) was shrouded in secrecy, that was not very different from the way cabinets and cliques made decisions even in Western democracies. The fundamental differences between the Soviet Union and the United States rested in the basis for distributing power, the nature of the economic system, and the extent that rule of law and constitutional protections were applied to citizens (or not). In some ways, penetrating the layers and disinformation in Washington was the most difficult factor in understanding what was happening in the Kremlin.

As we will see in great detail, using the Kennedy administration as one of many examples, the flaw was not in the absence of good, timely, and accurate information and intelligence on how the Soviets saw the world; the flaw was arrogance in dismissing that intelligence, as it made no difference to the plans the Kennedy team had in mind. The parallels between the Kosovo Campaign and Iraq are striking and reflect flaws that are present irrespective of party—and that are exacerbated by partisanship.

A Thumbnail History

Unlike China, American attitudes about and relationships with Russia were neither deeply rooted in history nor intimately involved with that nation until the 1930s, and then with World War II. The reasons were obvious. For the first 120 years that the United States existed, Russia was a sovereign and powerful state ruled by the House of Romanov. The United States was also preoccupied with the greater powers of the day, especially those such as Britain, France, Germany, Spain, and Japan, with whom it had more important interests or clashes.

Except for a few occasions, including the Tsar's *ukase* of 1821 that forbade foreign ships from coming within 100 Italian miles of Alaska (rescinded in a treaty with America three years later), and also including Russian repression of the revolutions of 1830 and 1848, America was generally friendly toward Moscow. Superficial similarities between the most advanced democracy in the new world and the absolute despotism of the old were, ironically, a contributor to these attitudes.

America and Russia were large, resource-rich states and were racially diverse. Both had freed millions of peoples in the 1860s—serfs in Russia and slaves in the United States. Both were faced with insurrection during those years. And because the two states were relatively isolated from each other, few tensions had developed.

During the American Civil War, in September and October 1863, the visits of two small Russian fleets to New York and San Francisco created the myth that these antiquated warships had been sent as a signal to the British and French to discourage their interference. That was not the case. The real reason was that war over Poland seemed imminent. The Russians did not want these ships bottled up in the Baltic or Far East, in the event of hostilities, by the more powerful Anglo–French fleets. Hence, their deployment to the United States (they were ordered home in April 1864) was not so much an act of friendship as an insurance policy to keep those ships out of harm's way.

Alaska had become a drain on Russia. Potentially valuable, the Tsar saw an opportunity to exploit the friendship garnered by the fleet visits. Approaching the United States with subtlety, in March 1867, the Russian Minister in Washington, Edouard de Stoeckl, offered Alaska to Secretary of State William H. Seward for $7.2 million. Despite the controversy over acquiring non-contiguous territory for a price, in April the Senate overwhelmingly approved the purchase, 37–2. However, it would be a year before fractious debate in the House ended with the appropriation approved 113–43 on July 14, 1868.

Nearly forty years later, as the Russo-Japanese War of 1904–05 exhausted both sides, American opinion initially favored Japan as the seeming underdog. Since Perry's opening in 1854, Americans had regarded Japan as a protégé and applauded what seemed to be Tokyo's support of the Open Door Policy. Even though Japan started the war with Russia with a surprise attack on Port Arthur, this action drew praise from American newspapers. President Theodore Roosevelt glowingly wrote: "Was not the way the Japs began the fight bully?" and regarded the Tsar as "preposterous little creature."

Convinced, however, that the defeat of either Russia or Japan could unbalance the Pacific, Roosevelt accepted the Japanese request to mediate the war. In August 1905, at Portsmouth, New Hampshire, Roosevelt prevailed and a peace agreement was reached. Ironically, Roosevelt won few friends in Japan, as the Japanese believed they could win the war—and little admiration from Russia on the same grounds. However, Roosevelt gained immensely in stature and was rewarded with the Nobel Prize for peace.

During World War I, Russia was an ally until the October Revolution in 1917 deposed the Tsar and ultimately placed Lenin and the Bolsheviks in charge after a bloody civil war. As George Kennan wrote in *Russia Leaves the War*, Americans resented the anti-capitalist excesses of the new regime. In 1919, a near-hysterical "Red scare" swept across the country, worsened by terrorist bombings that killed no one and never resulted in anyone's being brought to justice. The Russian revolutionaries were denounced as "assassins and madmen" and "beasts drunk from a saturnalia of crime." In 1920, the Wilson administration refused to recognize the Russian regime, in large part because the Bolsheviks had confiscated American property without compensation, repudiated legal debts, and later sent agents under the Comintern to recruit and convert Americans (and others) to communism and support of Moscow as the capital of the workers' paradise.

The Soviet Union was peddling an ideology antithetical to democracy and capitalism. At the same time, oil from the Middle East was generating great friction between the United States and Britain. By securing a mandate from the League of Nations for Palestine and Mesopotamia (now Iraq), Britain had cleverly positioned itself to access about half of the world's proven oil reserves. History may never repeat; it surely has interesting parallels, however.

The Great Depression ended the payment of debts and reparations due from the First World War. Cancellation, however, brought a change to the previous American policy of non-recognition of the Soviet Union. The American public had never been hostile to Russia and supported our relief effort in response to the gigantic famine of 1921–23 that swept through Russia; it had been hostile only to the Bolshevik government and its repressive regime. Be that as it may, in late 1933, the Roosevelt administration recognized the Soviet Union.

Moscow agreed to grant freedom of worship to Americans in Russia and to cease its anti-American propaganda campaign. The Soviets promised greater trade and investment, and then refused to deliver; nor did the anti-American propaganda cease. As a result, despite recognition, conservatives decried the Soviet Union as anti-democratic and anti-capitalistic. Liberals and socialists, especially in the 1930s as the depression worsened, idealized the Soviet Union and communism as better political alternatives, beginning the fascination of the American left with Bolshevism.

The Spanish Civil War of 1936–39 intensified the fascination of some Americans with both Hitler and Stalin and polarized the differences between the far extremes of the left and right. The pro-Catholic General Francisco Franco led the rebels in overthrowing the anticlerical Loyalist regime. Hitler and Mussolini openly supported Franco. The USSR aided the Loyalists. Several thousand Americans flocked to Spain to fight on the side of the Loyalists.

Pragmatically, antiwar sentiment in Europe prevailed and most of Europe stayed out of Spain's civil war. Given the Nazis on one side and the Soviets on Spain's other, no matter the winner, the democracies in Europe believed that there was little to gain. The tragedy was that these democracies allowed a fellow democracy to perish, and Spain proved to be a dress rehearsal for World War II.

In general, Americans did not like the Kremlin and Bolshevik repression, exemplified by the "show trials" of the late 1930s in which literally hundreds of accused "traitors" to the Soviet Union "confessed" their "sins." On August 23, 1939, Stalin amazed the outside world and America by concluding a non-aggression pact with Germany. In a secret annex, Stalin was assured of a slice of eastern Poland once war began just over a week later. As Nazi divisions poured into Poland from the west, Soviet troops from the east would occupy their share of that hapless country.

Stalin was following a cynical and pragmatic policy of siding with whomever best suited Soviet interests at the time. His thinking was that as the Germans and the democracies dissipated their strength against the other in the war, the Soviet Union would, by default, grow in power and influence. Stalin did not anticipate Hitler's military success in occupying Western Europe. Nor did Stalin believe that Hitler would turn against the Soviet Union and disregard the non-aggression treaty. However, on June 22, 1941, Hitler did both.

Operation Barbarossa launched the Wehrmacht east into Russia. Stalin reportedly was so shocked that he went unseen for days. While Russian peasants initially did not fear the invaders, Hitler ordered the Wehrmacht to treat the Russian civilian population as the enemy. The attack into Russia, and the just-mentioned order (which would turn any Russian against the invader, no matter how much they hated the Bolshevik rulers), were acts of colossal strategic stupidity that preordained Hitler's defeat, much as Japan's miscalculation over Pearl Harbor would do in the Pacific. One wonders if the decision to disband the Iraqi army by the U.S. Coalition Provisional Authority in Baghdad in mid-2003 will not prove an equivalent blunder.

Cold War Imperfections

Stalin had been an ally of expedience. Churchill said he would have made a pact with the devil, if doing so would have beaten Hitler. Many saw Stalin in the latter role. However, with Hitler fighting a two-front war, the Wehrmacht was overstretched. Russia would become a strategic quicksand pit in which to trap and destroy the Nazis. Too often, as the Allies were securing the territories around Europe's periphery in North Africa and the Mediterranean in preparation for the all-out assault on Fortress Europa, the crucial role the Soviet Union played on the Eastern Front was downplayed.

The historic meetings between Roosevelt, Churchill, and Stalin at Tehran and Yalta, and then at Potsdam after the war ended and Roosevelt had died and Churchill turned out of office, have been well reported. The fact was that Roosevelt had operated on the basis that by force of personality, he could strike a bargain with Stalin that would last beyond the war. What Roosevelt failed to recognize was the profound differences in aims that existed between the East and West.

Stalin was not about to repeat the lessons of the interwar years when the fragile and fledgling Soviet Union could not prevent intervention by the West, principally Britain, in the Russian Civil War. Nor was Stalin about to allow Germany in any form to have direct access to Soviet borders. Thanks to spies, Stalin was well aware of the American atomic bomb before Truman told him about it at Potsdam. And Stalin knew how weak the Soviet Union was, from the draining effort to repel and defeat the Nazis.

Hence, Stalin wanted, and would get, Eastern Europe as a buffer, as well as part of the Sakhalin Islands in exchange for declaring war against Japan following Germany's defeat. Not satisfied with a buffer, Stalin was planning to topple the Eastern European governments, replacing them with ones that could be controlled from Moscow. This defensive and indeed paranoiac mentality over protecting Russia from external attack was centuries in the making. Stalin had been given the opportunity, and he had the means.

From 1947 onward, the Cold War hardened. Churchill, of course, invented the term "iron curtain" in a great speech that he gave in Fulton, Missouri in 1946, warning of the danger from the east. The great alliance that defeated Hitler was dead and would metastasize into a four-and-a-half-decade-long political and ideological struggle seen in the United States as a replay of World War II, with good balanced against evil and democracy battling the newest tyranny in the form of communism.

In this battle, culture, crusade, and, later, partisanship dominated how America's political leaders ultimately viewed the threat and the policies necessary to contain that threat. At the beginning, the "wise men" such as George Marshall, George Kennan, and Dean Acheson understood the motives and intent of the men in the Kremlin. Containment, alliances, and nuclear deterrence were the tools created to prevent communist encroachment westward. Fueled by the "loss" of China, the Korean War, what appeared to be intense espionage and propaganda efforts, and Soviet intervention and bloody repression of the short-lived revolution in Hungary in 1956, Moscow was clearly seen as the enemy by a majority of Americans.

Eisenhower, having worked closely with the Russians during the war, was less persuaded of the absolute danger posed by the Soviet Union. The McCarthy years had so stigmatized any balanced or objective attitudes toward Russia as "anti-American" that public statements would necessarily maintain this atmosphere of belligerence. Eisenhower believed that Moscow could be contained, and he was able to implement his strategic "new look," with its emphasis on nuclear deterrence, on the grounds that no one in Moscow saw nuclear war as a desirable outcome. Ike also knew that the United States had substantial nuclear superiority and wisely played to that strength.

Objective assessment came to grief with the inauguration of President John F. Kennedy on January 20, 1961. Kennedy campaigned against the "soft" policies of Eisenhower regarding the Soviet Union and specifically the unfavorable military balance Ike had permitted to continue. The "bomber" gap of the late 1950s became the "missile gap" of the 1960 election. By implication and ironically, Richard Nixon, Ike's vice president and the Republican candidate with his well-known hardline anticommunist record, was attacked by the Democrats for placating and being "soft" on the Soviets.

Kennedy, of course, won by the narrowest of margins. That the bomber and missile gaps were imaginary made no difference. This was an administration that would enter office filled with idealism and activism. It was only fifteen years after World War II ended, and recollections of that war burned deeply in the new administration, as its members at all levels, by and large, had served actively in that conflict. Kennedy himself had been in PT boats and his boat, PT-109, had been cut in two by a Japanese destroyer. Anyway, aside from his brother Bobby, who had been too young to serve, his cabinet was steeped in the war and its lessons.

Taking office, Kennedy and his secretary of defense, Robert S. McNamara (an Army Air Force lieutenant colonel operational analyst during the war), set about strengthening the U.S. military. Several supplemental defense spending bills went to the Hill. The rates and numbers of U.S. bombers and missiles to be procured jumped dramatically. Military doctrine would shift from "massive destruction" threatened by nuclear war to "flexible response" that would create capabilities at all levels of combat, from unconventional war to strategic nuclear strike and missile defense. This was a muscular administration, and it believed in having more than soft talk and a big stick.

In April 1961, the administration approved a plan to use Cuban rebels to overthrow Castro, landing in Cuba at what would become the ill-fated Bay of Pigs. For any number of reasons, Castro's forces swiftly defeated the CIA-backed invasion force and the operation disintegrated into a foreign-policy disaster. In part, the promised American air support never materialized, as it was regarded as too risky. The combination of the U.S. defense buildup and the Bay of Pigs invasion sent shock waves through the Kremlin.

From the perspective of the Kennedy administration, the Soviet Union, as the Nazis before, could only and ultimately be contained by stronger military force. This was the lesson of Munich and World War II. "Godless" communism was little better than fascism. For freedom and democracy to prevail, a strong United States was essential. Part of America's strength lay in its superior ideology—although it was never called that—of democracy and freedom. It would become part of a crusade in Vietnam.

Unfortunately, the Kennedy administration completely disregarded the facts and the powerful intelligence that revealed Soviet purpose and intent, simply because that evidence did not conform with how the president saw the world. This was the classic and myopic combination of culture and crusade overriding reality and judgment. And it would lead not only to misadventure and tragedy in Vietnam; it probably extended the Cold War by years and resulted in huge and unnecessary defense expenditures.

How do we know that? By the late 1950s, Nikita S. Khrushchev had emerged as the *primus inter pares* in the ruling Presidium. Despite crises over Hungary and Suez in 1956, the scent of détente was in the air. The Soviets understood that Eisenhower's "new look" and emphasis on nuclear deterrence rather than expensive conventional forces was real. Peaceful coexistence was both possible and practical. As a result, a fierce debate began inside the Soviet Union over the shape and size of its military forces and the degree to which emphasis on nuclear capabilities provided the means for less defense spending.

From mid-1959 until late 1961, this military debate was well recorded and held in the pages of *Voenny' mysl'* (*Military Thought*), the top-secret journal of the General Staff. In later years, the debate would be chronicled in Marshal of the Soviet Union V. D. Sokolovskii's three editions of *Military Strategy*, published in 1962, 1966, and 1968. The reason we know about this debate was through a disgruntled GRU (military intelligence) colonel named Oleg Penkovskii. Not selected for promotion to general, Penkovskii exacted his revenge by turning traitor. The means was by photocopying *Voenny' mysl'* and passing the material to part-time journalist and MI-6 agent Greville Wynne, who was serving in Moscow.

Khrushchev and the "minimalists" won the debate. They argued that it was both safe and smart to emphasize nuclear weapons over conventional forces and allow defense cuts to be made, freeing up rubles for the civilian side of the economy. In January 1960, before Kennedy's election, Khrushchev announced major cuts in the size of the Red Army. He also spoke about "wars of national liberation." That phrase would provide, for the Kennedy administration, sufficient grounds for a major misjudgment of Soviet intent.

Through the presidential campaign and after assuming office, the Kennedy administration asserted that wars of national liberation were the means by which the Soviet Union would spread communism to the Third World. Vietnam would be the test case in point for this ideological battle. In fact, Sino–Soviet relations were nonexistent, and the two were engaged in a cold war of their own. Khrushchev intended the term as an assertion of the ideological superiority of Soviet communism over Chinese communism. The term was meant for the ideological struggle with the other Marxist-Leninist state, China. That was not how the "wars of national liberation" reference was interpreted in Washington.

Further evidence of the Soviet defense decisions came from the 21st Party Congress in the fall of 1959 and the "extraordinary" 22nd Congress held two years later that ratified these decisions. Understanding the Soviet military open press also provided important confirmation.

The military open press generally lagged behind the secret debate by about six to twelve months in publishing relevant articles. And it too began acknowledging the shift of defense thinking to the so-called "min-imum deterrent" posture, even though that deterrent would lead to tens of thousands of nuclear warheads. That debate would go on within the military press.

In the fall of 1960, as Kennedy was campaigning on a platform that accused Ike of being soft on defense and promising a major rearmament program, the Soviet Union was indeed scaling back its forces. Moscow acted on the belief that war was not inevitable and that both sides could operate on the basis of a minimum deterrent. Despite the embarrassing shootdown of Gary Francis Powers' U-2 over Russia in May 1960, which caused the cancellation of a final summit meeting between Ike and Khrushchev, Khrushchev believed that defense spending could continue to be reduced. The Russians also thought Nixon would win the November election and his policies would be extensions of Ike's. They were wrong on all counts.

The Kennedy team had access to this highly secret material. The CIA and its powerful counter-spook James Jesus Angleton thought the Penkovskii Papers could be disinformation, ignoring the other open-source material that supported or confirmed its content. With the profusion of "moles" and Russian spies from Kim Philby on, Western intelligence had good reason for skepticism. But, as happens more than occasionally, the presence of accurate intelligence was not relevant and made no difference.

Kennedy had made up his mind. World War II had ended only a decade and a half earlier. Kennedy, mindful of his first book, *While England Slept*, and the failure of Britain to take Hitler seriously, very much regarded the communist threat as a newer version of the fascists. In later years, in separate conversations with McGeorge Bundy, JFK's national security adviser, and Robert McNamara, who served as secretary of defense for six years, both acknowledged reading the Penkovskii papers. Both offered the same remarkable response: The Penkovskii Papers were discounted. President Kennedy had promised in his campaign to rebuild defense. He had decided; and the decision was irreversible, no matter what the facts may or may not have said.

Khrushchev was trapped. The ill-fated Bay of Pigs invasion in April 1961 confirmed to the Soviets the aggressive nature of the new Kennedy administration. Fighting a rearguard action, Khrushchev still persisted in his plan to shift money from defense to civilian needs. The 22nd Party

Congress affirmed his decision and probably approved what would become the strategic workaround to the American arms buildup: stationing nuclear missiles in Cuba.

For Khrushchev, the idea was inspired. The United States had ringed the Soviet Union with nuclear missiles. Why could the Soviet Union not do the same? Khrushchev and Kennedy had met earlier in the year over Berlin. Khrushchev believed that he had intimidated the young president (as FDR thought he had charmed Stalin) and that the Americans would have no choice except to allow Soviet missiles to remain in Cuba. With nuclear missiles within ninety miles of the American coast, Khrushchev reasoned that the Soviet Union would not need to field large numbers of long-range (and very expensive) intercontinental ballistic missiles. The Americans would be strategically outflanked. Khrushchev would win on both counts. He would counter the American buildup. And he could still shift spending priorities to the civilian—or soft—sector.

The Cuban Missile Crisis of October 1962 may have been the closest the Cold War came to becoming hot. The Soviets ultimately backed down, claiming to have won assurances from America over Cuban sovereignty and agreement by the United States to withdraw Jupiter missiles from Turkey, ironically fulfilling an order Kennedy had given much earlier and one that the system had failed to carry out. Sadly, the Cold War hardened. The U.S. continued its buildup. The Soviet Union reversed course and followed suit. Khrushchev's fate was sealed. Two years later, he would be deposed. By that time, the U.S. had become involved in Vietnam.

Clearly, culture and crusade in the form of the Kennedy administration shaped policy toward the Soviet Union. Oblivious to the facts, Kennedy had promised rearmament based on a flawed view of the adversary. The Soviets were embarked on the reverse track. That made no difference. The parallels between Iraq and WMD on the one hand, and the JFK perception of the Soviet Union on the other, are unmistakably clear. Hardened and predetermined decisions are resistant to change, no matter how much fact and intelligence argue otherwise. Perhaps the major difference was that Kennedy went to Harvard and Bush to Yale.

Nixon, and then Carter, carried on the policies of détente with the Soviet Union. Ronald Reagan's second term was able to improve those relationships. But while that history is important, it was the collapse of the Soviet Union that changed the shape of the world. Added to that, the tectonic changes in the Arab and Islamic worlds have redefined the nature of international politics. As we will see in Part III, the nature of American domestic politics likewise was altered. Partisanship and polarization have continued to harden both parties, making compromise still harder to achieve in ways that provide effective outcomes.

Friend or Foe?

American attitudes toward Russia are ambivalent. As Americans have been behind in understanding other cultures, this is also true with Russia. Common interests—such as maintaining stability in Eurasia, countering terror and proliferation, and reducing organized crime, along with illicit trafficking of all kinds—exist. Yet, these have not been sufficient to bring the two states closer. Russia is providing nuclear fuel to Iran, a further irritation with Washington. At the same time, the United States is expanding its ring of bases to the "stans" as part of the Global War on Terror, something the Russians do not like. Further expansion of NATO and ultimately what to do about possible Russian membership have been deferred to the distant future. Each can become a *cause célèbre*. Or each can become the reason for progress. Unlikely to become a close friend again, the best bet is a Russia that never quite becomes a foe—that is, unless the United States is prepared to make some fundamental course corrections.

Culture, Crusade, and Partisanship

From this brief review of history, it is stunningly clear that strategic analysis and objective assessment have not been central to American policies, with the major exception of Nixon's strategy of triangular politics with China. Nixon purportedly was a man from the right. Only a conservative, as Ronald Reagan showed a decade later with Gorbachev, had the political clout to make amends with former ideological enemies. But Nixon cared less about ideology. His national security adviser, later secretary of state, Henry Kissinger surely fit that mold. When Bill Clinton entered office, Russia was still evolving and Boris Yelstin had replaced Gorbachev as president. Those too were transitional years.

But, despite Watergate and the aftermath of Vietnam, culture, crusade, and partisanship, no matter how powerful in deflecting American policies to flawed directions, could be "righted" by the system. The problem and reality is that this righting function no longer appears viable or even visible. Given the complexity and the magnitude of the domestic and international issues and the critical question of whether the political process and those elected to serve in it are up to the task, there are grounds for considerable worry if American relevance and influence abroad and its dream at home are to be restored and protected.

Vietnam and the Greater Middle East

AMERICA'S RATIONALE AND CASE FOR the Vietnam War and the Bush 43 policies toward the Greater Middle East draw strikingly and eerily similar parallels. In both, the United States was bent on a crusade. In both, the White House manipulated facts and intelligence to support the case for war. In both, the White House failed to grasp and understand the cultural realities, assuming swift victory.

Consider the sense of crusade. President Kennedy was prepared "to pay any price and bear any burden" to defend liberty. South Vietnam was to be the focal point to stop what was perceived as the monolithic threat and spread of communism. If we failed, so the theory went, the rest of Southeast Asia would fall like a row of dominoes.

President Bush 43 saw Iraq as the opportunity to establish a democratic foothold in a region torn by violence. His crusade was to bring democracy to a region completely unfamiliar with it. The vision would produce a domino theory in reverse: a strategic transformation of the Greater Middle East, as a democratic Iraq would be contagious. Non-democratic states would topple, the domino analogy predicted. Of the two, Bush 43 was bolder and more aggressive in using democracy as a transformational tool. Kennedy saw involvement in Vietnam as a defensive move in the struggle against godless communism.

In both Vietnam and the Greater Middle East, our level of cultural understanding was deficient and our use of intelligence negligent. Kennedy exploited the so-called and erroneous "missile gap" brought home by the launching of Sputnik in 1957 to dramatize America's military weakness. After winning election, the administration embarked on a rearmament program of major proportions to close that gap, a gap that was non-existent, something that would be learned too late and would be repeated when Ronald Reagan entered office in 1981 determined to rebuild U.S. defenses. In Vietnam, America failed to recognize that the conflict was a civil war in the South between the Republic of Vietnam and the Vietcong or National Liberation Front (NLF) and the culmination of a long-term, nationalistic struggle waged by Hanoi to unify the country under its rule. We could not believe that an army that was technologically and physically inferior could outfight us. We also based our tactics initially on search-and-destroy, not physically controlling and pacifying huge chunks of territory, with the Americans doing the heavy fighting for much of the war and the South Vietnamese Army in support.

In Iraq, the case made by the Bush 43 administration for going to war was flawed. While it no doubt believed that Saddam had WMD and had surely flouted UN resolutions demanding that he disarm, there was no linkage between Iraq and September 11. More critically, while Western intelligence agencies all agreed that Saddam had a chemical and biological capability, no one argued that this threat was "imminent." And there was no debate or even public discussion of the larger context for war— using democracy as the means to transform the strategic landscape of the Middle East.

Hence, as in Vietnam, the rationale for war in Iraq proved as flawed as the missile gap and the domino theory. American cultural understanding of the region was negligent. Anticipation of the post-war demands was derelict. The administration made virtually every mistake possible, from disbanding the Iraqi army to demeaning international cooperation. The biggest distinction between Vietnam and Iraq, however, is the most important: Vietnam had no strategic consequences; Iraq does.

Finally, in both Vietnam and Iraq, the combination of culture and crusade run amok placed America at great peril. Vietnam was a powerful defeat. Iraq hangs in the balance. Although we failed in Vietnam, partisanship in the early 1960s could be contained regarding foreign policy. In Iraq, bitter partisanship has contributed to the mess. Whether that mess is reversible will be the lasting legacy of the Bush 43 administration. Writing in late 2005 and despite the large turnout for the December 15 elections, the chances that anything good for the long term will come from the Iraqi interlude do not look promising.

Vietnam: How We Got In and How We Were Thrown Out

What a team Jack Kennedy brought into his cabinet! These were the "best and brightest," chosen not on any political basis but on the basis of quality and character. In that regard, JFK deserved praise.

Virtually all of his senior team had served in World War II. Vice President Lyndon Johnson had been "master of the Senate" as majority leader, even if his Silver Star awarded in World War II was less than deserved. Dean Rusk had presided over the division of the Koreas at the end of the war as an Army lieutenant colonel. Secretary of Defense Robert McNamara was a "whiz kid" in the war and the first non-Ford to be president of that motor company. He and Treasury Secretary Douglas Dillon were nominal Republicans, to boot. McGeorge Bundy's bad eyesight had forced him to spend his time in uniform as an admiral's aide. And even Secretary of Agriculture Orville Freeman was a decorated and badly wounded Marine who had had part of his jaw shot away in an amphibious landing in the Pacific.

Many had written a book or two, or more. A proverbial dream team, representing the best America had to offer, was in place advising the young, dynamic, and bold-thinking president. How then could things have gone so badly wrong?

Consider the culture of the day. When JFK took office, World War II had ended only fifteen years before. Recollections of the war were still fresh. The main political lesson that the Free World drew from the experience was that evil could not be appeased. The West would not repeat the same mistake twice regarding the Soviet Union. The failure to halt Hitler's aggression was a powerful incentive to keep the Soviet Union contained and deterred.

In campaigning for office, Kennedy asserted that the Eisenhower administration was weak on defense. The launch of Sputnik in October 1957 was the "smoking gun" that proved the case. A "missile gap" confirmed by Sputnik threatened the United States and had to be closed (unlike the alleged "bomber gap" that had been proclaimed in the early 1950s, a gap that also did not exist).

There was no evidence or real proof to justify a "missile gap." Khrushchev, of course, and the Soviets were happy to use the American reaction as propaganda showing the superiority of Russian military technology, much as Saddam would create the impression that Iraq still possessed WMD. However, the perception among the public and the continued reference to Sputnik gave Kennedy the edge over his opponent. It was impossible for Nixon to disprove a negative, as forty-three years later it would prove impossible to counter the assertion that Saddam possessed WMD.

Kennedy's use of the missile gap was politics clear and simple, just as Bill Clinton would attack incumbent George Bush 41 in the 1992 campaign for cavorting with the "butchers of Beijing." The difference was that Kennedy meant what he said and immediately embarked on a military buildup, whereas the pragmatic Clinton embraced his predecessor's sensible policies toward China. At his second press conference, on February 1, 1961, Kennedy gave an insight as to what lay ahead. Asked about growing conflict in Southeast Asia, Kennedy answered:

> But I do think that the situation [in Southeast Asia] grows more serious. The Chinese communist strength increases, the intervention by the communists in these critical areas which I mentioned has grown greater, and therefore we have to consider whether, in the light of this conditional threat, the strength we now have—not only our nuclear deterrent, but also our capacity for limited war—is sufficient. It is not intended as a criticism of any previous action by any previous administration. It merely is an attempt to meet our own responsibilities at this time.[38]

A muscular yet cautious foreign policy was essential in dealing with the communists. In fact, the communist world was seen largely as monolithic, ignoring national security adviser Walt Rostow's prescience. Thus, the Democrats of that day adopted tougher policies abroad, along with socially responsible policies at home, something that Lyndon Johnson would make the centerpiece of his presidency in the Great Society.

America also favored crusades. The Cold War was not a replay of World War II. It was, however, a moral equivalent. It was the Free World, admittedly filled with its share of autocrats and dictators who supported us, versus the "totalitarian" Sino–Soviet bloc with their puppet states. And it was a world in which knowledge of the other side was always inferior to the general perception and public opinion that considered the Soviets and Red Chinese as totalitarian enemies.

The United States had been diplomatically involved in Vietnam at the end of the first Indochina war, when Ho Chi Minh and the Viet Minh were in the process of expelling the French. Indochina had been a French colony prior to the war, and FDR had been unwilling to pry it away from France after the war ended. War had broken out there in 1946. Ultimately, about 90,000 French lives would be lost.

With the war going badly, French General Henri Navarre decided to confront the Viet Minh army in one decisive battle. He baited a trap with a mountain fortress, in the northwest corner of Vietnam, named Dienbienphu. In December 1953, assured that the Viet Minh would be no match for French artillery and airpower, units moved into Dienbienphu. The Viet Minh took the bait. In March 1954, General Vo Nguyen Giap encircled the French garrison and, with artillery pieces that had been carried on the backs of his soldiers, pummeled the fortress into surrender. The French requested American air support, and there were rumors at the time that nuclear weapons might have been used to seal the passes cutting off the supply lines to Giap's forces. However, Eisenhower refused to use American forces without agreement from the Allies, particularly Britain. No agreement forthcoming, the fate of Dienbienphu was sealed.

After the crushing defeat, the French announced that they would withdraw from Indochina; and at the Geneva Conference in 1954, North and South Vietnam were created. The North, however, maintained ambitions to unite the two separate states. And the National Liberation Front (NLF) was to carry on that task in the South.

Kennedy made it clear that he intended to continue Eisenhower's policy of supporting the South Vietnamese government of Ngo Dinh Diem. He argued that if South Vietnam became a communist state, the whole of the non-communist world would be at risk. If South Vietnam fell, Laos, Cambodia, Burma, the Philippines, New Zealand, and Australia would follow. If communism were not halted in Vietnam, it would gradually spread throughout the world. This became the domino theory. Kennedy went on to argue: "No other challenge is more deserving of our effort and energy. . . . Our security may be lost piece by piece, country by country." Under his leadership, America would be willing to "pay any price, bear any burden, meet any hardship, support any friend, oppose any foe to assure the survival and the success of liberty."

President Charles de Gaulle of France warned Kennedy that if he were not careful, Vietnam would trap the United States, as it had France, in "a bottomless military and political swamp." However, most of Kennedy's advisers argued that with a fairly small increase in military aid, the United States could prevent a NLF victory in South Vietnam.

Kennedy initially had a good relationship with Diem, the leader of the South Vietnamese government, and in 1961 he arranged for Diem to receive the money necessary to increase the army (the ARVN, Army of the Republic of Vietnam) from 150,000 to 170,000. He also agreed to send another hundred military advisers to Vietnam to help train the ARVN. As this decision broke the terms of the Geneva Conference, it was kept from the American public. At that point, Kennedy had become enamored of the U.S. Special Forces. Created to fight behind enemy lines in Europe in the event of war against the Soviet Union, Special Forces units were trained in German, Russian, and other European languages. Many were trained to ski. None of these skills was applicable to Vietnam, where these forces would be deployed.

As the insurgency grew, in 1962 the Strategic Hamlet Program was introduced. For some time, the governments of South Vietnam and the United States had been concerned about the influence of the NLF on the peasants. To prevent that influence, local peasants were sent into new villages in areas under the control of the ARVN. Stockades and fortifications were built around the villages and patrolled by armed guards. This strategy failed dismally, and some observers claimed that it actually increased the number of peasants joining the NLF. Peasants resented working without pay to dig moats, implant bamboo stakes, and erect fences against an enemy that did not threaten them but directed its sights on government officials. In the majority of cases, the peasants did not want to move, and so the ARVN often had to use force. This increased the hostility of the peasants toward Diem's government. The peasants were angry at having to travel longer distances to reach their rice fields. Others were upset for religious reasons, for they believed that it was vitally important to live where their ancestors were buried.

Despite, or because of, the Strategic Hamlet program, the NLF had grown to over 17,000—a 300 percent increase in two years—and controlled over a fifth of the villages in South Vietnam. As a consequence, the United States chose to deploy more military advisers to Vietnam. By the end of 1962, 12,000 American military personnel were serving in Vietnam.

South Vietnam was also sent three hundred helicopters, and their American pilots were ordered not to "engage in combat," an order that was tactically impossible to guarantee. Gradually, the quagmire was building.

Distrustful of Diem's ability to lead the south, the Kennedy administration came to the view that another leader was crucial to winning the war. On November 3, 1963, a coup unseated Diem and he was assassinated. Nineteen days later, Kennedy himself was shot and killed in Dallas.

Lyndon B. Johnson was now in charge. At that time in late 1963, about 23,000 Americans were "in country" in Vietnam. Nine months later, on August 2, 1964,[39] the United States would become irreversibly committed to a war it would not win. The destroyer USS *Maddox* was on patrol in international waters off the North Vietnamese coast. Five North Vietnamese PT boats attacked her. A local commander believed that *Maddox* was part of a clandestine series of raids the United States had been conducting against the North. The reasoning for these raids was leverage to induce the North Vietnamese to cease their attacks in the south.

Two days later, *Maddox*, accompanied by the destroyer USS *Turner Joy*, returned to the patrol station and mistakenly reported they were under attack by North Vietnamese PT boats. There was no attack. On August 7, Congress passed, with only two dissenting votes in the Senate, the Tonkin Gulf Resolution, a de facto declaration of war that would engage the United States for another eleven years.

The Tonkin Gulf incident became a tragic excuse for escalation. The first attack was ordered by a local commander only, and the second never even took place. The clandestine operations America had been conducting were a clear violation of the Geneva agreement. But worse, the strategy was based on the erroneous argument that harassing pinprick raids could actually force the North Vietnamese to cease and desist their operations supporting the NLF in the south. The combination of deliberate deception—lying—and strategic stupidity proved fatal to 58,000 American servicemen and -women.

American forces would surge into Vietnam. In February 1965, an attack in the central highlands city of Pleiku would provide the excuse to send more forces into Vietnam. Air strikes pounded the North, as painful leverage to force Hanoi to quit its intent to unify the country. All of these would fail. Ho Chi Minh and his lieutenants would never win a battle against American military forces. But they knew that that was not relevant to winning the war. Persistence, patience, and attrition against the enemy would turn the tide of battle in the strategic center of gravity—American public support of the war.

Johnson was inextricably stuck. He could only escalate the war so far. He was fearful of Chinese intervention, as Truman had been in Korea in 1950. Plans to invade the North and cut it in two to neutralize the resupply south through the Ho Chi Minh Trail and force Hanoi to deploy its troops at home as it did at Dienbienphu, and mining the North's harbors, were rejected as too dangerous. So sending more forces and escalating air strikes were the only responses Johnson could make. Ultimately, a maximum number of some 535,000 Americans would be sent to South Vietnam. That would not be enough.

Painful and Expensive Lessons

Although the United States retreated from Vietnam over thirty years ago, that defeat was so stunning and painful that many of the lessons from that war have been ignored or neglected. The debate will always linger over what might have happened had Kennedy not been assassinated. The same question could apply to what might have happened if George H. W. Bush 41 had decided to march to Baghdad in 1991 or if George W. Bush 43 had chosen to let the sanctions, embargoes, and no-fly zones be the instruments of choice to contain Iraq, rather than the invasion and occupation.

Part of the American culture wrestles with an arrogance arising from its unprecedented power and wealth. Kennedy came to office with a campaign slogan that would become the foundation for his defense strategy. The missile gap had to be closed. Against the monolithic and aggressive communist threat, liberty and sovereignty of allies must be maintained, no matter the price to keep the dominoes from tumbling. Those assertions proved totally wrong. Yet there was no "righting" function to challenge them or to provide alternative views. And the public and Congress fully supported them. Under those circumstances, there is no alternative to failure.

The spirit of crusade was manifest in the Vietnam intervention. South Vietnam was anything but a democracy. That notion was a joke. As a Swift boat skipper serving there, this writer recalls two relevant incidents with sadness. The first was the opportunity for several young officers to brief President Johnson on this writer's war experiences in

1967. In fact, this was meant to be a morale-booster for the president, who met in the family quarters of the White House with several officers just back from the front. When Johnson heard highly pessimistic accounts and recommendations that we had two choices—take the war to the North with a ground campaign, or "train up" the South as quickly as possible and withdraw, which took all of two minutes to deliver—he and his senior advisers seized the moment to try to convince the young officers of how well the war was going and to tell them not to listen to contrary opinion.

The second was providing protection for Vice President Hubert Humphrey, sent to Vietnam to publicize the election for the South's president in 1967. This trip too was a bad joke. Reportedly, 90 percent of the eligible South Vietnamese voted. But voting made no difference. Democracy in South Vietnam was a figment of Washington's imagination. And the *raison d'être* for America's intervention, to keep the South whole and free against the determined aggression of the North and thereby prevent the inevitable spread of communism, was a fool's mission.

Hindsight is usually sounder than foresight. But this story of how the United States got Vietnam so wrong and was unable to change course has chilling overtones for the current engagement in Iraq. The question of whether or not this capacity for allowing flawed and superficial slogans to drive policy—the missile gap, the domino theory, and a dangerous amount of arrogance—is inherent in American culture will be answered to some degree in the Greater Middle East. Iraq is not Vietnam. But it could prove a lot worse.

Iraq: September 11, Epiphanies, and Consequences

When asked what he thought about the French Revolution of 1789, Chou en Lai, China's highly sophisticated and intelligent prime minister under Mao, replied: "It is too soon to tell." Since Iraq is an unfolding story, it is too soon to tell what its consequences will be. However, it is not too soon to dissect how and why the United States did what it has done in Iraq and how culture, crusade, and partisanship may be shaping the greatest foreign-policy disaster in the nation's history. That pessimism assumes that the administration's vision of transforming the strategic landscape of the Middle East by democratizing Iraq first was at best a pipe dream and at worst a catastrophe.

It is not a platitude to observe that administrations take on the character of their president and reflect his strengths and weaknesses. That this is so obvious is perhaps one reason why it is unstated and largely unreported. Part Three takes this argument further. The tenure of George W. Bush is a perfect example of how presidents shape their administrations.

Bush, like most of his predecessors, entered office inexperienced in foreign policy, as well as in other presidential responsibilities. The Texas governorship is not the most demanding elected office in America, by virtue of the limited responsibilities and authority granted to that office by the Texas constitution and precedence. The president's experience as an oilman and baseball-team owner was not as extensive as many of his business contemporaries. Perhaps the best experience he had was observing his father's twelve years in the White House as vice president and then president.

Bush also lost the popular vote in 2000 to Al Gore, in one of the nation's most contested and closest elections. It was only after the Supreme Court overruled the Florida Supreme Court, giving the state's electoral votes to Bush, that the election was finally decided thirty-seven days after the fact. Because of the closeness of the vote, Bush could have entered office as a compromise president anxious to operate along bipartisan lines and displaying a degree of humility. Instead, he chose to begin his presidency as if he had won a landslide victory. There was no uncertainty and an abundance of confidence as he took office.

If Jack Kennedy had a dream team in his cabinet of the "best and brightest," George Bush did one better. Vice President Dick Cheney had a superlative résumé and seemed better equipped for the presidency than the younger Bush. Brought into the White House by his mentor Donald Rumsfeld, Cheney had succeeded Rummie as chief of staff to President Gerald Ford when Rumsfeld moved to the Pentagon as secretary for the first time, back in 1975.

Cheney was then elected for five terms to the House from Wyoming, beginning in 1978. In 1989, following the Senate's rejection of John Tower as secretary of defense, George H. W. Bush 41 picked Cheney for the post. Cheney, of course, was part of the team that won the first Gulf War in 1991. Two years after leaving office, Cheney became chairman and CEO of Halliburton, a large energy and construction company. Following George W. Bush 43's nomination in 2000, Cheney headed the search team for the vice president.

As secretary of state, Bush had in Colin Powell arguably the most admired and respected man in America. A retired four-star general, Powell had served as President Reagan's national security adviser and President Bush 41's chairman of the Joint Chiefs of Staff. Powell had considered a run for the presidency himself, and decided against it for personal reasons. Had he run, given his popularity, many believed he might have won, irrespective of what party he chose.

Rumsfeld would have the opportunity to serve as the United States' oldest and youngest secretary of defense. A Princeton graduate and former naval aviator, Rumsfeld was elected to Congress at age thirty in 1962 and served four terms. He attempted a revolt against what he saw as the antiquated House Republican leadership and failed. With little future in the House, in 1969, he moved into the White House with the Nixon team to head the Office of Economic Opportunity. He later became chief of staff to his friend from the House of Representatives, Gerald Ford, in 1974 after Nixon's resignation, moving to Defense the next year. Rumsfeld also served as ambassador to NATO and as special envoy to the Middle East under Reagan, and chaired two panels on missile defense and space. In the private sector, he was CEO of two Fortune 500 companies and sat on a number of boards of directors. He had made an unsuccessful run for the presidency in 1988 and had a powerful reputation both in and out of government. He and Dick Cheney had been founders of the Project for a New American Century (PNAC) in 1997, the intellectual home for many of the so-called neoconservatives.

Condoleezza Rice had served in President George H. W. Bush 41's national security council and was the protégé of national security adviser Brent Scowcroft. She was an expert on the old Soviet Union, an academic who had been chancellor at Stanford University before taking on Scowcroft and Powell's old job as national security adviser. Her selection drew uniform praise.

Finally, George Tenet, a former congressional staffer and Bill Clinton's director of Central Intelligence, was retained at the CIA. Tenet enjoyed a fine reputation and had on-the-job experience that would provide continuity. All in all, the president and his national security team received excellent reviews and, based on their résumés, experience, and prior performance, deserved the accolades. Bush was commended for having these advisers to compensate for his own lack of foreign policy experience.

But as with John F. Kennedy, given this wealth of talent, how and why did the United States become enmeshed in Iraq, and how and why was that involvement so ineptly handled regarding the aftermath of the war?

Epiphanies and Character

After assuming office on January 20, 2001, the Bush administration got off to what charitably could be called a rough start. Displaying a certain cockiness, Bush had come to Washington promising tax cuts; a "compassionate conservatism" that would change the septic mood in Washington; and a plan for transforming the military for the twenty-first century, which included building a missile defense system and abrogating the anti-ballistic missile treaty. In short order, Bush killed the Kyoto Treaty on Global Warming that had been roundly rejected by the Senate; gave notice to the Russians that the ABM Treaty was to be abrogated; dismissed the International Criminal Court; and rejected the advice of South Korean president and Nobel peace prize winner Kim dae Jung in dealing with the North. The manner in which each of these was handled riled friends and allies abroad. In Europe, Bush was called the "Toxic Texan."

In April 2001, the knockdown of a U.S. Navy reconnaissance aircraft and its crash landing at Hainan created a mini-crisis in Sino-American relations. The Bush administration was foundering. Rumsfeld's tenure at Defense seemed in jeopardy, as reports leaked from the Pentagon showed a department in disarray in coming to grips with transformation. Around Labor Day, *Time* magazine ran the question on its cover, "Where has Colin Powell gone?" This was clearly an administration in trouble.

September 11 may not have changed the world. It did, however, profoundly change Bush and his administration. There are several parts to this story. In understanding how culture, crusade, and partisanship coalesced in creating flawed policy, two of those parts are most important: the character of the president, and the influence of the so-called neoconservatives and their vision of democratizing the Greater Middle East.

By his own admission, George W. Bush had experienced two epiphanies. At his fortieth birthday party, his intoxication on that occasion and alcoholism generally finally forced his wife Laura to deliver an ultimatum: give up drink, or else. By an act of sheer willpower, Bush did that, and apparently did so without counseling or the standard treatment alcoholics undergo to break the addiction. The second epiphany stemmed from the first: In beating his addiction, Bush, according to his often and proudly repeated "admission," embraced Christ and was "born again."

September 11 became his third epiphany. The destruction of New York's Twin Towers and a part of the Pentagon now gave the new president a transforming *raison d'être*. His mission and—given his passionate embrace of religion—his sacred duty was protecting America from future attack. The character of the administration would change literally overnight by the need to fight and to win the Global War on Terror. And the character of the president was further affected by another factor.

Bush is reportedly dyslexic.[40] If that is true, the symptoms of his particular form of dyslexia can be debated. However, from how he has approached his presidency, it would seem that Bush tends to think in a linear and consecutive fashion by solving problems one at a time rather than by creating a strategic or comprehensive approach that relates individual problems to a larger whole. Whether related to dyslexia or not, his thought process is quite germane to policymaking.

Furthermore, his successful battle with alcoholism also affected his leadership and management styles. Recovering alcoholics generally need, and rely on, a support structure of friends and other recovering alcoholics to help fight the addiction. Bush therefore is especially dependent on people he has known for a long time. Hence, he picks people who fit that category. His closest confidants, including Karl Rove and Karen Hughes, have been with him for years. Harriet Miers, his general counsel, was an example. Her selection as a candidate for the Supreme Court reflected Bush's reliance on trusted friends. That she withdrew her candidacy does not change his preference. While many appointments were made on other bases, for the most important decisions Bush relies on this closest circle of associates.

His dyslexia or his preference for taking problems head on and in sequence ostensibly obviates the need for a broad strategic framework. Hence, his sloganlike pronouncements that become policy or strategy, such as "the best defense is a good offense"; "we will stay the course"; and "you are either with us or against us," demonstrate his thought processes. In a flurry of coincidental and profoundly negative criticism of his Iraq policy, separately, Brent Scowcroft, Colin Powell's former chief of staff Colonel Lawrence Wilkerson, and former Secretary of Defense Melvin Laird complained of the dysfunctional decision-making process of the administration.[41]

Wilkerson identified the "Cheney–Rumsfeld cabal" as the center of decision-making authority that bypassed the rest of government. Wilkerson accused Rice of weakness in not providing balanced advice to the president. In fact, there is probably a more accurate explanation. Cheney, Rumsfeld, and especially Rice understood how the president operated. Rice, in reality, was the trusted friend on whom Bush especially depended. Realizing what the president wanted, Rice simply operated on that basis. This was intolerable for the other participants, who would attend meetings and believe that a decision had been taken, only to learn later that that had not been the case.

In other words, this decision-making process was exactly what this president wanted, and his most trusted aides carried out that preference. It was not by accident that on a number of occasions, when asked why a certain decision was taken, Rumsfeld responded that it was "above his pay grade." Given Bush's character and experiences, as well as the likely effects of his recovery from alcoholism and his dyslexia, this description appears accurate. Of course, there is the possibility that can only be proven some time well into the future, when full access to these proceedings and decisions is granted, that the White House has been in disarray and Colonel Wilkerson is correct that a "cabal" was indeed at work.

The Siren's Song

After September 11, Bush faced a monumental test and challenge. Unlike the Clinton administration, which had favored a "minimal response" to acts of terror, from the attempted assassination of Bush 41 by Saddam in 1993 to the bombings of the Khobar Towers in Saudi Arabia in 1995, U.S. embassies in Africa in 1998, and USS *Cole* in 2000, Bush was bolder and more aggressive. Warned by a bevy of former senior officials, including past secretaries of State and Defense, that American credibility was on the line throughout the world, Bush was advised to take a strong, military response. This was not quite a domino theory of collapsing states, but the fear was that American leadership and influence would be severely damaged if Bush chose only to unleash even a barrage of Tomahawk cruise missiles.

From a number of sources, as the administration wrestled with responding to September 11, Iraq was proposed as a potential target for retaliation. For some, this was a mixture of revenge and finishing business left over from 1991. Saddam was ripe for removal. To others in the so-called neoconservative camp, Iraq presented the perfect opportunity to resolve, in one fell swoop, many of the running sores that made the Greater Middle East such a dangerous and vital region.

The argument went like this: Deposing Saddam, already a non-binding resolution passed by Congress in 1998, would lead to installing a democracy in Iraq. A democratic Iraq would have many salutary consequences. Local powers would take note. Iran would be warned. Egypt and Saudi Arabia would be induced to move toward more democratic forms of government. And with Iraq democratized, Israeli security would be advanced on the grounds that democracies do not make war on other democracies.

Proponents of this neocon thinking ranged from Deputy Secretary of Defense Paul Wolfowitz, who had Wilsonian impulses of idealism that motivated his passion, to Richard Perle, chairman of the Defense Policy Board, a group of prestigious and highly influential outsiders who provided their wisdom directly to Rumsfeld.[42] Perle saw Iran as a candidate for regime change, arguing that Tehran was the locus of terror and support of Hezbollah (a Lebanese terrorist organization of radical Shiite groups). Much of the thinking in the neocon school stemmed from the Project for a New American Century noted earlier, and many of its members went on to high office in the Bush administration.

George W. Bush ultimately was taken by this bold strategy. It was, in his mind, "one-stop strategic shopping." Ending Saddam's regime and establishing democracy would bring stability and order to the Middle East. It would put a huge dent in Osama bin Laden's network and would also induce the Saudis to slacken their external support of Wahabi charities. Ultimately, a ring of democracies might spawn another revolution in Iran, this time a democratic-, not Islamic-, based overthrow of the ruling mullahs. Indeed, many neocons believed that the time was right for a student-led revolution to end the repressive rule and argued strongly that the United States needed to encourage that outcome far more strongly. Ironically, Bush was embarking on a reverse of the old domino theory. In this case, the theory went, the dominos in the Middle East would fall in our favor.

Given Bush 43's penchant for linear thinking, the line of argument proposed by the neocons probably sounded perfectly reasonable. The response to terror would be bold and direct. It would kill many political birds with one stone, if that is an acceptable metaphor. The critical question was whether or not Saddam, presumably armed with WMD, could be overthrown and Iraq occupied relatively quickly and with minimal casualties to both sides. If that could be done, then the notion of democratization could be implemented. As Bush 43 would learn to his later regret, many of the neoconservatives had been taken with Ahmed Chalabi, head of the Iraqi National Congress (INC), and his passionate arguments that installing a new regime would go swiftly. These same neos also believed the argument of émigré Iranians that the fundamentalist regime there was ripe for a revolution and that the majority of Iranians would prove supportive.

Before turning to Iraq, there was a first stop. It was Afghanistan, the home of the Taliban and of Osama bin Laden and al Qaeda. Immediately after September 11, all the evidence pointed toward al Qaeda. Retaliation was not merely appropriate; it was necessary and justified. Afghanistan would be the proving grounds—the modern equivalent of Spain during its Civil War. And, the United States had received the redounding support of the rest of the world in fighting terror after the attack. For the first time in its history, NATO invoked Article V that says an attack against one is an attack against all. NATO joined the war. And in France, *Le Monde* ran the headline "We are all Americans!"

Operation Enduring Freedom was launched on October 7, 2001. Despite the pundits and critics who could not see how the ruling Taliban could be defeated without deploying large numbers of ground forces, repeating the failure of the Soviet invasion twenty years earlier, dazzling American technology and indigenous Afghan forces loosely organized as the Northern Alliance shocked and awed the enemy, supported by U.S. Special Forces and CIA paramilitary units. The Northern Alliance moved south, routing the Taliban. In December, Marines were deployed 800 miles inland—Afghanistan is landlocked—and seized an airbase at Kandahar. U.S. airpower, from modern F-18 Navy Hornets and F-14 Tomcats to forty-year-old B-52s, fired deadly accurate and lethal ordnance from altitudes above the range of Taliban missiles and antiaircraft guns.

In a remarkably short time, the Taliban were routed. U.S. ground forces unsuccessfully hunted for bin Laden at Tora Bora near the Pakistani border. However, in military terms, the operation was inordinately successful. While Hamid Kharzai was elected president and Afghanistan made the transition to a democratic form of government, sadly, the political realities on the ground dramatically shifted.

Replacing the Taliban rule outside Kabul, tribal warlords have become inordinately powerful. Poppies and the drug trade have flourished, making Afghanistan into a narco-state. Drugs now account for an estimated half of Afghanistan's GDP. While NATO has deployed to Afghanistan and is the process of taking over the bulk of military missions there, Kharzai is more the mayor of Kabul than the president of the country. Drugs and criminal activity could halt the transition of Afghanistan to a whole, stable, and functioning country. That said, the mission to end Taliban rule and eliminate the al Qaeda network is still broadly supported by the international community, even as Afghanistan is ridden with an epidemic of illicit drug manufacturing, with an estimated 90 percent of the trade going to Europe.

With the success of Enduring Freedom, the Bush administration looked toward expanding the war on terror to Iraq. In early 2002, Central Command, headquartered in Tampa, Florida, and assigned as its principal theater of operations much of the Greater Middle East and Southwest Asia, began planning for what would become Operation Iraqi Freedom. That story is well known and need not be repeated in detail. The original Iraqi contingency plan developed by the former Central Command commander, General Anthony Zinni, envisioned a force of three to four hundred thousand troops, required not only for fighting the war but dealing with the peace. Zinni also had plans drawn up to deal with the likely post-war period and rebuilding and reconstructing Iraq.

His replacement, Army General Tommy Franks, had been directed by Secretary of Defense Rumsfeld to incorporate lower force levels in drafting the war plan.[43] As planning progressed, the general strategy was to use the Army's Third Infantry Division and the Marine Corps's First Division in a two-pincer assault along the Tigris and Euphrates rivers, with Baghdad the objective. Other units, including the 82nd and 101st Airborne Divisions along with Special Forces, would be deployed in the north and west and in a position to seize the oil wells before Saddam could set them afire. From the west, the Army's Fourth Division, its most technologically advanced, would attack from Turkey. Unfortunately, the administration failed to win Turkish approval, and the Fourth Division did not arrive in the fight until much later.

On March 19, 2003, the war began with a decapitation strike against Saddam. Saddam survived, but his army did not. Three weeks later, Baghdad had fallen and the American military campaign was one of the most brilliant and well executed in history. However, with all wars, it is not the military campaign but the political and strategic objectives that determine who ultimately won or lost.

The Real Battle

Ironically, success or failure in Iraq will prove to have been largely determined by the pre-war deliberations made by the Bush 43 administration. With the success in Afghanistan as evidence of the capacity of the American war machine, the question was not whether to attack Iraq but how to make the strongest argument. The point when Bush himself decided that war was inevitable probably occurred in early 2002. However, the debate inside the administration revealed how culture, crusade, and partisanship conspired in creating huge fault lines and flaws in planning for Iraq and the future.

Bush was convinced of Saddam's links with terror and the danger the dictator presented. Bush also embraced the neocon argument that democratization was the strategic key to transforming the region. But how to make the case? That debate would go on until September 2002.[44]

Dick Cheney and others believed that "regime change" was the aim and that neither UN nor Congressional support was necessary. The president, post–September 11, already had that authority, the argument went. This was a very go-it-alone view—"coalitions of the willing" rather than reliance on traditional allies and alliances in the fight against terror.

But these views were not shared by friends and allies abroad, nor by Colin Powell. The reaction to Bush 43's unilateral declarations against ABM, Kyoto, and the International Criminal Court and the lip service given to NATO's invocation of Article V turned from disbelief to animosity. Critics at home who counseled caution would be labeled as unpatriotic. Critics abroad, particularly Germany and France, would become regarded as opponents. As Bush 43 stated frequently, "you are either with us or against us."

This arrogance was largely dismissed by the certainty of the administration and the president that he was doing "the right thing." It was clear, however, that regime change would not suffice as grounds for war. Without support from the UN and Congress, the political underpinnings could collapse.

Cheney and Powell both must have recognized that fact from their experience in the first Gulf War when, in late October 1990, a letter signed by a number of Democratic members of Congress warned Bush 41 that if he pursued war against Iraq without authorization, he faced impeachment. Bush 43 would certainly have been aware of that warning. Yet his confidence in the strength of our cause initially outweighed the need to obtain broad support.

British Prime Minister Tony Blair and his foreign secretary Jack Straw saw the case differently. Regime change, according to Blair's attorney general, had no standing in international law. The stronger argument was weapons of mass destruction and Saddam's flagrant disregard of UN resolutions requiring disarmament and certification by UN inspection that had been carried out. Powell agreed.

By the time Bush was to speak before the UN in September, the administration reluctantly had accepted the argument for compelling Saddam to comply with UN resolutions or face the consequences. That required UN approval if force was required. And one way to motivate UN action was for Congress to pass a resolution authorizing the use of force. Bush probably was indifferent to the rationale. Deposing Saddam was vital. The reasons were less important.

Saddam was a villain, guilty of crimes against humanity. He had used chemical weapons against Iran in the long war with that country, and also against his own people. He had ambitions to acquire nuclear weapons. It was irrefutable that Iraq possessed stocks of chemical and biological agents that after the first Gulf War were to be destroyed. But Saddam disregarded UN resolutions and, in interfering with UN inspections, acted as if Iraq still had WMD. No one disputed these facts.

In the fierce debate and criticism that erupted over the failure to uncover WMD and indeed the realization that Saddam actually had allowed their destruction, for all of the investigative commissions and reports, one critical issue was missed. It is true that U.S., British, French, German, and Italian intelligence believed that Saddam had WMD. George Tenet proclaimed that "it was a slam dunk." It is possible that the White House pressured the CIA to reach conclusions it otherwise might have regarded as uncertain. But be all that as it may, no one in the intelligence community believed that Saddam posed an "imminent" threat. In other words, sanctions, containment, and no-fly zones had worked.

In October 2002, shortly before Congress was to vote on authorizing force, Rumsfeld invited Director Tenet to the Pentagon to meet with the

Joint Chiefs of Staff. Tenet presented his case. Two of the members asked the more polite equivalent of "Is that all you have, George?"[45] Had Congress asked any military commanders to testify on the WMD conclusions and the imminence of the threat, it is not likely that the resolution would have been approved.

History will provide a more balanced and less politicized answer to the questions of how much the White House manipulated intelligence; and of how much the basic facts of Saddam's history and his activities to impede inspections made it practically impossible to conclude that there were no WMD. More importantly, why then did the administration fail to plan adequately for the post-war period, and why did it assume that political power could quickly be turned over to the Iraqis? That the administration was wrong over WMD could be an understandable—if not forgivable—error. But the post-war bungling and the failure to provide credible arguments to the American public outlining the strategy and future steps were totally inexcusable. However, in these times, accountability is still missing in action.[46] And so far, the American public has not demanded an accounting.

The record is unambiguous, and books such as Larry Diamond's *Squandered Victory* and George Packer's *Assassin's Gate* detail the litany of errors and missteps.[47] The assumption made by the administration was that after defeating Saddam, U.S. presence would be required for a short period. The post-war plans that were made were for the purposes of responding to such things as humanitarian disasters, firing of the oil wells, and other contingencies that did not materialize. While the State Department produced a huge study for the rebuilding of Iraq, it was categorically rejected by the Pentagon, who had been assigned the responsibility for Iraq by the White House.

The chain of command was also bizarre. After the president, who was in charge of Iraq? Rumsfeld was in nominal charge. Both Central Command and the reconstruction effort would report to him. Rumsfeld assigned the overall responsibility to Under Secretary of Defense for Policy Douglas Feith. The day-to-day duties fell to the operational commander on the ground, Lieutenant General Ricardo Sanchez, who reported to General Franks and later to General John Abizaid, who replaced Franks as Central Command commander. As Iraq began to disintegrate, the White House became more deeply involved, and former Ambassador to India Robert Blackwill assumed that portfolio. In a classic sense, it was unclear who was in charge, and the relations between the civilians and CentCom were poor.

The Office of Reconstruction and Humanitarian Assistance (ORHA) was established to lead the aid effort, headed by retired Army Lieutenant General Jay Garner. Garner was told to expect a short stay, telling associates he fully intended to be home by August. He was correct. Unsurprisingly, ORHA did not work and Garner was replaced by the Coalition Provisional Authority (CPA), headed by Ambassador L. Paul (Jerry) Bremer. Compounding the problems, the CPA was staffed by volunteers who rotated in and out on a short basis. If the twelve-month rotation in Vietnam helped lose that war, a rotation of only 90 to 120 days made continuity impossible.

But despite the administration's assumptions about a short stay, there was no one in Iraq ready to assume the reins of power. Chalabi, who would fall out of favor, had been secretly sent back to Iraq after Baghdad fell. However, the INC was in no shape to run the government. Then Bremer made a catastrophic misjudgment: He ordered the disbanding of the Iraqi army and, later, a program of de-Baathification.

The Iraqi army was in disarray. Hence, the view was that it no longer existed. Disbanding it, however, created an automatic increase in unemployment by some 350,000, as the former soldiers had nowhere to go to seek work. The program of de-Baathification meant that any and all members of Saddam's Baathist Party, with few exceptions, were not eligible for government jobs. These two actions deprived the government of the more capable Iraqis who understood at least something about administration, and accounted for more than their fair share in offending and angering many Iraqis.

Many other errors plagued the post-war effort. Saddam had about two thirds as much weaponry and ammunition as the United States did. AK-47's, RPG-7 grenade launchers, and artillery shells by the millions lay unguarded in ammunition dumps throughout Iraq. Because the ground war had been fought with fewer than 200,000 troops, not enough soldiers were around to guard these dumps. Hence, every Iraqi had access to extensive weaponry.

When looting broke out in Baghdad after Saddam's fall, U.S. troops stood idly by. The political consequences were devastating, and Baghdad seemed—and was—ungovernable. Understanding that religious, ethnic, and tribal factions were central to implementing a successful peace, the

United States incredibly did not reach out to many clerics, particularly the Ayatollah Ali al Sistani, arguably the most important Shiite in the country. As of this writing, no American official has yet met with him.

The United States rejected a real international coalition. Its "coalition of the willing" resembled Lyndon Johnson's attempt to recruit allies in Vietnam. When a contingent of Filipinos arrived in Vietnam, Johnson remarked: "They were the best allies money could buy." The tiffs with Germany and France over their opposition to the war continued. French fries were renamed American fries, and there were boycotts of French wines (although sales of Mercedes, VW's and BMW's did not decline).

In October 2003, Congress appropriated $18.7 billion for reconstruction and rebuilding. Unfortunately, the law required the letting and awarding of contracts to follow the U.S. federal acquisition regulations, a bureaucratic nightmare of redundant, confusing, and time-consuming requirements. Iraq, unaffected by the information age and still primitive in terms of how it administered government, was incapable of coping with these rules. As a result, the bulk of those monies did not go to reconstruction. Much of it went to paying for security necessitated by the growing insurgency.

Rather than being received as "liberators" as Vice President Cheney had predicted, Americans became perceived as "occupiers." Iraqi sentiment began turning against the United States as such basic services as electricity, water, and sewers failed to return to pre-war levels. The insurgency mounted and shifted from an anti-American campaign to Sunnis fighting Shias.

Despite the administration's positive spin on Iraq that persisted through the summer of 2005 and the record of achievement in opening schools and hospitals and in beating back the insurgency (Cheney also claimed then that the insurgency was in "its last throes"), the facts were otherwise. The Iraqi elections in January 2005 to choose an interim government, the October 15 referendum that approved the constitution, and the December 15, 2005 elections for a permanent government were hailed as signs that democracy was working. But, despite the courage of Iraqis in voting and attempting to rebuild a demolished country, reality was different. Here is the heart of the matter: Iraq was never a cohesive, homogeneous nation, having been artificially constructed (along geographic lines) by Winston Churchill and the British in the 1920s. Its religious, ethnic, and tribal divisions have no real common bonds; in fact, they were held together in the past by force—and often brutal force at that.

Iraq: What Lies Ahead

Eventually, all wars end. The Gulf War of 1991 lasted 100 *hours*; a war that began in the fourteenth century in Europe, 100 *years*. At some stage, the insurgency in Iraq too will sputter and expire. The question is when. By most accounts, including that of the Department of Defense, "when" means considerably in the future. But suspend disbelief for a moment.

Suppose the October 2005 vote in Iraq to approve a constitution (or the December 15 election to choose a new government) had produced an astonishing political effect, as did the tsunami in late 2004 that amazingly induced the Indonesian government and the rebel province of Aceh to reach a ceasefire. Suppose the Iraqi vote had "removed the oxygen" from the insurgency. Would such an event lead to the results promised by the Bush 43 administration for a democratic Iraq? And would a government made legitimate by the ballot box, in which the rights of minorities were protected and the rule of law assured, sustain a whole, democratic Iraq?

The simple answer is no. The reasons show why bringing freedom and democracy to that part of the world is an exceedingly difficult, if not unworkable, aim and why measuring success in terms of military action is less relevant. For democracy to succeed in Iraq and for the centrifugal forces that could fracture the country to be contained, it is important to understand the obstacles blocking the way.

First, whether Iraqis approved the constitution or not (and they did), as with all constitutions and our own in particular, there are inherent contradictions, flaws, and gaps that must be reconciled by the ensuing political process and by the new government. In our Constitution, for example, it took a civil war to resolve the clash between state and federal rights and powers. And Americans still do not vote directly for their president, as the 2000 election so forcefully reminded us.

Within the Iraqi constitution, contradictions, flaws, and gaps abound. The balance of power between the provinces and the central government has not been well defined. With the degree of federalism and central control in question, will any government be capable of striking a politically acceptable balance between regions seeking autonomy and the need for some control by the center? The conflicts among Sunnis, Shias, and Kurds, exacerbated by the insurgency, remain huge impediments and obstructions. Even if the insurgency stopped tomorrow, these obstacles and realities would remain intense and resistant to resolution.

Second, the relationships between sharia (religious) and civil law remain unsettled. The constitution gives both priority. But the region where one lives will determine which law will prevail over the other. The Shia south is rapidly becoming a fundamentalist state. Sharia law will dominate there. The same is not true in other regions; therefore, the administration of law will not be consistent throughout Iraq, provoking further challenges for the central government and contributing to centrifugal forces that could divide the country.

Third, the division of oil revenues had not been determined. The Kurdish north and the Shia south contain virtually all of Iraq's oil reserves. The Sunni center contains hardly any. Given the tensions over federalism and Saddam's legacy of harsh minority Sunni rule, ending hostility and resentment among the various religious and ethnic groups, even if the insurgency stops, cannot happen quickly. Human nature is not that forgiving.

Finally, in light of these issues, the role of women in society also requires careful definition. That twenty-five percent of the seats in parliament are reserved for women is a good start and something that has no counterpart in the United States. But beyond that, the mechanisms for defining and legitimizing the role of women are by no means obvious. And in a state that has no experience in democracy other than the past two years, the absence of government and public mechanisms to deal with these political issues fairly, consistently, and effectively adds another serious obstacle to making democracy work.

Returning to reality, the insurgency is not going to dissipate soon. The destruction of the Golden Dome Mosque in Samarra in February 2006, Shia's second most holy site after Najav, nearly precipitated a civil war. Reportedly 1,300 Iraqis died in the violence between Shia and Sunni following the bombing. On a proportional population basis, that figure would be equivalent to about 15,000 Americans or five times the number of those killed on September 11.

The Bush 43 administration finally began admitting the immense and formidable challenge posed by rebuilding and democratizing Iraq. The administration's expectation is that the training and fielding of Iraqi security forces are beginning to pay off. As those forces grow in numbers and ability, the logic insists that the insurgency will gradually falter.

The insurgency, however, is not the critical factor in determining Iraq's fate. The outcome of a free and whole Iraq will rest on how well or how badly Iraqis resolve these political contradictions and ambiguities. The question to ask is what the United States can do, if anything, to facilitate that process and ensure a favorable outcome. Or is it too late?

Iraq is almost certainly headed for a de facto partitioning. Roughly 80 percent of the population are Shia or Kurds. Sunnis have governed for centuries. The north has already become a largely independent province. The south is turning into an Islamic republic, and ties with Iran are almost certainly going to improve. Given the extraordinary threat ("Israel should be wiped off the map") delivered by Iran's president Mahmoud Ahmadinejad, any Iraqi-Iranian rapprochement will worry the United States.

The Sunni center is likely to be racked with violence for years. If the 1920 British occupation of Mesopotamia is any guide, the insurgency is unlikely to dissipate. With the added impetus of al Qaeda and other jihadists seeking to establish a base and even a junior caliphate in Iraq, the future does not look good. Should the Kurds move too quickly to establish an independent Kurdistan, Turkey will not sit idly by, as it will not tolerate any support given to its Kurdish populations, who are already engaged in an insurgency against Istanbul. The scenario noted in Chapter Two could too easily play out in a fragmented and violent Iraq.

Culture, Crusade, and Partisanship: The Dangers

Common threads have run throughout American history. American culture has reflected the rise of American power and influence in the world scene. It has also induced a certain arrogance and nurtured a certain lack of understanding of other cultures and peoples, both politically and strategically.

At the same time, a spirit of crusade has permeated the culture and the public mood. Abandoning George Washington's legacy of avoiding permanent alliances, we have seen the impact of crusade in the wars the nation has fought since the Spanish–American conflict in 1898. In each, there was a moral cause, and we were on the side of right.

Finally, and as Part Three will show, the emergence of bitter partisanship has contributed to making the political process dysfunctional.

Unless that trend is reversed, it is doubtful that the political process and those elected to serve in it will be able to cope with challenges at home and threats abroad.

Vietnam and the current situation in Iraq are tragic examples of how culture and crusade sent us down tunnels that did not necessarily have any light at their end. That both Vietnam and Iraq were motivated by flawed assumptions and manipulated intelligence and "fact" is of more than passing interest. Iraq will have strategic consequence. Whether it will be as much of a failure internationally as Vietnam was domestically hangs in the balance.

PART III

RESTORING AMERICA'S PROMISE

GOVERNMENTAL PERFORMANCE IS POTENTIALLY THE most cata-strophic fault line in America today. To be sure, not all of government is failing to carry out its responsibilities; the nation is blessed with many fine, able public servants in the best sense of the term. However, good people can only do so much if the system in which they work is not fully functional. And ours is not.

The greatest danger to the public's welfare and security is provoked by the systemic incapacity of government to cope with the huge and complex array of challenges, crises, and problems facing the nation. Several of the main causes of this dysfunctionality—specifically, Constitutional contra-dictions, a super proliferation of special-interest groups and powerful single-issue constituencies, and the excessively adversarial nature of the political process—cannot be corrected easily, quickly, or simultaneously.

The best chance of repairing this major fault line of failing governance is through attacking the cumulative and negative impact of the dark sides of culture, crusade, and partisanship. Culture, crusade, and parti-sanship have shaped American history for good and for ill. Applied in excess or wrongly directed, the consequences for the United States of this evil alchemy have been harmful and occasionally very dangerous. Certain parallels between Vietnam and Iraq are painful reminders of how culture and crusade can precipitate tragic consequences. One significant difference between the two is how much more intense, distorting, and dangerous partisanship has become in today's political environment.

Big Ideas to Fix Big Faults

Some argue that "leadership" and a "great person" will make things right. My own sense is that without a catastrophe or event of sufficient magnitude to enable powerful leadership to carry the day, such thinking is unlikely to prove prescient. And the cataclysmic event could prove so destructive as to neutralize the capacity of even the greatest individual of the greatest generation.

Hence, in my view, to repair or narrow this and other fault lines, big ideas are needed. These ideas must be powerful and attractive enough to shift opinion and thought, not merely tinker with solutions at the margin. As the Declaration of Independence and the Constitution were based on big ideas that set the nation on an extraordinary course, a vision is crucial. That vision must apply both domestically and internationally. It constitutes the first big idea.

The second big idea is to create the means to engage the public more directly in their government. The means is through a system of universal voting described later, national town hall meetings and referenda, and "question time" for the president.

The third is to force accountability on government, drawing legislation to that end for the private sector in the form of a Sarbanes–Oxley Act for Congress and the presidency.

The fourth big idea is to propose two changes in Congress that can radiate outward to reduce the harmful aspects of culture, crusade, and, most of all, partisanship.

The fifth idea is to remedy the injustices and catastrophic reactions to the treatment of enemy combatants captured in the war on terror.

And the sixth idea is the means to make the public aware of the huge and growing gaps between the promises, expectations, and obligations of government and the money to pay for them in order to impose fiscal and financial discipline on a political process largely incapable of making those tough choices.

From these ideas, additional actions can follow to rectify the deficiencies that must be repaired within government, especially in terms both of dealing with people who serve and of making the interagency process work.

I hope that my judgment regarding the future of the United States and the dysfunctional state of its government will prove to be overstated. But I fear not. However, even if does, these ideas and actions will still help us strengthen, if not reinvent, our democracy.

For those who are looking to this book for specific solutions to "fix" social security, health care, energy, and environment, as well as proposing new economic plans for alleviating debts, deficits, and liabilities, you will be disappointed. The solutions offered are meant to clear away the impediments and obstacles that prevent implementation of policies. The dilemma is that it is far easier to invent solutions than to implement them.[48] Hence, the big ideas focus on implementation, facilitating or coercing government to take the tough decisions that have become so difficult to resolve.

For readers who are interested in specific recommendations, I modestly suggest reading my earlier books or my columns in the *Washington Times* called "Owls and Eagles." The specific organizational and other plans must be worked out within the political process under this broader vision.

Returning to the fears and concerns of Americans, many people sense that the foundation for the American promise is at risk. Others may believe it is crumbling. In any economy, but particularly a global one, cheap labor will displace more expensive competition. Throughout the world, health-care and medical costs are surging. The American population is graying. Pension plans, Social Security and others, are grossly underfunded. Current account (i.e., trade) and budget deficits, along with the nation's debt, are exploding for the long term. Each of these must be addressed. The nub of the problem goes beyond the inertia and obstacles within the political system that make it virtually impossible to impose reform or change until disaster or crisis forces action.

A further dilemma is that many actions intended to repair these deficiencies have made the problems worse.[49] Social Security and health care are in worse financial shape today than they were a year ago. No effective policy on energy and environment is in place, long after gas prices soared above $2.00 a gallon and reached over $3.00 in mid-2005. Immigration policy in the wake of September 11 and the justified preoccupation that illegal visitors could be part of the terror network, has proven too tough to resolve. The reason is that the political system is currently constitutionally incapable of responding to these crises with effective and lasting solutions.

To deal with these issues and correct the fault lines, a higher level of abstraction is essential. What must be done if government's failure to perform is to be reversed is not to focus on the tactical level of specific interests that attract considerable public involvement; instead, the public must be engaged more broadly. If the public is to be aboard for the landing, then surely it must have a say in the takeoff. Public opinion and involvement are the only sure ways to counter the negative effects of the influence and dominance of special-interest groups and constituencies with agendas that reflect individual rather than national needs.

The most perfect response of an imperfect system will not overcome imperfection. The answer is not to have smarter people working in a flawed system; rather, the task ahead is to reduce these imperfections.

For that to happen, the people are the crucial ingredient. Hence, by focusing on fixing the fault lines, beginning with the failure of government to function commensurately with the challenges, it will be possible to create recommendations and ideas for preserving America's promise and, hopefully with public support, to implement them.

Partisanship and Paradox at Home

Partisanship, Relevance, and Influence Abroad and the Dream at Home

Politics is about governing. Governing is about power, authority, accountability, and responsibility for making decisions under the rule of law and within the bounds of the consent of the governed. Profound differences of opinion will always exist, and solutions will never be perfect. However, maintaining the consent of the governed is critical to the legitimacy and credibility of the governors.

Here is a central paradox of democracy, certainly as it is practiced in America. Majority rule, with the sole exception of the Senate, where the minority can override the majority through the filibuster, is the defining measure of the political process. But when increasing numbers of issues are decided by the slimmest of majorities, say 50.1 percent to 49.9 percent, it is very difficult to gain the consent of the minority in such a close-run thing.

To a greater degree, this paradox is what makes reaching the goal of a stable Iraq so elusive. For stability to take hold despite decades of repressive rule by the Sunnis and Baathists, the majority Shias and Kurds must respect and protect the rights of the minority Sunnis; the Sunnis must also respect the rights of the majority. Until those conditions obtain, the political outlook in Iraq is grim.

So, with such tightly decided issues and standoffs between majorities and minorities in America, reconciliation is inordinately tough to achieve. The issue of "big" versus "small" government, tax and fiscal policy, free versus regulated markets, distribution of wealth, incentives for growth, rectifying ills that lead to unequal treatment of citizens, social responsibility for the underprivileged and less fortunate, and the balance between individual liberties and the broader public safety—all have polarized attitudes and opinions. In a society predicated on freedom of expression, this kind of debate is usually healthy. Around these differences of opinions, political parties have emerged or attracted popular support.

But in the current environment, these differences have been hardened both by the power of special-interest groups and by the adversarial "campaignization" of almost every political issue. The presidential campaign of 1992 was a defining point for this adversarial practice of politics, even though the antecedents had long been present (Bush 41's 1988 use of the Willie Horton issue—a convicted black who was released by Governor Michael Dukakis and then raped again—is often cited as illustrative of the most negative type of campaigning). The Clinton campaign for the nomination and the Clinton–Gore ticket for the White House made the "war room" approach to politics famous. This so-called war room spewed out all manner of campaign propaganda. It did so through every conceivable outlet—fax, press release, word of mouth, phone, radio, television, E-mail, and paid advertising.

When the Bush–Quayle ticket ran an ad or released a statement, the Clinton war room immediately counterattacked. The Republicans fired back. In the heat of battle, facts and truth counted for less than winning a particular skirmish. In those conditions, partisanship sometimes spiraled out of control. What was different was the formalization of the attack–counterattack mentality and the instant availability and access to literally millions of people through information technology.

Nearly fifteen years later, technology and public access to information, often unfiltered, have improved by orders of magnitude. Cell phones, Internet use, and blogging have become ubiquitous. The conduct of politics has very much become dominated by the war-room mentality and the attraction of attack ads and negative campaigning. Left alone, these adversarial trends will grow—despite some encouraging results from the 2005 elections, particularly the election of Virginia's governor Tim Kaine (in part because Kaine was Mark Warner's lieutenant governor [and Warner had a 70 percent approval rating], and because Republican opponent Jerry Kilgore was hurt by a popular backlash against his negative ads). Still, partisanship is getting generally worse, not better.

Who or what exactly is a partisan? A partisan is an adherent or supporter of a party or cause, and often a zealous advocate. The Oxford Dictionary goes further. A partisan may be "prejudiced, unreasoning, or a fanatical adherent." Hence, the phrase "partisan politics," while often associated with strong opinions, should convey a greater sense of radicalism and irrationality. This is where partisanship has become harmful.

Cynics will argue that it has always been thus. Politics is a system that is characterized by "adversarial" proceedings that originally were central to jurisprudence and have since spread to other facets of society. Nations routinely face inherently difficult choices, ranging from war and peace to determining what constitutes fair and equitable treatment of its citizens. Hence, it is natural and part of the human condition for highly divergent and deeply divided positions to attract intense and often ugly dissent and debate. However, over the past few decades, partisanship and polarization have spilled over to virtually every issue, whether large or small, profound or trivial.

Today's politics has become "adversarial" in the extreme. The adversarial nature of proceedings works well in a courtroom in which there are laws, procedures, and a judge to command the proceedings and keep them from getting out of hand. Extremely adversarial politics works less well, if at all, in a free and open society that ultimately requires consent of the governed and a measure of civil discourse and civility if it is to function at all.

Tracing this evolution of partisanship and politicization, while interesting, is of less importance than redressing the causes and returning a certain civility to politics. If that can be done, the chances are greatly enhanced that the accumulation of today's challenges and crises will find more effective solution. The alternative is a parliamentary type of government in which the party in charge and the executive leading that party, as in Great Britain, have the authority to act as a modern-day benevolent dictator, still operating under the rule of law—but of laws that he or she may change.

Destructive Partisanship

The most bitterly divisive issues have always been part of politics, no matter where they were practiced. Two hundred and thirty years ago, the debate over whether to declare independence from the crown or win the de facto rights enjoyed by other English citizens led to the Revolutionary War. Fourscore and five years later, ambiguities over federal versus state powers, exacerbated by the free-or-slave debate, resulted in a civil war. Isolationism and internationalism clashed most pronouncedly during the inter–World War years, before Pearl Harbor finalized that debate. A hundred years after the Civil War, civil rights still divided the nation and required forceful action by the federal government in guaranteeing that all Americans were indeed equal under the law.

World War II had been a great and entirely non-partisan victory from which America emerged as the sole superpower of its day, militarily and economically. Wartime destruction spared the continental United States. Creating the arsenal of democracy produced a gargantuan economy accounting for about half of the world's total GDP. Had FDR been a Republican, because of the war he probably still would have been re-elected for a third and a fourth term. (Wartime presidents have had a distinct advantage—they win elections. Wilson, FDR, Johnson, and Bush 43 fared well. The first Gulf War was long over when Bush 41 lost, the result of Ross Perot's third-party candidacy that took votes from the incumbent, not from Mr. Clinton.) However, amongst the fruits of electoral victory lay the seeds of future perverted partisanship.

After World War II, vestiges of isolationism were not completely dead in America or in the Senate. But as the Soviet Union consolidated power and occupied Eastern European states behind the Iron Curtain, Moscow's actions forged a bipartisan foreign policy and, using the cliché of the period, politics stopped at the water's edge. Republicans and Democrats could generally agree on foreign policy. Many members of Congress had served in the war (or World War I), making that service a bond. Presidents Kennedy, Johnson, and Nixon had all served in the Navy.

With the onset of the Korean War and the 1952 election, both parties made a bid for Dwight D. Eisenhower's candidacy. Ike was on leave from his post as president of Columbia University to serve as NATO's first supreme military commander. As common to officers of his generation, Ike had no party affiliation. (Interestingly, many officers of that vintage refused to vote in presidential elections on the grounds of avoiding a potential conflict of interest with the commander-in-chief. If their man lost, would it be disloyal to serve the winner? And if their man won, would objectivity be questioned in carrying out future orders? By today's cultural standards, in which retired military officers routinely support candidates as well as run for office themselves, non-affiliation may have seemed quaint.)

There was, of course, no truce that prevented the perversion of politics of the day. Joe McCarthy instituted a reign of terror with his communist witch hunts based on personal gain, not on fact, an antecedent to some of the more bitter forms of partisanship that have since emerged. However, after his election in 1960, Kennedy came up with about as apolitical a cabinet as was imaginable, not even realizing, for example, that Douglas Dillon, his pick for Treasury Secretary, was a Republican.

The return of excessive partisanship began with the escalation of the Vietnam War in the 1960s. While that war had no real strategic consequence in global terms, it had hugely debilitating effects on domestic politics and laid the foundation for excessive partisanship. The war also detracted from the goal of Lyndon Johnson's Great Society, which was to bring the American Dream to all Americans, irrespective of race, ethnicity, or gender. The Great Society and the Voting Rights Act of 1964 would have another weighty political consequence: Over time, the Democratic South would become a Republican bastion, as old-time Democrats converted to the GOP in disagreement with this "liberal" legislation.

The Vietnam War and the Watergate affair ultimately destroyed public trust and confidence in government. Richard Nixon promised voters that he had a "plan" for ending the war. No such plan existed. In its stead, the Americans began a "Vietnamization" of the war, turning as many military operational responsibilities over to Saigon as possible. Nixon did, however, widen the war in an attempt to deprive the Vietcong and North Vietnamese of the use of "neutral" Cambodia as a sanctuary and pathway into the South. In 1970, the American military was ordered into what had been "off limits" in Cambodia to clean out the enemy. This so-called secret war, which included bombing raids in Cambodia, was no secret to the North Vietnamese, although the Nixon administration initially withheld that information from the American public, on whose support the war rested.

The antiwar movement in the United States was in full gear. As reports of the Cambodian intervention leaked, the country was shocked by and filled with massive protests. At Kent State University, untrained and frightened Ohio National Guardsmen panicked and shot and killed four students who had taken part in campus protests over Cambodia; this became known as the Kent State Massacre. Despite the huge antiwar sentiment, Nixon still crushed antiwar candidate Democrat George McGovern in the 1972 elections with 47 million votes to McGovern's 29 million.

The Watergate break-in, however, did more than end the Nixon administration; it cemented the foundations for the excessive sides of partisanship.

The Last Three Decades

Time often overcomes the poison and bitterness of the past. It is easy for many of us to forget Nixon's enemies list and the dirty tricks that led to the bugging of the Democratic headquarters at the Watergate. It is easy to forget President Gerald Ford's pardon of Nixon, which provoked a polit-ical firestorm and probably cost Ford the 1976 election. But politics in the United States were profoundly and irretrievably changed by Water-gate. Neither government nor the Republicans were to be trusted by a growingly cynical public, further battered by the fall of Vietnam in 1975.

With the presidential accession of Jimmy Carter and then Ronald Reagan, the practice of politics was changing. Campaign financing was becoming more prominent as an issue, as more and more money was needed to buy expensive television airtime. What was different was the extent of fundraising. After all, when George Washington won his first election (in 1758, to the Virginia House of Burgesses), he reportedly did so by providing enough whiskey to change the minds of a majority of voters—an imaginative and effective use of campaign funds.

By 1979, it was clear that the Shah of Iran could no longer hold on to power. The revolution that overthrew him installed as supreme leader the septuagenarian Ayatollah Ruhollah Khomeini, who had been in exile in Paris. On November 4, Iranian mobs, allegedly angered by the U.S. deci-sion to allow the Shah to receive medical treatment in the United States, overran the U.S. Embassy in Tehran and took fifty-two American hostages, who ended up being held for 444 days. The capture of the embassy was the low point for American power since the fall of Saigon four years earlier. Aside from sending several aircraft carrier battle groups to steam in lazy circles in the Indian Ocean and using the law to freeze Iranian assets, the Carter administration was unwilling to respond more forcefully. Worse for the president, and despite the arms-limitations agreements with Moscow, the Soviet Union intervened in Afghanistan and would stay there for nearly a decade until it was so bloodied that it had to retreat. Carter, to many observers, was weak and indecisive.

When Reagan took office on January 20, 1981, he brought to Washington the Reagan conservative revolution. His program was threefold: cut government, cut taxes, and strengthen defense. The economy was suffering from the grip of the infamous misery index—the sum of unemployment and inflation. Foreign policy had not gone well. Despite Carter's Panama Canal Treaty, which transferred the territory back to Panama; further arms-limitation agreements with the Soviet Union; restoring relations with China; and the historic Camp David Peace Accord between Egypt and Israel in 1978, Iran and Afghanistan had proved disastrous for the president.

Reagan assumed office, reinforcing and reflecting the nation's move to the political right. Reagan had his share of controversy and failure—the Strategic Defense Initiative for missile defense (known somewhat derisively as "Star Wars") in March 1983, which was not universally welcomed, either in America or abroad; the October 1983 bombing of the Marine Barracks in Beirut, and the invasion of tiny Grenada that same month to protect American students there who had never been in danger;[50] and, in his second term, the Iran–Contra scandal, in which arms were sent to Iran in exchange for the release of Americans held hostage and the money recycled illegally to support the Contras in Central America. Had Reagan not been so personally popular, impeachment or other punitive action could easily have occurred.

There was, of course, no absence of hugely partisan fights on these and other issues. However, while Reagan was a conservative, he was also pragmatic. As a result, he was not inflexibly wedded to ideology. After Iran–Contra, he had the capacity to admit publicly that he had erred. His relationship with Mikhail Gorbachev in his second term and the breakthrough in arms agreements strengthened Reagan politically and absolved the president of much of the blame over Iran–Contra. And the Soviet Union still existed as the ultimate "righting" element and major threat, against which the nation could largely agree.

George H. W. Bush's election brought to the White House a president who seemed uniquely qualified and born for the job. Elected to the House, de facto ambassador to China, Director of the CIA, and chairman of the Republican Party, Bush spent eight years as Reagan's understudy. With the demise of the Soviet Union and the smashing victory in the first Gulf War, Bush seemed electorally invincible.

The 1992 presidential campaign was a watershed in the deepening of what would later disintegrate into seemingly irreconcilable partisan differences in American politics. While the roots of bitter partisanship go back to the first days of the Republic, a combination of factors elevated and altered the manner in which these divisions would widen. The end of the Cold War removed that unifying threat. The entry of a third-party candidate into the race, while by no means anything new (among many others, John Anderson had made an unsuccessful bid in 1980, and Colin Powell would consider it in 1996), with a personality and character as strong as Ross Perot's, alienated many Republicans and would result in greater future party discipline, meaning greater partisanship the next time around.

The Clinton adoption of war-room campaigning, a singularly brilliant political tactic, would prove strategically catastrophic when copied in later elections, bringing a meanness and victory-at-all-costs mentality into politics. With the Internet and "blogs" (Web logs) to carry the message, this ruthless attack-and-discredit mentality became the *modus operandi* of politics. The bitter fight waged today between the two parties over the Iraq war reflects both this mentality and the march of technology. One may speculate that if the Internet and blogs had been around in 1968 or 1969, the United States might have left Vietnam a lot earlier. And the racial unrest and riots in major American cities might have ignited much greater widespread violence and chaos, as happened in France in 2005.

After Bill Clinton's election in 1992, partisanship took on a new hue. In 1992, the vestiges of the Cold War still persisted. That both East and West had exercised constraints on the centrifugal forces in politics for five decades would take time to dissipate throughout the rest of the world and in the former alliances. The passage of the Cold War would bring new perplexities, challenges, and threats to what President Bush 41 called the "new world order."

In this seemingly safer world, the new president's political skills and acumen, although blemished by continuing rumors and stories of sexual and financial wrongdoings, provided the ground zero for attacks by Clinton's many political opponents and enemies. The disastrous health-care initiative begun early in the administration destroyed a great deal of his credibility. And in his second term—the great curse for successful politicians—there came a further "explosion of bimbos," a reminder of the tawdry side of the presidential campaign and the stories that plagued it.

From the Whitewater investigation over a real estate deal that allegedly made the Clintons some fast money, to the suicide of Clinton confidant and White House aide Vincent Foster, to the affair with White House intern Monica Lewinski that led to Clinton's impeachment, the administration was awash in grand juries and special counsels. One result was to coalesce both political parties around defending or attacking the president. War rooms on both sides spun stories and facts to support their case. The result was a mean, unsavory, uncivilized, and distorted nonstop series of exchanges to harm or damage. Impeaching the president is deadly serious—or should be. The gravity of the moment unfortunately brought forth man's meaner impulses. Most Americans, what Richard Nixon called the silent majority, whether appalled or simply nonplussed, watched, not realizing that this practice of war-room politics was debasing the process and hardening the partisan differences between Republicans and Democrats over issues that had, at best, razor-thin majorities.

In a different context, Oscar Wilde famously remarked that the reason politics in academic life was so sharp was because the stakes were so small. In contemporary politics, the stakes are often huge. However, the irony is that partisanship has become so sharp because the differences in policies and actual actions are often so small. For example, Clinton's China-bashing and the narrowness of real national-security policy differences in the 2004 Bush–Kerry contest (or the sleazy accusations about prior military service of both) are illustrative. Hence, to make the most convincing case, not only must the opposing view be discredited, it must be totally repudiated. This is one of the central fault lines in American politics—a negativism that has become destructive and a fault line that grows only wider.

Consider how this adversarial condition has played out. Most Americans are of the political center and are generally not activist. Activists, on the other hand, tend to cluster around single issues—pro- or antiwar;

right-to-life or pro-choice; for or against gun control; labor rights—and aggressively move to advance or defeat those interests. Hence, the smaller vocal minority, especially those with deep pockets, has tremendous cumulative influence on the process. This led to greater polarization, partisanship, and often vindictive motives. Getting mad was replaced by getting even.

Democrats became furious and vindictive with Republicans for the impeachment of Bill Clinton. Earlier, what was perceived as autocratic behavior in changing the rules in Congress after the GOP won control in 1995 provoked great hostility. However, the 2000 election case-hardened the negative aspects of partisanship. Vice President Al Gore won by about half a million popular votes and lost Florida's then 25 (now 27) electoral votes and the election after a five-week legal battle resolved by the Supreme Court in Bush's favor by a 5–4 vote on party lines. Animosity over that election has fueled the harsher sides of partisanship.

For better or worse, beyond the fault line created by the paradox of majority rule and the minimal majorities or pluralities that decided issues, George W. Bush widened the partisanship divide. Coming to office on the strength of the above-mentioned Republican-appointed Supreme Court majority, Bush exuded confidence and a degree of cockiness certainly not to be expected of a president who had lost the popular vote. This confidence reflected his personality and the political judgment that the best means of overcoming any perception of weakness, given the election, was a show of strength. Perhaps the president overcompensated.

Bush also promised "compassionate conservatism," a term never defined, and to change the mood in Washington, presumably to a more civil one. But in the first eight months of his term, prior to September 11, the administration was adrift. By its actions and despite the presence of many experienced "old hands," it quickly alienated friends and allies at home and abroad.

Abroad, Bush policies, from abrogating ABM to Kyoto and the International Criminal Court, drew substantial criticism. At home, his policies drove Vermont Senator Jim Jeffords out of the Republican Party, costing control in the Senate. With a 50–50 tie in the Senate, Vice President Cheney had theoretically provided the deciding vote. But with Jeffords's defection to independent status and decision to caucus with the Democrats, the Republicans became, by a 49–51 vote, the minority.

For reasons that remain unclear, the White House persisted in its pursuit of extreme secrecy in arriving at its decisions and usually ignoring and discouraging broader counsel, including from members of its Congressional delegation. That history has yet to be written. Yet these characteristics were part of the decision process for invading Iraq, handling enemy combatants, and authorizing the NSA to carry out what it called "terrorist surveillance" within the United States. In conversations I had with senior members of the administration from the first-term Congress, dissenting opinions were not welcome. A common complaint, reported often in the press and a staple of Sunday-morning television talk shows, was about the secrecy, inflexibility, and closed-mindedness of the White House.

The critiques rendered by former secretary of defense Melvin Laird, former Powell chief of staff Lawrence Wilkerson, and twice national security adviser Brent Scowcroft each raised profound concern over the tight little circle of advisers who made the key decisions. This penchant for—and perhaps even obsession with—secrecy, the active discouragement of seeking wider counsel, and the unwillingness to admit mistakes did not make friends or attract new supporters.

The unwavering way the administration went to war in Iraq—so certain of Saddam's possession of WMD, his links with terrorists and al Qaeda, and the immediacy of the danger—brought these traits into into high relief as, one by one, they were proved dead wrong. With the mistaken assumptions over the ease and pace of the reconstruction and political rebuilding of Iraq and the human and dollar costs of those efforts growing, the president's credibility and popularity clearly was going to go in no direction except precipitously downward. These deficiencies were exacerbated and reflected by the "outing" of CIA operative Valerie Plame in the attempt to discredit Ambassador Joe Wilson; the subsequent indictment of vice presidential chief of staff I. Lewis "Scooter" Libby; and the withdrawal of White House counsel Harriet Miers for nomination to the Supreme Court after a firestorm of protests from the right wing of the Republican party, all noted earlier.[51]

Ironically, Bush 43 managed to "change the mood" in Washington as he promised, but not for the better.

It does not take a political genius to recognize that under these circumstances, partisanship took on a further, bitter, and even destructive edge. Private (though not off-the-record) conversations between the author and senior Republicans in Congress reflect this divide and anger with the White House. Several senators, who use the code "We are where we are" in Iraq as shorthand for a series of huge White House errors and mistakes, privately blame Bush for an aloof style of hands-off control and an all too evident lack of experience for the post. Yet, what is the alternative? If the White House refuses to change course or admit error, what options outside impeachment are open? This is the crux of a major predicament facing the nation and further reason for the failures of government.[52]

A signal moment occurred in November 2005 when Senate minority leader Harry Reid cleared the chamber of visitors to demand that his colleagues on the Intelligence Committee expedite the long-overdue second part of the investigation of September 11. This was a little-used tactic; it reflected the complete dissatisfaction of the Democrats with what was seen as unwillingness on the part of the Republicans to hold the administration accountable for the intelligence failure associated with September 11—a not-unreasonable objection, had partisanship not been an issue.

Majority Leader Bill Frist not only called the move a "stunt"; he also said that he could no longer "trust" Reid. Meanwhile, some of Frist's Republican colleagues silently supported Reid's action. The degree of how far partisanship has descended finds no better indicator than in the Senate, a body that has prided itself on colloquies and civility and has often attempted to stand above the fray of dirty and excessively adversarial politics.[53]

For critics of the president, it is tempting and simple to use the precipitous decline in American relevance and influence abroad and the pernicious consequences of partisanship as reflective only of this administration. Had Al Gore won in 2000 or John Kerry in 2004, would we have been in a similar position? Well, the answer is a qualified "yes."

How Al Gore would have responded to September 11 is unknowable. What John Kerry might have done to get the ship of state on a better course is also impossible to know. But that is why history is useful. Irrespective of September 11, the United States has been largely oblivious to the two revolutions sweeping through the Arab and Islamic worlds. These were readily visible from the mid- to late 1990s, when Al Gore was vice president. The Clinton administration chose to ignore those revolutions and to regard terror largely as a criminal matter, not one of national security. Those were errors of judgment. Of course, Clinton was preoccupied with his own misconduct in *l'affaire* Lewinski, a very unfortunate situation, as it turned out, for the nation.

At the same time, both parties were coalescing around the more extreme ends of the political spectrum. In the Third Way report cited earlier, by that time religion had reasserted itself and began playing a larger role in politics. Those Americans who regard themselves as religious, as measured by attendance at services, increasingly aligned with the Republican Party. For all of the separations between church and state that are guaranteed by the Constitution and precedent, religion can be divisive and destructive. Deeply felt religious views can intensify partisan differences.[54]

The composition of Congress is of direct relevance to the increasing influence of partisanship. In the Senate, since World War II, the Democrats controlled all but the 80th and 83rd (1947–49 and 1953–55) until the 97th (1981–83) and then regained power from the 100th to the 103rd (1987–95). Since then, the Republicans have been in control except for the 107th (2001–03 when Jeffords crossed over). In the current 108th Congress, the Republicans hold a 55–45 majority in the Senate. That Jeffords left his party is another commentary on the administration's penchant for secrecy, its allergy to outside counsel, and how its often abrasive actions have an inadvertent effect that does real damage to the White House.

From FDR's first term, the House had been a Democratic bastion. The Democrats held the House from 1933 until 1993 and the "Gingrich Revolution," except for the 80th and 83rd Congresses (1947–49 and 1953–55). The Republicans have been in control since, and currently have a 229–205 majority in the House.

In 1989, the Democratic speaker of the House, Jim Wright of Texas, was forced to resign over allegations of ethics violations concerning sales of books he had authored. The culprit or the hero, depending upon one's view, was Representative Newt Gingrich of Georgia, who pursued the charges and the attack on Wright. The bad blood created then between the parties would have a long half-life. And Gingrich was on his way to launching the Republican "Contract with America" that would return the GOP to control for the first time in 38 years. Gingrich himself would later stand down as Speaker to avoid ethical problems.

To assemble and sustain a Republican majority, party discipline was vital. The Democrats followed suit. In the ensuing years, especially in the

House, rules and procedures were rewritten to empower the majority and exclude the minority—a de facto form of parliamentary rule. The Democrats complained, correctly, that they were increasingly denied power and access. Holding committee meetings without Democrats in attendance and attaching amendments to bills that had already been voted on were cited as evidence of bad faith. But were the Democrats in charge, could the Republicans expect fairer treatment? And turning the House into a de facto Parliament, with the majority granting few rights to the minority, was not the best way to dampen partisanship.

A final word on partisanship makes a broader point. A paper presented by a Princeton University professor revealed consistent differences in "patterns of real pre-tax income growth under Democratic and Republican presidents since World War II."[55] Unsurprisingly, perhaps, Democratic presidents have produced "slightly more income growth for poor families." Republican presidents have produced "a great deal more income growth for rich families . . . resulting in a subsequent inequality." As wealth accumulates with the super-rich, the consequences, if any, for social cohesion are uncertain yet troubling. And this further gap demonstrates the growing partisan divide in constituency politics.

Relevance and Influence Abroad

The simple and sorry fact is that the United States has no effective plan for public and preventive diplomacy. In a February 2006 address to the Council of Foreign Relations, Defense Secretary Rumsfeld underscored that failure, calling for a major effort to rebuild how the United States communicates with the outside world. Public diplomacy is the way the United States is presented to, and seen by, the rest of the world. Preventive diplomacy is the means to resolve potential problems now, before they become crises. The time, for example, for taking actions that can prevent a future Islamic revolution in Nigeria is now, not during or after an insurgency has started.

By most indicators, from Pew to Gallup polls and as recorded by the media, the reputation and status of the United States abroad are held in low regard, perhaps even contempt. The reasons relate to more than policy, culture, and style. Because of its power and stature, the United States considers itself the world's remaining superpower. However, does that status have any meaning when there are no other competing superpowers? Or does the term "sole remaining superpower" alienate lesser powers who are resentful, jealous, or fearful of the overwhelming American power? Does it serve to confirm the implied or actual arrogance and superiority that it conveys?

None of America's major allies, except Poland for a short time, showed popular support for the war in Iraq. Germany and France were particularly critical. France's President Jacques Chirac warned of the dangers of the peace. His counsel was dismissed. The Europeans, with some 20 million Muslims living among them, had grounds for concern. Extensive riots by Muslim youths, angered by lack of jobs and exclusionary polices that isolated them from French society, swept through France in early November 2005, turning dissatisfaction into violence.

In the Arab and Islamic worlds, largely because of what has been perceived by Arabs and other Muslims as America's unilateral and unfair support of Israel at the expense of the Palestinians, public opinion is harshly opposed to U.S. policies. The war in Iraq has exacerbated those sentiments, as the United States shifted from liberator to occupier, at least as far as most Muslims were concerned. While there has been some improvement in the North African Maghreb, specifically Algeria and Morocco, toward the United States, those are exceptions. As late as November 2005, following the suicide bombing of three hotels in Amman killing fifty-six, 80 percent of those citizens surveyed in Jordan, a close U.S. ally in the Middle East, strongly opposed American policies in the region.

In early 2006, a wave of riots and protests swept through both Arab and Islamic states over a dozen cartoons that had been first published in a Danish newspaper in the fall of 2005. These cartoons featured different characterizations of the Prophet Muhammed. One portrayed Muhammed with a bomb emerging from his turban. The cartoons were enormously offensive to Muslims, whose religion disallows any portrayal at all of the Prophet. The magnitude of the reaction caught the West off guard and raised a profound contradiction that showed why this clash of civilizations can be intense.

The cartoons brought into conflict the Western value of freedom of speech and of the press and the religious beliefs of a faith numbering over a billion practitioners. Clearly, only a small fraction of Muslims would respond violently. However, the volatile and explosive reactions, in part a reflection of attitudes in which the West and the United States are held, demonstrated the challenges that lie ahead for public and preventive diplomacy.

In September 2004, a largely unnoticed, unclassified report drafted by an important and mostly invisible Pentagon advisory group—the Defense Science Board (DSB)—contained surprisingly strong criticism of the Bush administration's approach to the global war on terror. The report was titled "Strategic Communication." In plain English, that means waging and winning the war of ideas between the United States and Islamic extremism. The blunt conclusion of this group of outside experts was that "U.S. strategic communication must be transformed" because it "is in crisis." In plainer English, in the global war on terror, the United States is simply not communicating its message at home or abroad and is losing this contest of ideas.

The report also challenged key administration foreign-policy assertions. Americans have been repeatedly told by the Bush 43 administration that terrorists are out to kill us because they hate America and its democracy. But the report observed that "Muslims do not 'hate our freedom'; they hate our policies" and, in particular, "what they see as one-sided support in favor of Israel and against Palestin[e]." And the optimistic assessments offered by the administration of post-war nation-building in Afghanistan and Iraq were countered by: "*in the eyes of Muslims*, American occupation of Afghanistan and Iraq have not led to democracy there but only more chaos and suffering" [italics in original].

The DSB report further observed that the U.S. "is engaged in a generational and global struggle about ideas, not a war between the West and Islam" and the fight is "more than a war against the tactic of terrorism." Hence, DSB chairman William Schneider advised: "To win . . . [this] . . . global battle of ideas, a global strategy for communicating those ideas is essential," a requirement senior government officials clearly understand.

So why then are we losing this battle? The answer rests in three fault lines. First is a failure to understand reality as it *is*, not as we might like it to be. This flaw was central to the 9/11 Commission's critical finding that "group-think" produced intelligence misjudgments over Iraq's possession of weapons of mass destruction. Second is the difficulty in holding senior officials accountable for policy choices that go wrong. No one was fired or reprimanded for either the intelligence or the strategic communication failures, nor for that matter for the handling of the post-war reconstruction of Iraq. Third is the "dysfunctional" character of the U.S. government's national security organization, a character that often prevents rational decision-making and certainly confuses it. The failure of the interagency process, discussed earlier, to produce an effective communication strategy for winning the war of ideas is further evidence of a fault line that must be repaired.

Seven recommendations followed in the DSB report. The first called for the president to issue a directive for strengthening the nation's capacity for conducting strategic communication. The second proposed a strategic communication structure within the National Security Council headed by a deputy national security adviser for strategic communications supported by an independent, non-partisan Center for Strategic Communication "think tank–like" organization. The remaining five recommendations specified changes within the State and Defense departments regarding public diplomacy and planning for strategic communication, including a tripling of resources (personnel and funding) for strategic communication in the Pentagon.

This report mirrored the work of the 9/11 Commission, whose recommendations were enacted into law after heated debate in Congress. Intelligence suffers from similarly dysfunctional effects of government. The reality is that our security structure is still stuck in a time warp. Even with the new Homeland Security Department, the National Security Act of 1947 and the vestiges of the Cold War still largely define our strategic instincts and national security organization. And "group-think" has not been eliminated.

The DSB report ended by predicting that we will lose this war of ideas "if we tinker at the margins." And we are tinkering. The fact is that the administration does not have a comprehensive plan yet for dealing with these challenges.

The president's November 2005 visit to Argentina to improve trade and commerce provoked highly negative responses from within the region. Unsurprisingly, Venezuela's president and Bush 43 nemesis Hugo Chavez led the anti-American rallies. Earlier that fall, Pat Robertson, a well-known televangelist and one-time independent presidential candidate, suggested that Chavez ought to be assassinated, creating a small firestorm (particularly since the suggestion comes from a putative Christian). One wonders what the response in the United States would have been if Chavez had returned the favor.

The loss of relevance and influence is made clear in a range of negotiations, such as those with China to devalue the yuan and tighten up intellectual property protection. Marginal gains have been made. North Korea probably believes that the United States is so bogged down in Iraq that it is powerless to use force against Korea. In the Middle East, regional friends are unlikely to confront the United States, but they say publicly that United States influence is in decline. The Saudi foreign minister made that case.

In NATO, where American leadership has been critical, senior military officers are worried that because of the decline in its relevance and influence, many of the important initiatives to transform NATO, such as the NATO Response Force, are becoming moribund. Opinions can change quickly. However, to Europeans and despite NATO having invoked Article V after September 11 to come to America's aid, why has not a single European state and public taken the "Global War on Terror" as seriously as the United States? The answer is because these states believe that America does not understand either the nature of the danger or the damage by its policies in the Middle East and in that war on terror.

American public and preventive diplomacy, instead of being mainstays in providing for the safety and security of the nation, are fault lines that must be repaired. As Chapter Nine shows, beyond the need to change policies that are flawed or wrong, the absence of clearcut lines of authority, responsibility, and accountability are major causes of the dysfunctionality of these programs. The question is whether the divided nature of government will ultimately allow rationality to be brought to bear in conducting public and preventive diplomacy, as well as most other programs.

The American Dream

What is the American Dream? Fifty years ago it was college, home ownership, two or three children, and a comfortable retirement. Health care was less a problem, as it was relatively less costly. There was also a sense of hard work being the great equalizer. America surely had social classes. However, mobility was not perceived as rigid. And unions provided protection for working-class Americans.

Today, that dream probably has no equivalent and common perception. However, just examine its basic tenets. Today, America faces an education crisis that is still largely invisible and is paradoxical. Certainly at the university and graduate-school levels, the United States has the finest programs in the world. However, its citizens are not using this asset as they must if the United States is to retain its economic advantages.

In this vastly more competitive world, American advantages rest on innovation and ideas, not production. Virtually every panel and commission on education has made similar findings. America is lagging in science and mathematics. Today, about 28 percent of all Americans have college degrees. The number is declining. Worse, it appears that over 40 percent of all teachers who take first jobs at elementary and secondary schools leave within five years. With a similar amount, nearly 40 percent, of today's teachers having more than twenty years' service and therefore beginning to approach retirement age, the potential shortage of teachers could have epic proportions.

Home ownership is, of course, a marvelous incentive and reward. But what happens when or if interest rates return to the high double digits of the late 1970s and early 1980s? Many owners who borrowed using adjustable-rate mortgages will have to scramble to pay higher interest costs and may not be able to afford them. Would that plunge the housing market into free-fall, as houses at lower prices are sold because owners cannot pay the higher mortgage rates?

Retirement and health care are obviously of great concern. As more Americans live longer, the graying of the population will change the retiree-to-worker ratio dramatically. In 2025, it is estimated that the percentage change in ratio of elderly to working-age adults will increase by about two thirds. That means that far fewer workers will be supporting far more retirees. In 2001, there was about one person over age sixty-five for every 5.2 people of working age. In 2025, there will be one elderly person for every 3.1 working-age adults.[56] The Congressional Budget Office (CBO) further estimated that if changes are not made, health care, which now accounts for about 16 percent of the GDP, when Medicare and Medicaid are added, will grow by 2050 to about 50 percent of GDP.[57] 2050 is a long way off, of course, but indicative of the trends.

Demographic changes will have profound effect on health care, pension funds, social security, and productivity, as well as on the cultural norms of an older society. The arrival of more immigrants of younger age can help, but the problem with this is the broader issue of illegal immigration and tighter controls required to screen out potential terrorists. The year 2025 is two decades away. With compounded interest rates, the accumulating debts and deficits from not taking early action are frightening.

Finally, unions no longer have the power they once possessed. Whether that is good or bad is not the issue. As retirement and health-care costs grow and American corporations must match them, the competitive cost edge is lost. Management and unions must find a new grand bargain to deal with these realities. General Motors is one example of a former industrial titan caught in this dilemma. But the past expectation of cradle-to-grave care, both for union and non-union workers, can no longer be assumed as part of the future American Dream.

Obviously, a new definition of the American Dream is needed. That is a challenge for politicians of both parties, as such redefinition has been ignored or overlooked. In creating a new definition of the American Dream, it is crucial to understand certain realities.

As the international scene continues to roil, the fabric of America is also changing. The social, economic, financial, demographic, religious, and political contours are in transition. The obvious is known. Globalization has led to cheaper foreign goods replacing those made in America and to a growing current account imbalance for the United States. Low interest has replaced traditional means for savings and investment, with both borrowing and a heated-up housing market. For example, as of December 2005, the Dow Jones Industrial Average of thirty of America's largest corporations had not regained the 11,000 level from 2001 when George Bush 43 took office. (It finally crashed through that barrier on February 15, 2006.) However, American wealth has accumulated through appreciation of real estate.

The backbone of America is its infrastructure—highways, airports, telecommunications, railroads, medical services, financial institutions, power generation and distribution, media, and much more. The prior division of infrastructure used for vulnerability assessment applies here. There are two huge issues.

The first, discussed in detail, is vulnerability. The second is modernization and replacement. Infrastructure lasts only so long. Highways have been maintained and built under the National Security Transportation Act of 1954. Obviously, many of them are in disrepair. As we saw in Hurricanes Katrina and Rita, port facilities and levees throughout America are far from perfect. So there is a massive need to improve the infrastructure on which everyone's dreams and standard of living depend. The costs for replacement will run into the tens and possibly hundreds of trillions of dollars.

Voltaire wrote that there are lies, damned lies, and statistics. Figures esti-mating debts, deficits, and liabilities are at best estimates. In October 2005, the Congressional Budget Office projected, in billions of current dollars:

	2004	2005	2006	2007	2008	2009	2010	2011	2012	2013	2014	2015	total
on budget	-567	-507	-503	-528	-554	-556	-564	-479	-347	-355	-344	-335	
off budget surplus	155	176	189	203	219	234	248	261	269	275	278	279	
total deficit	-412	-331	-314	-324	-335	-321	-317	-218	-78	-80	-66	-57	-2,110
GDP (trillion)	11.5	12.3	12.9	13.7	14.4	15.1	15.8	16.6	17.3	18.1	18.9	19.7	162.6
Debt (trillion)	7.33	7.91	8.55	9.19	9.85	10.52	11.2	11.8	12.3	12.8	13.2	13.7	
Interest on Debt (billion)	322	352	385	426	479	521	561	597	627	652	678	703	5,629
Social Security	482	519	546	574	602	634	670	709	753	801	852	907	7,047
Medicare	297	332	385	437	462	491	527	574	606	665	722	785	5,653
Medicaid	176	184	192	203	221	239	260	282	305	330	357	387	2,775

In a separate document, OMB estimated that if the original Bush tax cuts were sustained with a 10 percent cut in rates, the ten-year added deficit would be $1.6 trillion per 10 percent cut. By current estimates, in 2015, Social Security will be paying out more than it is receiving. At that point, about $20 trillion out of a cumulative GDP of $163 trillion will be spent on interest, health care, and social security, about 15 percent by government. In 2005, that percentage was about 11 percent of GDP. Four percent seems a tolerable increase. But that requires fiscal discipline unlikely to be imposed and continued economic growth that cannot be assumed. Other estimates suggest that 20 percent or more of GDP will be going to interest payments, health care, and social security (as noted, by 2050, if there is no change, 40 or 50 percent of GDP will go to Medicare and Medicaid). And unadded are the costs of infrastructure replacement that will go into the trillions. Hence, the gap between expectations and money will almost cer-tainly grow much larger. Therein rests the dilemma that challenges the American Dream. Retirement and health-care programs must be changed or GDP grown at an unprecedented rate to make up these differences.

Beyond these rising costs and deficits, another phenomenon is occur-ring: The rich are getting richer, and the super-rich even more so. Figures on the distribution of wealth in the United States are approximate at best. It is the trends that are informative. Consider some of the data: Less than 10 percent of the population is estimated to own over 85 percent of the real estate in the country, and about the same percent of stocks and bonds; 2 percent accounts for about three quarters of the total wealth. According to a Federal Reserve September 2003 report, from 1989 through 2001 Americans with wealth (in current dollars) of $1,000,000 or more went from 4.7 percent to 7.0 percent. Meanwhile, the poverty rate for minorities increased. By another measure, in 1960 CEO's were paid on average about forty times the average worker's salary. But forty years later, that ratio has increased to over 200 times, a fivefold jump. The reasons for these disparities rest in the fact that equity, bond, and real-estate markets, areas in which families with wealth tend to be invested, clearly grew far more quickly than wages and income.

Two problems are present. The first is the perception of disparity; the second is actual disparity. Clearly, if the public at large believes that the rich receive disproportionately favorable treatment, animosity and resentment can follow. The windfall profits of oil companies in the fall of 2005 precipitated an outcry of price-gouging and Congressional hearings. Somehow, energy companies were to blame for higher energy prices and for obscene profits.

The reality is more complex—and no less damaging. Exxon Mobil's third-quarter results are representative. Net income went from $5.68 billion in the third quarter of 2004 to $9.92 billion in the third quarter of 2005, a 75 percent increase. Earnings went from $6.23 billion in all of 2004 to $4.14 billion in the third quarter of 2005, a 33 percent hike. Profit margins remained around the same, and capital and exploration expenditures rose 25 percent, from $3.63 to $4.14 billion.[58] Income taxes rose from $3.85 to $6.3 billion in the same period.

The question becomes, then, what is perceived as "fair?" Earnings soared, as did taxes. Gross margins did not. Microsoft, for example, makes a 22 percent return, more than double that of the average energy company. Is it possible to delineate these numbers in political terms? The answer is no.

To some, that growth for the energy companies is obscene. To those with a business background, this is the marketplace at work. The beneficiaries are the government, which received an additional $2.5 billion in tax revenues, about a week's costs of the war in Iraq, and exploration and capital improvements, which received another $500 million. Reconciling these divergent views—a recurring theme of politics, no matter the era—is never easy. And when partisanship tends to accentuate class, economic, and wealth-distribution disparities based on gross numbers, not analysis, public interest is rarely served.

Accountability

The nature of divided government makes assigning accountability extremely difficult. Elections still manage to re-elect incumbents to Congress at a high percentage. In time of crisis when things go wrong, there are few resignations. Carter's secretary of state, Cyrus Vance, offered a rare resignation over the Iran hostage raid in 1979, but only because he was not consulted beforehand, not out of any sense of accountability.

The preference for divided power certainly confounded the command structure in Iraq after the war ended. Who, for example, was in charge of post-war operations? Nominally, the secretary of defense sat atop the Coalition Provisional Authority (CPA) (Ambassador Bremer replaced by Ambassador John Negroponte) and CentCom (General Franks, then Abizaid with Lt. General Ricardo Sanchez, the ground commander, replaced by General George Casey). But while there were attempts at coordination, what was the role of the Department of State? And who made the tough decisions when CPA and CentCom disagreed? The answer was usually no one. It was not for naught that many military officers, frustrated with the CPA, nicknamed it "Can't Provide Anything."

In a brutal critique of the abandonment of central control and the vacillation of the political leadership, unhelped by some senior military leaders failing to intervene, author F. J. (Bing) West's *No True Glory* describes the Battle for Fallujah and the on-again, off-again orders to attack, withdraw, and re-attack that completely ignored the tactical realities on the ground and the strategic consequences of indecision.[59] Where was the accountability?

In 2004, very visible awards of the Presidential Medal of Freedom, the nation's highest civilian honor, were made to three of the chief architects of the war in Iraq and its aftermath—the Central Command commander, retired General Tommy Franks; former CIA Director George Tenet; and the head of the Coalition Provisional Authority, Ambassador L. Paul Bremer. Franks was indeed responsible for a magnificent victory in the war. But he retired shortly thereafter. Surely some of the failure to prepare for the peace rested with him.

George Tenet proudly proclaimed a "slam dunk" in guaranteeing the existence of Iraqi WMD. Colin Powell was so unforgiving of the intelligence he was given that led to his February 5, 2003 address to the UN, which surely convinced many doubters that Saddam was armed and dangerous, that he still chooses not to speak to Tenet. The CPA did many things; however, putting Iraq on the correct track was not one of them.

FEMA Director Michael Brown was in the process of resigning his post before the Katrina fiasco hit. And Scooter Libby had no choice but to resign after he was indicted. The point is: Who was accountable? And who was accountable for oversight in Congress? The answer can be written on a very short list indeed.

Given the difficulty of obtaining good people to serve and the extraordinarily long time the clearance process takes, reluctance to the firing of high-level individuals for poor performance—or to asking for their resignations—is understandable. Many errors may not be the fault of the individual in charge. The complicated rules and divisions of authority may not allow the individual to have the necessary power to carry out his or her duties.

But suppose the United States were a public corporation called USA Inc. Further suppose that American citizens were majority shareholders. And finally suppose that analysts in Wall Street and foreign bourses were completing their year-end analyses of USA Inc. in preparing "buy, sell, or hold" recommendations for clients before the corporation's annual general meeting on January 20. How might those recommendations turn out, and what should bother or please shareholders most?

Highest on any analyst's checklist is corporate financial performance. 2005 revenues for USA Inc. totaled over $11 trillion. But the operating arm, U.S. Government LLC, spent about $800 billion more than it took in. Off-budget expenses that were not included on balance sheets, some of which went to the hostile takeover noted below, piled up almost an equal amount of red ink. Trading imbalances between imports and exports hit record deficits and raised the combined debt level to over one trillion dollars of operating loss. Ten-percent loss is sustainable for the short term, even though the combined debt/deficit is projected to grow larger in the future, as must borrowing to close the financial difference, a nontrivial issue.

The balance sheet listing assets and liabilities is of greater concern. Assets are vast. But liabilities are causes for alarm. Health and pension plans are underfunded by tens of trillions of dollars. The CEO of USA Inc. has made pension reform his top priority, calling it social security for employees. However, the most dangerous financial wolf closest to the sled, the health plan called Medicare, has been deferred to the future. Shareholders hope he has good reason for this priority.

In 2003, USA Inc. undertook a successful hostile takeover of a Middle East consortium called Saddam Systems. USA Inc.'s top management, convinced that Saddam Systems' main asset represented an explosive competitive danger to the corporation, saw the takeover as an act of corporate survival. Hundreds of billions of dollars and immense amounts of prestige were invested to seize control. And the reason for the takeover turned out to be dead wrong, a product of colossal misjudgment and Saddam's successful corporate PR.

And there was a second flaw.

The intent was to make Saddam Systems a partially owned subsidiary and turn management quickly back to local executives whose vision of the world corresponded with USA Inc.'s own view. That did not work out either. The initial success was replaced by extreme levels of hostility. As a result, hundreds of thousands of USA Inc. employees are now working throughout Saddam's old empire to make that takeover work, a task confounded by many of Saddam Systems' former employees going on the warpath in protests ranging from strikes to wholesale destruction of corporate property to outright violence against the temporary management.

USA Inc.'s directors, another interesting topic, apparently exercised little oversight, either of the corporation's financial condition or of the takeover. In part, that is because USA Inc.'s CEO has unique authority to reward and punish his directors, often by cash contributions that help or hurt winning re-election to the board. The board is large, with 535 individuals, many elected for reasons eccentric to managing the company. Indeed, many directors have interests in direct conflict with the company and regularly flout them. Once elected, and assuming that they do not offend management, directors by and large serve for as long as they wish. Oversight is exercised in accordance with the idiosyncrasies of the directors, not with shareholders or share value in mind. Take audits, for example.

Sarbanes-Oxley, the law passed in 2001 to deal with corporate malfeasance and greed in the wake of financial scandal on Wall Street and in boardrooms of Enron, WorldCom, and other now-fallen giants, established audit committees as independent of corporate governance, to protect the public and provide it with reliable and verifiable accounting data. But USA Inc. has no independent audit committee. In fact, it probably has some fifty to a hundred committees and subcommittees, each with specific jurisdiction and authority. And the CEO is not bound by any rule or regulation to certify, as his colleagues in the private sector must, the accuracy of balance sheets, budgets, and financial data.

The management of USA Inc. also dispenses dividends uniquely. Business practice is always to assign a set amount per share. But, for USA Inc., dividends are proportioned not by individual share but by the number of shares individuals hold, meaning that the wealthiest collect the lion's share of the spoils.

USA Inc. is purposeful fiction. But there is one other distinction between reality and invention. Corporations can seek protection from bankruptcy under Chapter 11 of the law. Clearly, governments cannot. So where is the accountability?

Just the Facts, Ma'am

Continuing in this line, what happened to facts and truth in government? In the 1950s, the phrase "The facts, ma'am, just the facts" was the recurring plea of police sergeant Joe Friday on the hit television series *Dragnet*. The line became famous, underlying a public sentiment then that fact and truth were inseparable, despite the occasional outrages of a Joe McCarthy. But that was a long time ago.

In the poisonous political atmosphere that shrouds debate in Washington today, facts have fallen on harder times. Either they are noticeably missing in action, or they are tortured and bent to tell a "truth" based on preconceived or preferred notions of a world as it might be, not as it is. From social security to tax reform and from the size of pension fund liabilities to what we are actually spending on the Global War on Terror, getting "just the facts, ma'am" and therefore the truth is elusive and often illusory. Ask those who believed Iraq possessed Weapons of Mass Destruction.

Several disparate yet relevant stories suggest the fate of facts in contemporary politics and reinforce these points: getting the facts right doesn't always count; getting the facts wrong doesn't always matter either; and on some (or even many) big issues, facts are not relevant at all.

In the spring of 2005, the so-called Downing Street Memo was purposely leaked and published in London's *Sunday Times* just prior to the British general elections; it unequivocally proved that the British government got the facts right about Iraq and about American intentions to deal militarily with Saddam nine months before the war was launched in March 2003. The memo, classified "secret and strictly personal—UK eyes only," summarized the July 23, 2002 meeting of Prime Minister Tony Blair and his "war cabinet."

The memo revealed a stiff warning to Blair by his intelligence chief that "military action [by Washington] was now seen as inevitable" and would be "justified by the conjunction of terrorism and WMD." "But," the memo acidly noted, "the intelligence and facts were being fixed around the policy," not the other way around, and there "was little discussion in Washington of the aftermath" and consequences of going to war in Iraq.

The memo quoted a skeptical British attorney general advising Blair that "the desire for regime change was not a legal basis for military action," and concluding that only a UN Security Council resolution would suffice. As a result, Blair and his key advisers would shortly persuade the Bush administration to take the UN route because Saddam's egregious violation of UN resolutions was the only sellable case for war.

The facts won out and, despite the "dossier" Blair had prepared to document Iraqi WMD, the memo reflected doubts over the existence of these weapons. In 2005, the British voters, reacting against the war, took no notice. In their minds, deed was more important than fact. But while Blair won an unprecedented third term, his majority in Parliament was drastically cut.

Regarding wrong facts (beyond the failure to find Iraqi WMD), in its May 9, 2005 edition, *Newsweek* magazine's "Periscope" section reported that U.S. guards and interrogators at Guantánamo Bay intimidated prisoners by flushing a copy of the Koran down a toilet. Few took note. Given prior abuses in Abu Ghraib and elsewhere, the story was plausible.

Eleven days later, riots broke out in Afghanistan and then Pakistan over the alleged abuses. Fortunately, no Americans were killed. Withering under fierce criticism from the administration, *Newsweek* embarked on a frantic damage-control program and repudiated the story. It turned out that Korans had been desecrated, but not where *Newsweek* alleged. However, the White House had intimidated the magazine into submission.

That *Newsweek* got the some of the facts wrong made no difference to the outbreak of these riots. Had the story been totally true, the outcome would have been similar. Indeed, it does not take much imagination to ponder what disinformation or outright lies our adversaries may concoct to discredit the United States and its friends by exploiting the anti-Americanism resident in the Arab and Muslim worlds. That point was driven home in February 2006 over the riots and protests throughout the Muslim world precipitated by a handful of cartoons first appearing in a Danish newspaper lampooning the Prophet Muhammed.

Last, when it comes to "big" political issues, such as the "nuclear option" in the Senate over preserving or eliminating the "filibuster" regarding judicial nominations, the absence of fact is obvious. This is a case where there may be no relevant "facts" to bring to bear, other than understanding tradition, precedent, and the consequences of ending de facto minority rule through terminating extended debate.

The political world of today is one in which facts no longer appear to matter, or matter little at best, overshadowed by ideology, pummeled by cavalier attitudes toward the truth in a rush to prosecute the war on terror, and driven by normative values not of how things really are but of how we would wish them to be. Whether the day of "the big lie" looms or not, it still will be a very long time before a future Sgt. Friday can plead for "the facts, ma'am, just the facts" and expect to get them.

Losing the Moral High Ground

With malice aforethought, the Introduction made reference to the treatment of "enemy combatants," the authorization of electronic surveillance of U.S. citizens by the NSA (in possible circumvention of the Foreign Intelligence Surveillance Act), and the hugely destructive moral consequences for America that those abuses have had at home and abroad. The tension between adherence to the Constitution and the priority of public safety is not theoretical. It is very real.

There are no easy solutions and answers. Debate over "cruel and unusual punishment" has been present since the Constitution was drafted. The death penalty is the most obvious example of this chronic question. However, in the war on terror, when virtually all of the detainees and suspects are Arab or Muslim, treatment of enemy combatants was and remains an issue of the most volatile and potentially dangerous nature.

America's treatment of these combatants captured in the global war on terror and detained at Guantánamo, Abu Ghraib, and other secret prison locations, along with secret "renditions" (sending criminal suspects, generally suspected terrorists or supporters of terrorist organizations, to countries other than the United States for imprisonment and interrogation) that moved detainees across national borders and without judicial oversight, provides a brutally candid pathology of how these very difficult issues exceed the capacity of government to act without provoking unintended and highly destructive consequences to our interests and our democratic values. No matter the intent, the Bush 43 policy toward enemy combatants has turned into a national disgrace and has done irreparable damage to the United States abroad. The damage has been worsened by allegations that the new Iraqi government has illegally detained, tortured, and executed Iraqis without any form of due process, resorting to the practices of Saddam. In reaching its policy toward enemy combatants, the Bush 43 administration could have based its deliberations and findings on balancing the Constitution, due process, and the Bill of Rights against the exigencies of protecting the public from terrorist attack. It could have sought a wider circle of advice and counsel. But it did none of those things. It deliberated largely in secret and, until forced by public disclosure, did not share its reasoning with the American people. And, as it failed to plan remotely adequately for the peace in Iraq, it grossly underestimated the explosive reactions that its treatment of enemy combatants would spark.

The administration reasoned understandably that because terrorists chose to operate outside legal norms and targeted innocent civilians, any standing or protection under the laws of war and, indeed, under the U.S. Constitution was forfeited. Terrorist detainees were classified as enemy combatants, who are not covered by the Geneva Convention in the same way that prisoners of war are.

The policy further authorized and directed indefinite confinement, tribunals, and aggressive interrogation of these prisoners. Torture is prohibited by U.S. and international law. But aggressive interrogation of enemy combatants was justified under this policy as crucial to yielding information that otherwise was not obtainable and conceivably could save many thousands of innocent lives, particularly if such methods prevented the ultimate nightmare of a terrorist-delivered nuclear attack.

Americans will determine whether "water-boarding" (simulated drowning), sleep deprivation, and exposure to intense temperature changes constitute torture and are expressions of America's values.

If the handling of enemy combatants yielded information that saved lives, why then not extend this standard to suspected (civilian American) criminals and suspend the presumption of innocence? Murderers, drug lords, rapists, arsonists, pedophiles, and other violent criminals are, in the main, no different from terrorists. After all, Timothy McVeigh was a terrorist and a murderer who killed 168 innocent Americans. Why not treat these felons as "enemy combatants"?

The answer is that a nation of laws and values cannot suspend these protections except under the most extreme circumstances, such as Lincoln did with habeas corpus during the Civil War and Wilson during World War I. Lincoln of course went back to Congress for approval. If there are to be exceptions requiring suspension of certain laws, and if a case can be made that, if a detainee has vital information that could save tens or hundreds of thousands of innocents, extreme methods might be justified, then there must be some legal safeguard or oversight. Perhaps under those circumstances, approval of judicial authority such as Supreme Court justices or judges in the appellate courts might be required, but with Congressional oversight. However, none of those safeguards was considered or even suggested; and, as far as the record shows, there has been no independent oversight conducted on the treatment of enemy combatants other than within the executive branch, which is not exactly what is meant by the concept of oversight specified by the Constitution. And since upwards of a hundred prisoners reportedly have died during detention, a number made public by Col. Wilkerson, oversight is surely needed.

The administration acknowledged that the eight appropriate members of Congress were informed of its policies toward detainees. But the details of that process are just becoming public; what real oversight, if any, Congress performed has not yet been disclosed. Whether Congress will hold full hearings on these matters has not yet been decided. The initial absence of public interest and outrage was not a good sign regarding the health of the republic.

In the end, due process was purposely revoked for at least two American citizens who have been detained as enemy combatants, to many observers bypassing the Constitution. In *Hamdi v. Rumsfeld*, the defendant was an American citizen captured in Afghanistan and declared an enemy combatant. The Supreme Court, on a narrow basis, found for the administration, arguing that commander-in-chief authority in time of war permitted that. However, now retired Justice Sandra Day O'Connor pointedly argued that "no president is above the law," a reminder that limitations on presidential power still existed.

No matter how Americans may feel about the handling of enemy combatants and the tensions between protecting civil liberties and civil society, the result has been destructive to the reputation of the nation abroad. The moral high ground America usually commanded in defense of freedom, liberty, and democracy was abandoned on the pragmatic grounds of protecting the public, presumably at all costs. Clearly, similar thinking prevailed during the Civil War and with regard to the internment of Japanese-Americans in World War II. But the war on terror was neither the Civil War nor World War II.

The reaction against these policies has been devastating to the administration and to the country. The Republican Senate voted 90–9 to prevent "cruel, inhuman, and degrading" treatment, a rebuke of the first order. Senator John McCain, himself a victim of torture during five and a half years of captivity in Hanoi; General Colin Powell, one of the most admired of Americans; and a bevy of other distinguished citizens strongly objected to these policies, along with an overwhelming majority of the public.

Abroad, the backlash was and remains titanic. By every poll, gross mistreatment of prisoners at Abu Ghraib has done more damage to America's reputation in the Arab and Muslim worlds, through humiliating Arab and Muslim captives, than any other single event during the occupation of Iraq. America's commitment to democratic values and human dignity has been repudiated and in some instances destroyed. America's integrity, honor, and status as a great nation may not have been shattered; but, paraphrasing Wellington's remark after defeating Napoleon at Waterloo in 1815, "It is a close-run thing." When the investigations and inquiries end and further stories leak and emerge, the fallout and consequences of America's treatment of enemy combatants could conceivably be as destructive for the United States as the Tet offensive in Vietnam in 1968 was for LBJ's administration.

There is a further, hard reality. Whether one advocated or condemned these policies and, as important, the way they were made, the treatment of enemy combatants has no simple solution, no matter what these prisoners are called. In an age of mass-destruction weapons, the dilemma of permitting or banning extreme interrogation measures in exigent circumstances cannot be casually dismissed. The ultimate disposition of detainees, as with incorrigible criminals, must consider the likelihood that release would afford—or even guarantee—future attack by the perpetrator once freed. However, in any deliberations, the Constitution and American values must play decisive roles in determining policy. That was the fatal flaw in the Bush administration's actions.

Because of the negative reactions and the steadfastness of Senator McCain, backed by huge majorities in both houses, the president relented. In a well-scripted December 2005 Oval Office scene, Bush 43 graciously welcomed McCain and Senator John Warner, chairman of the Senate Armed Services Committee, and agreed to the ban on "cruel, inhuman, and degrading treatment." But whether this inglorious chapter is finally closed will depend upon how well the policies are implemented.

Repairing the Rifts

THE TWO MAJOR FAULT LINES that should preoccupy Americans most are the current inability of government to deal with these accumulating and explosive issues—many of which do not have obvious or even satisfactory solutions, let alone the means to implement them—and the unwillingness of the public to engage with their leaders. Every political system has huge imperfections. We rightly criticize the response of government at all levels to Hurricane Katrina. It took two days for the president to react, at least in a very public manner. In France, it took President Jacques Chirac eleven days before he addressed his nation over the riots that had spread throughout his country in November 2005 fueled by disaffected Muslim and Arab citizens of France.

Churchill observed that all forms of government were bad; democracy was just the least so. Unfortunately, that categorization no longer fits, if government must come up with answers that are acceptable to the governed.

The United States faces immense challenges and crises. If it fails to produce even short-term solutions to health care, social security, immigration, energy, growing debt and deficits, and education, it is the public, not the government, that will bear the brunt of the pain. If al Qaeda and the jihadists prove not to be temporary phenomena, spreading their ideas, ideology, and intent throughout the 1.3 billion-strong Islamic world, the consequences are nightmarish. A radical Iraq, Saudi Arabia, or Pakistan or some combination with an Iran that is already hostile to the U.S., armed with nuclear weapons and huge oil revenues, would irreversibly change the international balance of power.

A hostile China or India or a recrudescent authoritarianism in Russia are not out of the question. A more belligerent North Korea is not out of the question, nor a nuclear Iran. If any of these contingencies occurred, a rearmed and nuclear Japan could not be discounted, with grave implications for destabilization and conflict in the region given the unhappy history among the key states in East Asia. Similarly, a rollback of democracy in Latin America would increase America's security burdens, even when Fidel Castro finally dies (he'll be eighty in a few months, as this is written).

The list of contingencies is endless. Unfortunately, unlike the Cold War, when the two superpowers and their allies provided a large measure of bipolar stability, there is no structure that is in place to impede the centrifugal political forces at work today. In that light, the leadership and presence of the United States is critical. The question is whether or not we can lead, and lead well enough.

At War with Islam?

Smaller—yet strategically placed—fault lines crisscross American understanding of the threats, dangers, and uncertainties that challenge us. For the first three or four years in the war on terror, elected leaders have told the public that the enemy hates America's values and democracy and attacked us for those reasons. But that simply is wrong. Americans were also informed that the United States was not at war with Islam. However, that truth collided squarely with how relevant American policies are perceived in the Arab and Islamic worlds. From an Arab perspective, American policies call for one-sided support for Israel, prolonged occupation of Iraq, and gross maltreatment of enemy combatants. Inadvertently, the United States has created the impression that it *is* at war with Islam.

Western leaders, and particularly President Bush 43 and Prime Minister Blair, properly regard Islam as a great religion and the vast majority of its practitioners as peaceful, law-abiding people. However, the same leaders remain silent on the powerful tensions and turmoil within Islam and inside the Arab world, and what danger these twin revolutions augur for the West and what must be done to minimize those consequences.

If the West is not at war against Islam, with whom *is* it at war? The failure to recognize the true adversary is another fault line. And what happens when the terrorists are homegrown American Muslims—a nasty problem, given that the fastest-growing religion in the United States is Islam and the largest group of converts is largely African-American former and current prison inmates?

Regarding terror attacks, America had its September 11, Madrid its March 11. On July 7, 2005, terror reminiscent of Germany's World War II Blitz revisited London. Four suicide bombers hit three subway trains in the Underground and a London bus. Nearly sixty people were killed, and hundreds were injured.

The shocking fact for Britons was that three of the bombers were British-born Muslim citizens of Pakistani descent. Indeed, one of the bombers was highly proficient in that most English of games, cricket. Each had been seduced by the siren's song of radical Islam and the cult of jihadist martyrdom that, in this case, leaped borders as readily as Superman soared over tall buildings. That this suicidal conversion occurs is something that most people cannot comprehend.

The bombings in London in July 2005 and the riots that swept France later that fall raised the stakes. While the riots in France were not the result of al Qaeda or other terrorist organizations, clearly their impact and potential for future disruption were not lost on these jihadist groups. In both cases, the main cause for this violence is the failure of society to assimilate its Islamic populations.

To a point, history repeats. Between the world wars, communism and Nazism attracted their share of acolytes. Many of today's fiercest American neoconservatives seriously flirted with socialism and communism. Celebrities such as Charles Lindbergh and the Duke of Windsor found much to admire in Hitler's Germany. Fortunately, that appeal had limits. Jihadism may not.

The use and attraction of suicide bombing against innocents who often are Muslim (as is occurring in Iraq) raises an interesting question. Is the West at war *with* Islam? For the moment, "with" means alongside, not "against." In other words, do jihadist tactics offer a means for engaging Islam more closely?

Change—fired in part by globalization; political, social, and economic disenfranchisement; injustice; the Arab-Israeli-Palestinian conflict; American, British, and Western intervention in Iraq and Afghanistan (and U.S. support for Israel); and other powerful forces—is engulfing the region and the religion. One consequence could be Islam's first reformation in centuries. Or darker outcomes could follow.

As Islam struggles to define relationships among religion, clergy, and state; fundamentalism and how much is acceptable or mandatory; the place of women; and how to deal with, embrace, or reject radicalism, these challenges spill over and hold powerful sway on huge chunks of geography and people. Islam is vast, stretching over an area from the western tip of Africa to the eastern end of Indonesia containing about 1.3 billion souls. That scope alone complicates and confuses how and where these tectonic changes will play out.

Against this context, Osama bin Laden and others like him seek to steal political power, along with control of Saudi oil and Pakistani nuclear weapons. Meanwhile, jihadists see autocratic regimes in Egypt, Saudi Arabia, Pakistan, and elsewhere struggle to retain power by repressing, usurping, or exiling many who are or could become warriors in this jihad. And from Baghdad to Tel Aviv to London, suicide bombers have become foot soldiers in this jihad, with scores of madrassas and radical mosques to relay and amplify the message.

At home, tough questions loom. How many "sleepers" are hiding in the West, where millions of Muslims reside? How do we identify potential jihadists to prevent future attacks without resorting to infringements on civil liberties such as during World War II, when Japanese-Americans were incarcerated in detention centers, or today, when the administration authorized electronic surveillance of U.S. citizens without court order? Where might jihadists strike next? Will they obtain weapons of mass destruction? These questions must be answered—and soon.

The more serious challenge rests within Islam. This ongoing war means that Americans and the West are in this conflict alongside mainstream Muslims. Their success or failure is ours. A jihadist republic armed with nuclear weapons, a chronic condition of possibly ubiquitous disruptive terrorist attacks, and the fear and anxiety arising from these threats are all dangers and nightmares to be avoided or prevented. Hence, as Islam and the Arab world find themselves in this sea of change, it is essential for the West to understand this reality and engage. It is in the West's vital interest to win this colossal fight for the heart, soul, and mind of both a religion and a crucially important region.

But how do we win, and what constitutes "winning"? Can people be contained who are sufficiently humiliated, desperate, or disgruntled to heed the jihadist message and turn to suicide and terror? Can the jihadist message be invalidated and eliminated? The only answer is to mitigate the causes of jihadism. So far, the Bush 43 strategy has been to address the symptoms, not the disease, by eliminating the terrorists rather than the reasons for the terror. A different intellectual and political strategy is critically needed. If this strategic transition cannot be negotiated, the West can find itself not at war *with*, but at war *against* Islam. That would be a true disaster.

Another Fault Line of Misunderstanding: Suppose the Adversary Isn't Crazy

Consider a loaded question that carries on from the question of who the enemy is. Suppose Osama bin Laden's reasons and strategy for confronting the United States were fully rational and that he was not a crazed fanatic, as many people assume he is. After all, he helped drive the Soviets from Afghanistan, ultimately leading to the great collapse of the Soviet Union. And further suppose that the case, put forth by the White House and uncritically endorsed by both sides of the aisle in Congress, that bin Laden was simply out to destroy America and all that it stood for because of hatred of our values, society, and embrace of liberty and freedom—was as flawed as the conclusion that Saddam Hussein possessed WMD. Would that revelation change our policies and induce us to deal with al Qaeda and the threat of radical Islam differently?

Imagine presenting this case to President George W. Bush and large slices of the American public. At best, the reaction would be disbelief, scorn, and disparagement. After all, September 11 and suicide bombers bent on martyrdom are about as far from rational behavior as one can get, aren't they? Bin Laden is clearly a nihilist using terror and destruction as the means to impose a radical form of fundamentalism on Muslim society. Women and children, as well as other innocent civilians, are acceptable targets. "Look at Israel, the poster child for how Islamic terrorists operate," they would add.

In response, a careful review of bin Laden's pronouncements and statements reveals a remarkably consistent message. Bin Laden has detailed a list of grievances against the United States. These reflect attitudes widely accepted throughout the Arab and Muslim world as to why American policy is disliked and opposed, even by so-called moderates. From them arise major demands, including the end of U.S. aid to Israel; the elimination of the Jewish state and replacement with an Islamic Palestinian one; withdrawal of Western forces from Muslim territory; restoration of Muslim control over energy; replacement of U.S.-protected so-called Muslim regimes that however do not govern according to Islam; and the end of U.S. support in the oppression of Muslims by the Russian, Chinese, Indian, and other states.

These demands are categorically unacceptable to any American government. But, in terms of each grievance, they were no greater or lesser than, say, those our forefathers levied against England, igniting our Revolution. However, to state this publicly would evoke a firestorm from all directions by citizens deeply offended by any comparison with al Qaeda, even though King George III branded the American rebels as "terrorists."

Two questions raised in this discourse are particularly interesting. First, in the toxic and partisan-charged atmosphere that shrouds Washington, can the notion of a rational bin Laden even be suggested and seriously discussed? Or would it be laughed out of town? Second, if this case actually *could* be made, what, if anything, does that mean for American policy?

The first question is unanswerable (although most of us could probably come up with what seemed like a pretty strong presumption) until someone has the courage or recklessness to launch this proposition. As for the second, there are some possibilities that deserve further exploration. If these grievances are genuine foundations for bin Laden's strategy and planning, then surely America would be well advised to determine where their impact on the Muslim world can be blunted and reduced, so, as the worst case, Muslims may empathize with but not join with al Qaeda in jihad. Better understanding could also accelerate attempts to bring peace to the Arab-Israeli conflict as an urgent step in containing and destroying al Qaeda by removing one of its principal attractions for legitimacy.

And there is another immediate benefit. Terrorists are often lumped into one category, in which the only remedies are bullets, bombs, or incarceration. In other words, the terrorists are impervious to anything other than brute force. But if there is a measure of rationality present, then perhaps that insight can be applied to the dozen or dozen and a half Sunni terrorist organizations operating in Iraq today. Many are not jihadists and are fearful or resentful of a Shia-controlled state, or reflect tribal and other rivalries. Hence, negotiating with some or many of these "terrorist" subgroups and adjudicating their grievances, if possible, might dent and derail the insurgency and expedite the transition to a pluralistic and law-abiding society.

The larger question of whether bin Laden might have reason to seek some form of dialogue or even negotiation with the West, as Nixon and Kissinger held with China and with North Vietnam and the National Liberation Front during that war, is premature even to suggest. However, perhaps someone should start thinking about that possibility, no matter how distant and reckless it may look today.

What's in a Name?

Language can also be a fault line. President Bush 43 was both praised and condemned for the term "axis of evil"—the tri-state villains of Iraq, Iran, and North Korea. The war on terror knocked out one major member of the axis. The question is whether it is now time to phase out the expression "axis of evil" and, in so doing, gain advantage. In other words, to do with the two surviving axis members what President Ronald Reagan did with the Soviet Union—the original "evil empire"—and his challenge to "take down that wall, Mr. Gorbachev!"

The administration still treats Iran and North Korea as pariah states, grimacing while negotiating through surrogates and multi-lateral fora. If Iran, with a proud, intelligent, and skilled population of nearly 70 million, chooses to build nuclear weapons, there is nothing the United States can realistically do about it, short of using force. From its view, Iran has genuine interests in the region that we can ignore or deny, but to what end? And, no matter how the war turns out in Iraq, a big winner will certainly be Iran, as southern Iraq becomes more and more a "little Iran" and a series of mini Islamic Shia republics.

Iran has its reasons to oppose Israel, support Palestine, and expand its peaceful nuclear-power programs in spite of its energy reserves. The White House categorically disagrees with this policy. It is time to break this impasse. In the nuclear area, a transparent inspection regime is critical to ensuring that weapons programs do not emerge. That is the basis for a direct negotiation and, if successful, the implicit incentive of a moratorium on membership in the "axis of evil" and further talks on other divisive issues. In late 2005, it was reported that America's Iraqi Ambassador, Zalmay Khalilzad, was authorized to have informal contacts with Tehran.

Whether Kim Jung Il is a nut case or a cannier, politer, and informed-if-not-enlightened ruler, as former Secretary of State Madeleine Albright was surprised to learn when she visited North Korea five years ago, the test is separating Pyongyang from its nuclear-weapons ambitions. The six-power talks on that subject may or may not succeed. However, it is not clear that "loathing" Kim and labeling him a murderer of millions of his fellow citizens will be conducive to success. If it is, then by all means proceed at full speed.

Surely, Kim is after recognition. One could quip that an invitation to dinner at the White House would probably make him an unwanted friend for life. So to escape from the axis, a peace treaty finally ending the Korean War and a verifiable guarantee not to pursue nuclear weapons would seem a fair bargain, even if that means the North retains some nuclear power plants. Should these steps fail with Iran and North Korea, then the administration would have done everything in its power to seek peaceful resolution. That alone would immensely strengthen its hand with the international community, and subsequent actions to contain Iran and North Korea would no doubt be easier to put in place and enforce.

Concerning Iraq, the administration's plan is a perfect sound bite. As the Iraqis stand up, we stand down. The constitution will resolve the intractable political issues, bring the Sunnis aboard, and, ultimately, peace, stability, and prosperity will follow. The December elections for a new government eased the transition. But while that sounds good, it is not something on which to bet the ranch, in Crawford or elsewhere.

As noted, the administration finally announced a "strategy for victory" in Iraq. However, with the drumbeat on Capitol Hill growing, as 2006 progresses, the administration will have to come up with details for how and when it plans to exit. If it continues to do so in secret and in keeping with its steadfastly optimistic views of Iraq, then, when that "rosy scenario" does not work out, future options will surely range from bad to worse.

Humanitarian Response

In August 2005, a giant tsunami wrought almost unimaginable devastation and suffering in South Asia, with a loss of life that extended well into the hundreds of thousands. That calamity should give us pause to think about disasters of all kinds, both natural and manmade, and what we should be doing about them that we are not.

Then, less than three months later, an earthquake devastated Pakistan and parts of Kashmir.

Tragically, the response to Pakistan's disaster was far more modest than that to the tsunami. Geography, altitude, and weather were partially responsible. The tsunami-struck regions were all accessible by sea and air. Pakistan and Kashmir were not. And winter's setting in at altitude handicapped relief efforts. The disaster also has put President Musharraf's leadership at risk. As happened with Katrina and the riots in France, the chief executive will be held responsible for dealing with the aftermath of those events.

First, an obvious point: no matter how far technology and science progress, like stopping the sun from rising, humankind's ability to prevent natural disasters is limited at best. Early warning of tsunamis and other quickly developing storms can be improved. However, as President Bush 41 learned following a sluggish government response to Hurricane Hugo, the international community must have better structures and procedures in place to generate more immediate action to catastrophic disasters, even at holiday time and no matter how infrequently they occur.

As happened after Hurricane Hugo, the apparent failure to have timely responses in place this time around is inexcusable. This is one area where even the nearly two hundred members of the United Nations should agree unanimously and take effective remedial action.

Second, while most natural and manmade disasters in which many innocent human beings perish too often receive Admiral Lord Nelson's "blind eye" treatment, only disasters and direct threats to sovereignty or nationhood freely open national treasuries, irrespective of the level of carnage or destruction. Nations will always maintain the right to defend themselves regardless of the size of loss. At Pearl Harbor, about two thousand Americans (1,921 servicemen and few civilians) died in the attack that stunned a passive nation into sparing few resources to win a world war. In 1982, Britain sent its forces 10,000 miles to retake the tiny and strategically irrelevant Falkland Islands after Argentina's surprise invasion, at huge relative cost (although, in fairness, that demonstration persuaded the Soviet leadership to take Britain's modest nuclear deterrent more seriously). And current American military operations in Afghanistan and Iraq continue to show this inversion between actual loss and magnitude of response.

By further comparison, somewhere between fifty and a hundred times more people perished in the tsunami's wake than the nearly 3,000 who were killed in the disaster of September 11, 2001. Yet, as an extension of the importance of national security, it will come as no surprise that the United States will spend possibly a hundred times more money on the global war on terror than will go to coping with rebuilding in South Asia. Human suffering, however severe, lacks a political constituency, another harsh fact of life.

Third, beyond the fury of nature there are manmade disasters. Consider genocide. Hitler's extermination of millions of Jews and East Europeans was no secret even during the war. The allies could have taken some form of preventive action to at least try to save lives. They did not. In the 1970s, the international community stood idly by while the Khmer Rouge slaughtered a million or so Cambodians in the infamous "killing fields." Rwanda in the 1990s and Sudan today are grim evidence of human cruelty and the reluctance and inability of either the global community or individual nations to take decisive action to prevent mass murder.

Last, it is easy to argue that comparisons between different categories of disasters and levels of response are simplistic. Sending half a million Americans or other troops to Africa to prevent genocide is not going to happen. But more than half a million Americans were stationed around the world during much of the Cold War to contain the Soviet Union, a Cold War in which virtually no one died in combat against the Russians; and a similar number did fight in Vietnam and served in the first Gulf war to liberate Kuwait in 1991. So what does this mean?

The tsunami should be a further warning to look more seriously at other possible natural calamities about which greater or more immediate attention is needed now. Dramatic climate change (popularly expressed in the debate over global warming), and HIV/AIDS and other diseases and possible pandemics are among the candidates for consideration. However, once the water and the television crews recede and the dead are buried, almost certainly the urgency of thinking about disasters will dissipate until the next one strikes.

There is, however, one form of disaster where we can and should act preemptively. That pertains to genocide. It is about time to take seriously the laws and declarations made to oppose mass murder. Conventions will not prevent future tsunamis and hurricanes from wreaking great damage, as coastal residents understand. But when it comes to humans killing other humans in significant numbers, blind eyes are no longer conscionable. We can only grieve and offer aid and succor to the victims of this latest disaster. We can, however, do something about Sudan and other places where death and violence are preventable.

What About the Threat?

To many people, that al Qaeda or jihadist extremists have not re-attacked the United States since September 11 seems quite surprising. The administration and Republicans in Congress argue that the measures the United States adapted, from airport security to forming a Homeland Security Department to carrying the war on terror to distant shores, have been responsible. That is an understandable and possibly accurate view.

But on February 16, 2005, in open session before the Senate, America's intelligence chiefs sounded a chilling alarm. CIA Director Porter Goss bluntly testified that "it may only be a matter of time" before a terrorist group "attempts to use chemical, biological, radiological, and nuclear weapons" against us. In his written statement, the acting Homeland Security secretary, retired Coast Guard admiral James Loy, perhaps with the anthrax attacks of 2001 in mind, seconded that warning, telling senators that "any attack of any kind could occur at any time." Neither specified whether his time frame for this potential attack was days, months, or decades.

What are Americans to make of these warnings? Are they credible or not? If they are credible, is government doing its reasonable best to protect the nation against this threat? Or is this business as usual—a partially declared war on global terror admittedly being waged with huge sums of money, but one that suffers from the ills of a sclerotic government struggling to get its act together? The 9/11 Commission strongly supported the latter judgment.

Alternatively, should Americans be skeptical about these warnings? After all, this is the same administration that was absolutely certain that Saddam Hussein possessed weapons of mass destruction and that we would find them in Iraq along with direct links to al Qaeda. Could they be as mistaken here in their certitude about a future attack?

The prudent answer is that no one can predict with certainty when, or if, we will be attacked next. But it would the height of folly to behave as if we are immune from terror. After all, it is painfully true that al Qaeda and other extremist groups who have perverted Islam as ideological cover to advance their own political agendas have every intent of opposing the United States with all their might, whether or not we are attacked at home. So how should the nation respond to these latest warnings, beyond what is already being done?

First, despite the hundreds of billions and possibly trillions of dollars that have been spent on defense and homeland security since the Twin Towers came crashing down, who knows if this massive effort is following a coordinated and sensibly integrated master plan government-wide, or whether a coherent approach is absent? The only way to get an answer is to look, and look hard. That means establishing another "September 11–type commission" before another September 11 occurs, with a far broader mandate to examine all aspects of national and homeland security. Its purpose would be to conduct an incisive and thorough assessment, in essence grading ourselves, of how effective the effort to defend the nation really is; what we should be doing that we are not; and what we are doing that we should not be.

The criterion for another such examination is that the government is still failing to carry out its responsibilities. Any nation is inherently vulnerable. No nation can ever be entirely safe much, let alone all, of the time. The question is how well we are proceeding along that path. The results could be as worrisome as Goss's testimony. Almost surely such a commission would reaffirm the 9/11 Commission's finding that the government is still not properly organized for the task; that there is no coherent national architecture for self-defense; that coordination between and among federal, state, city, and local authorities is lacking; and that an electronic or cyber communications "backbone" to link these crucial yet disparate organizations in a sensible way still has not been built.

Second, none of this can work unless Congress is part of the solution. This means that profound change is needed within that body. There are simply too many committees and subcommittees, too much overlapping authority and jurisdiction, and too little time for serious debate. For there to be constructive change, the president or the public must demand and pressure its Congressional representatives to take such steps.

Third, as the Pentagon's Defense Science Board concluded in 2004, we can never win the global war on terror unless we win the war of ideas. In simplest terms, this means understanding the enemy far better than we do now. For that purpose, some time ago, the creation of an entity that drew from the Manhattan Project and Bletchley Park was urged. The former built the A-bomb; the latter broke the Axis codes during World War II. This entity would possess both the hard and soft science skills necessary to break the thinking of the enemy, and would have the capacity to invent new ideas, tools, and means to defeat it.

Fourth, the interagency process that brings all pertinent departments and agencies together for national and homeland security is, like the government itself, badly broken. It is about time that it was finally repaired. But, as with reforms for intelligence and law enforcement, invention of solutions is not equivalent with implementation. A big idea for reversing this block will follow.

Americans can make no mistake. Protecting the nation against determined enemies, many of whom are prepared to martyr themselves in the process, is deadly serious. Government may be doing the best it can. However, it is the duty of citizens not only to trust but, as Ronald Reagan said in a different context, "to verify" that its government is effectively engaged. And verify we must, if we are to be safer.

The Most Important Element of Security

About making the nation safer from terror attack, there is one deficiency so glaring that it is hiding in plain sight. That failure pertains to people. The Marine Corps attracted recruits by calling for a "few good men" and, dare we say, women. One of America's first naval heroes, the redoubtable John Paul Jones, understood that, in estimating the fighting power of a man-of-war, "men are more important than guns in the rating of a ship." So, as Congress spent the back end of the long hot summer of 2005 wrestling with the 9/11 Commission's recommendations for intelligence reform, what was done about the most important component of national security—people?

The answer is: not much. We revamped our security structure as well as overseas deployments. Yet government seemed indifferent to considering how to attract, retain, prepare, and reward sufficient numbers of good people to serve in the broad defense of the nation. The military is a prime example. With over 40,000 National Guard and Reserves serving in the Gulf, many active-duty forces involuntarily extended and the Army badly stretched, the fact is that the ground force portion of the all-volunteer force, once a positive result of the Vietnam War, is now broken or close to it. And the dialogue about how it will be "fixed" or replaced is not focusing on long-term and major fixes.

What about manning the other agencies of government that play an equally important role as the military in protecting the nation? Customs inspectors, embassy counselor officers, emergency services personnel, law enforcement, intelligence agents, and countless others now man the front lines. The United States has never had a professional civil service as have other states such as Britain and France. The time has come to ask whether this policy would make sense and whether the nation needs a professional national security civil service.

Finally, for instant depression, ask what the government is doing about educating—not merely training—its national security workforce in this brave and frightening new world, from the president and members of Congress all the way down the line. Take the rationale for the threat. Many members of Congress and the executive branch assert, as has been mentioned above, that the reason al Qaeda targets America is simply because they hate us, not that they are advancing a political agenda through using terror. That claim is naïve, and its persistence will not bring victory. And officials of any administration often take office with little up-to-date understanding of current issues and events, particularly if appointments are made for reasons of politics or patronage.

The 9/11 Commission gave new life, however short, to reform. Why, then, not convene another national commission to examine the nation's security needs regarding people? Analyses of the all-volunteer force and alternatives would be a key function. State and local requirements for national-security personnel could well be included. Weighing the merits of a national-security civil service corps would be another task. And planning how to educate and prepare our people for these demanding tasks can no longer be deferred.

A Further Warning

On the current course and despite the Bush 43 administration's vociferous dissent, the United States cannot be guaranteed to win the Global War on Terror unless it attacks the causes—not only the symptoms—of what motivates the opposition. Until that happens, Americans will not be made appreciably safer or more secure than even a few years ago. And the effort to democratize Iraq and make the Middle East more stable will surely fail unless three things happen:

First, Americans must recognize the full extent of our adversaries' ambitions. Currently, we do not. We see the danger largely and simplistically as radical Islamic terrorists out to kill or harm us because they hate democracy and freedom. But our adversaries have far more expansive goals in which terror is a tool, not an end in and of itself.

Second, despite establishing the Homeland Security Department more than four years ago and enacting legislation driven by the 9/11 Commission to "reform" intelligence, our government is still not properly organized to win the fight against this enemy. The 2001 Hart–Rudman National Security Strategy Commission/21st Century report made this clear, concluding that our security organization remains "dysfunctional." In some ways, particularly regarding the role of Congress, this condition has worsened. The report of the House of Representatives on the response to Hurricane Katrina by DHS was a scathing critique showing just how dysfunctional this department was and is.

Third, in the nearly five years since September 11, beyond fighting wars in Afghanistan and Iraq and damaging al Qaeda, we have not constructed a comprehensive global strategy to cope with these broader threats, dangers, and vulnerabilities. By comparison, during roughly the same time period following the hardening of the Cold War, NATO and the Marshall Plan for economic recovery in Europe and Japan had been created and the concepts of deterrence and containment melded into a strategy to counter the Soviet Union and "monolithic" communism. Those achievements have not been matched in the current Global War on Terror.

Why there has been little public outrage over this, let alone the failure to find weapons of mass destruction or plan effectively for post-war reconstruction in Iraq, is a question that begs an answer. Instead, Presidential medals of freedom, rather than "pink slips," were awarded for those outcomes. If we are ever to be safer, we must react to the breadth of the danger, take bold steps to fix our security posture, and fashion a global strategy for attacking not merely the symptoms of terrorism and violence but, more important, the causes.

The root of the danger is political: Our principal adversaries are out to seize power in the Greater Middle East. Saudi Arabia with its oil, and Pakistan and its nuclear weapons, are key targets. As Lenin used communism a hundred years ago and Hitler employed Nazism in the 1920s to establish their authoritarian regimes, today's enemy has hijacked Islam to justify its radical agenda. Other Islamist extremists with different aims and similar targets for terror reinforce those ambitions.

The damage and costs that will be inflicted on us will not be the massive destruction of society, as thermonuclear war with the Soviet Union would have wrought. Yes, weapons of mass destruction can do great harm, but they cannot end our society. The new threat is the massive disruption of society, such as the attacks of September 11 here and March 11 in Spain produced. Fear, pain, and huge economic loss are the levers that our enemies will exploit, intensified by Americans' preference for a risk-averse, creature-comfort-oriented society.

That the United States has not overcome its "dysfunctional" national-security organization is made obvious by the failure to assign accountability, authority, and responsibility across government. Who is really in charge of the war on terror, Iraq, and many other security matters? Homeland Security chief Michael Chertoff still reports to eighty-eight separate committees and subcommittees of Congress, a clearly unworkable arrangement. Despite promises of reform, Congress has not streamlined or modernized many of its "antique" processes. Yet, where are the serious critics and voices of protest? They are as missing in action as is Congressional oversight of many national-security responsibilities.

Regarding a global response, the target must be the causes of violence and instability, not only the perpetrators. This means imposing some form of peace on the Palestinian–Israeli conflict if the warring parties cannot do it themselves. It means implementing a new version of the old Marshall Plan, not just to better the lives of millions, but to win the war of ideas against radical Islam. It means creating a framework for working with China, Russia, India, Pakistan, NATO, and Europe to prevent the use and spread of nuclear weapons. And it means taking Africa and Latin America more seriously now, to prevent current problems from exploding into future crises.

Until the American public demands that its government act comprehensively to deal with these three crucial issues, we will not be safer. Failing that, will it take another September 11 or December 7, possibly with nuclear or biological agents, to provoke the necessary remedies? Can we afford to wait? The next chapter goes into specific recommendations to these ends.

How About "Question Time" for the President?

Presidents largely control how and when they address the public. The time has come to consider regularizing those appearances. Here, British politics have some particularly interesting traditions. In Britain, there is no written constitution. But prime ministers face mandatory "question time" in front of Parliament. Members of the opposition, if clever and determined enough, can use that time to pepper the PM with all manner of questions. Given the level of debate and discourse, those proceedings are often useful in better understanding the policies and intentions of the government.

Clearly, no such institution exists here. Presidents have news conferences, photo opportunities, and scripted interviews where they may or may not choose to answer questions. Daily press briefings in the White House and the various departments provide what is usually pretty toned-down material, although Secretary of Defense Donald Rumsfeld's briefings have tended to be interesting exceptions to these rules.

So with debate raging over Iraq, the war on terror, responses to hurricanes Katrina and Rita, and many other issues, how about a real question time for the president? And if the chief executive is to bare his breast, so to speak, should there also be question time for Congress? To extend the idea, is there any reason why the Supreme Court should be exempt? Hearing the justices respond to questions about cases and decisions would be of real public interest.

Of course, none of this is will ever happen. In the first place, where would the president hold question time? He isn't about to place himself in front of Congress, most likely on prime-time television, and suffer the slings and arrows of either dissidents of his own or the opposition party. And inviting members of Congress to the White House for a public inquisition of the president is an idea whose time will never come.

It is tempting to imagine question time for congresspersons, where the majority and minority leaders and chairman and ranking members of every committee would undergo some form of inquiry by colleagues. This would be time-consuming and potentially very embarrassing, as the temptation to use question time to score debating points and make the other side look foolish would likely prove irresistible. Of course, there are soliloquies in the Senate and debates in the House. But these are not the same as parliamentary question time. And members spend much of their time with constituents, answering questions and conducting town-hall meetings as well as in hearings.

Finally, what about the Supreme Court? Under what conditions would justices ever hold press conferences and publicly discuss specific cases and decisions? And who would ask the questions—members of Congress, cabinet officers, or others? Hence, question time for the brethren, however interesting to ponder, is also not going to happen

Members of the executive branch routinely testify before Congress. Indeed, the amount of time certain cabinet officers spend on the Hill is often excessive. For example, Michael Chertoff has some seven dozen committees and subcommittees to whom his department reports. Question time there is not lacking, and clearly must be reduced, if only to allow the secretary some slack to manage his large and now very overworked department.

Given the political, logistical, and even legal obstacles to imposing some form of question time on the president, Congress, and the high court (protecting executive privilege, for one), a better question is whether the nation would benefit from this type of interaction and exchange—and, if so, under what conditions?

So here is an idea to kick around. Question time for Congress and the court is probably neither necessary nor appropriate. But that is not the case for the chief executive. During past presidential debates, the town-hall meeting format has brought both candidates into contact with so-called "average" Americans and their specific queries. To some degree, in speeches and visits, presidents have engaged in milder forms of this type of give-and-take.

With many critical issues, from the nuclear intentions of North Korea and Iran to the raft of domestic matters of economic, financial, and social importance, a regularized series of townhall–type meetings, televised nationally, would provide a useful opportunity for the president to respond to the public at large. Some presidents, such as John F. Kennedy, Ronald Reagan, and Bill Clinton, would have found these settings ideal to project their plans and personalities; others perhaps less so.

For this to work, townhall meetings could not be staged affairs. On February 17, 2006, Bush 43 held a televised town hall meeting in Tampa, Florida. Virtually every questioner was pro-Bush and nary a tough query was posed. Holding partisan "pep rallies" to celebrate and congratulate any president rather than pose legitimate and tough questions would degenerate into a waste of time. That implies certain political risk as well as the need to introduce a measure of civility into the questioning. Both are worthwhile aims.

While transplanting question time wholesale into the United States would never be as easy as importing Scotland's great game of golf, having presidents consent to attend townhall-style meetings on some basis would bring benefits and a certain discipline to the answering of the tougher questions through these exchanges. And such meetings would afford presidents useful platforms and bully pulpits from which to inform and motivate the nation. Maybe this idea's time has finally come.

History Still Counts

August 15, 2005 marked the 60th anniversary of Japan's surrender ending World War II, a surrender precipitated by the atom-bomb attacks on Hiroshima and Nagasaki the week before and made official in the solemn ceremony held on the teakwood decks of the battleship USS *Missouri* in Tokyo Bay on September 2, 1945. As in most great conflicts, a lot may be learned. From World War II, there are some lasting insights that apply to the twenty-first century and the latest conflicts, principally America's global war on terror.

First, wars do not begin as isolated events. Wars do not spring full-grown from the head of Zeus as mythology describes that Athena, the goddess of war, did. Wars have antecedents and causes that go back decades, often centuries.

Second, strategic decisions entail cultural, political, and ideological components that can substitute perception and belief for reality and fact.

Third, while war generally produces "winners and losers," the same distinction need not apply to peace. Under certain conditions, peace might yield only winners, in other circumstances only losers.

Fourth, that a society may engage in suicidal behavior does not mean that such extremes are a permanent or irreversible condition.

Consider the relevance of these observations to the twenty-first century.

Wars Beget Wars

The origins of World War II date back to World War I, and some would argue to 1815, the Congress of Vienna, and Napoleon's final defeat. Following the Napoleonic Wars, peace would more or less last in Europe for nearly a century. For that century, the major European states were embraced by a balance of power in which no one nation was really supreme. Rivalries, however, were projected onto other continents. Hence, there were races to colonize Africa and Asia, as Latin America remained shielded by the United States and its Monroe Doctrine that discouraged new foreign intervention.

In Asia, China would be divided up under the "Open Door" policy publicly enunciated by American Secretary of State John Hay. Japan, despite its feudal heritage and unlike China, would embark on a profound industrial and military modernization program launched by the arrival of Commodore Perry's "black ships" in 1854 and the threat of Western intervention and domination. So successful was Japan in rapidly modernizing that she defeated a hapless China in 1895, occupied Korea, and one hundred years ago last February sent the Russian fleet to the bottom of the Tsushima Straits in the 1904–05 war.

The great power rivalry in Europe that lasted for so long was inherently unstable, however, and war became inevitable. Even though the Central Powers, principally Germany, lost World War I, the carnage, slaughter, and cost bankrupted most of Europe, "winners" and "losers" alike. There were no real winners in the peace. Indeed, from that war came the makings of World War II, as Lenin and the Bolsheviks turned Russia into the Soviet Union and Hitler and his Nazis created the Third Reich in Germany. In Asia, Japan ascended to great power status, accelerated in the late 1920s and the 1930s by a political shift to fascism and militarism. Thus, from the First World War came the seeds and roots of the Second.

That World War II would produce a Cold War is now well known. Despite the promise, in the decade and a half since the Soviet Union imploded, the future is no clearer. In part because Islam never underwent a reformation or revolution as did Christianity, and in part because most Arab and Islamic states are autocracies or monarchies, many of the more profound political changes in the Arab and Islamic worlds were taking place below the surface and invisibly, at least until September 11, 2001 and the attacks on the World Trade towers in New York City.

Globalization is a painfully complex force that, like Janus, can have polar opposite effects on states and individuals for good or ill, improving, complicating, or impeding progress. Along with the profound pressures within the Arab and Islamic worlds intensified by the Arab–Israeli–Palestinian conflict and the presence of the bulk of the world's fossil fuel reserves in the Greater

Middle East, and exacerbated by America's global war on terr
dations for violence, conflict, and instability have been sec...
Each, as in previous conflicts, stems from historical and long-standing
causes.

Cultural, Ideological, and Psychological Components of Strategy

Foreign policy and national strategy tend to be viewed through some
form of a rational prism, whether one of balance of power or of national
interest. Too often, the cultural, ideological, and psychological factors
that affect, influence, and can dominate major decisions are discounted
and ignored. Yet these inputs are critical to a sound understanding of
problems, causes, and solutions. For example, Japan's decision to attack
Pearl Harbor was based less on strategic and military considerations
than on a deeply flawed perception of how America would behave and
respond when faced with military force.

Following Germany's invasion of Poland in September 1939, under
President Franklin D. Roosevelt's leadership, the United States would
finally come to the defense of England. But given the power of isolationism that persisted in the country and public opinion that opposed
war, Roosevelt had to maneuver slowly and carefully. This he did, with
the carefully concealed intent of ultimately going to war against Hitler.
But Japan was also a problem as it sought to expand its empire
throughout China and Southeast Asia by military force.

The Americans imposed embargoes against Japan on oil, iron, and
other materials that could fuel Japan's war machine. Japan's leaders,
fully recognizing the paucity of these resources in the home islands and
the consequences of not having enough, were determined not to be
denied access to these vital materials. But the U.S. Navy posed a potential threat.

The Japanese high command, dominated by Army leadership, concluded that if the U.S. Navy were eliminated as a threat, the American
people would be shocked into inaction and would choose not to fight.
Instead of war, a truce or peace could be negotiated. On that basis, the
plan went forward. But as Admiral Isoroku Yamamoto feared, the reverse
effect was created: The sleeping giant was awakened.

Today, the danger is that the impact of the cultural underpinnings of
the Arab and Islamic worlds has been ignored or dismissed by the United

States and some who side with her on the global war on terror. Islam, a variegated and disparate religion, is far from united. However, the tectonic changes that have been occurring under the surface have been liberated and exposed. This may or may not be a sleeping giant. However, it does pose considerable problems.

Winners, Not Losers

Fortunately, unlike the aftermath of World War I, it turned out that the defeated World War II powers became winners. With the Marshall Plan, named for its creator, U.S. Secretary of State General George C. Marshall, the Axis powers embarked on a remarkable road of reconstruction and democratization. Today, Germany, Japan, and Italy are the embodiments of successful industrial democracies. In every category, each is a winner. Thus far, the same is not true in the states that are the battleground in the Global War on Terror.

Afghanistan lurches from the opportunity it had, once the Taliban were defeated, to become a functioning state, to a nation that faces further conflict, instability, and disenchantment over the pace of promised aid for reconstruction. Exacerbated by a combination of drug trafficking, which provides the largest share of Afghanistan's GDP (50 percent) and a recrudescent Taliban and greater violence, Afghanistan has not yet emerged a winner. And it may not for some time, if at all.

Iraq is more difficult and strategically critical, because of geography and energy. In the heart of the Greater Middle East, Iraq borders on virtually all of the key states and is proximate to the others, from Iran and Turkey to Israel and Saudi Arabia. The loser in two past Gulf Wars, it now faces losing the peace. The question of which will prevail—the historic model of post–World War I and subsequent conflict, or the model of post–World War II and great success—is unanswerable. Indeed, either case could apply with disastrous consequences if the 1920–39 period is recreated, even in remote form.

Reversing Suicidal Behavior

Sometime in the fall of 1944 (most likely by late 1943 for most intents), the United States knew that it and the Allies would win the war. But no one yet knew the costs of victory, particularly in the Pacific. Operation Olympic was the code name for the plan to invade Japan. That plan estimated a million Allied—and tens of millions of Japanese—casualties.

The reasoning was clear: Japan would resist to the death. And that resistance would demand suicide by its soldiers and possibly by its civilians. Japanese kamikazes had inflicted serious damage on the American fleet at Okinawa, and very few prisoners were taken in the advance along the island chains of the Pacific. At Saipan, women, children, and old men jumped off cliffs to sure death to escape capture. Japan was cut off from all supplies by the naval blockade. The B-29 firebomb raids killed hundreds of thousands in Tokyo, Nagoya, Haruna, and many other Japanese cities. Still, Japan would not surrender.

On August 6, a B-29 named Enola Gay, the first names of pilot Colonel Paul Tibbets's mother, dropped the first atomic bomb on Hiroshima. Three days later, Nagasaki was similarly bombed. Six days after Nagasaki, Japan announced its surrender. From an unyielding posture of suicidal resistance, the Japanese transformed to total surrender. One key reason was that while most Japanese could understand how 100,000 could perish after an all-night or all-day attack by hundreds or even thousands of bombers, the concept of one bomber, one bomb, and one city gone was too extreme to comprehend. Japan's psyche had been profoundly affected and changed.

That lesson is clear. While no one is suggesting the use of nuclear weapons to change the minds of radical or fundamental Muslims and terrorists such as Osama bin Laden, the fact is that at least one society that embraced suicide as part of resistance was disabused of that belief—and for the better, as it turned out. There may be no parallels for today. However, before all notions of negotiations and discussions with the adversaries in the war of terror are dismissed, a little history should be remembered.

To forget history is to risk repeating past errors and blunders—a cliché, but one with relevance. The sixtieth anniversary of the end of World War II in the Pacific is a demarcation point worth remembering. From it, there are many sobering lessons, some of which apply today.

Then and Now

As a last point to contrast the world then and the world today, when the war ended, what did our most senior commanders do? The top ones stayed on to finish the job. Having masterminded the war, Army Chief of Staff General George C. Marshall was persuaded to go to China to negotiate a truce and form a coalition government between the Nationalists and the communists in November 1945, later became secretary of state, and then, after retiring from the State Department in 1949, was called back in 1950 to serve as secretary of defense.

Having fought his way across the Pacific, occupying more territory with fewer casualties than anyone else in history, General Douglas MacArthur became Supreme Commander Allied Powers Japan and was largely responsible for the extraordinary transformation and democratization of that defeated power until the Korean War and his relief.

After commanding D-Day and defeating the Nazi army in Europe, General Dwight D. Eisenhower became Army Chief of Staff until 1948, and then took leave from the presidency of Columbia University to serve as NATO's first commander before being elected president in 1952.

Those days were different. There were no huge fees for writing autobiographies (although Eisenhower was well paid for *Crusade in Europe*). It is interesting that by comparison, General Tommy Franks retired shortly after his monumental victory, choosing a highly compensated civilian career over commanding what turned out to be a difficult peace in Iraq. Of course, the current system probably would not have allowed him to stay well beyond retirement age. He reportedly received a $3 million advance for his autobiography.

Franks had every reason and right to want a comfortable retirement after long service. That he took it, and that his predecessors after winning a greater war chose to serve, is a measure of the differences between then and now. The culture then was one of service. After all, those officers had all served in the lean years between the wars. The crusade was far greater in World War II than in Iraq, and far nobler. And while partisanship always existed, the memory of World War II and the first years afterward, despite the deathly low popularity ratings of President Truman, seemed less a handicap then.

C H A P T E R   T E N

Big Ideas

HERE IS THE ESSENCE OF America's quandary. Even if instability in Iraq and the war on terror were to disappear (which they will not), America cannot ignore or defer addressing the rapidly accumulating challenges and crises it faces domestically and internationally. Nor can it change the profoundly difficult and complex nature of these issues and escape from the dual realities: that even brilliant solutions may not rally broad consensus and, if they do, implementation may still prove impossible.

The Constitutional contradictions, the impact of single-issue interest groups, and the profoundly adversarial content of the political process are totally resistant to immediate and probably long-term correction. But reversing the downsides of culture, crusade, and partisanship is not. The big ideas to improve the working of government must attack these ingredients of the evil alchemy that is producing this dysfunctionality.

Internationally, jihadists pose a threat of potentially unprecedented magnitude. Lacking a conventional army, jihadists are using ideas, ideology, and terror as highly effective surrogates for weapons. Conventional means, which succeeded in the past against more potent military enemies, are not sufficient to defeat this current-day adversary. Countering that adversary, given its inextricable association with the Arab and Islamic worlds and the changes occurring in both, is made far more difficult by the low standing and disregard with which the United States is held in that part of the world and the diminished credibility of its word and reputation. The recent riots in protest over the Danish cartoon characterizations of the Muslim prophet Muhammed provide another example of a political weapon that can be wielded with great effectiveness against the enemies of jihad.

Furthermore, jihadists have inadvertently provoked a profound moral contradiction for the United States. The revelations about the mistreatment of enemy combatants, the debate over what constitutes "torture" and what does not, will continue to do unprecedented damage to America's democratic values and the democratic system on which freedom and liberty depend, particularly overseas and how others in the Middle East view us.[60] Even the release several years later of photographs showing the earlier mistreatment of prisoners in Abu Ghraib caused riots in the Arab and Islamic worlds.

Domestic issues, including health care, social security, gun control, women's right to choose/right to life, and the place of religion now have a seemingly permanent and unresolvable place in political debate. The fiscal reality is that within the next decade or so, promises and obligations made by the government will have so far outstripped the revenues it will collect that the only choice will be to cut budgets and raise taxes, probably massively, further demolishing American expectations. Even if culture, crusade, and partisanship were to stop at the water's edge, which they do not, solutions to tough problems still will be based at best on winning a plurality, not a majority, of support or approval. Absent a strong majority or broad public consensus, the result is a perpetual fight over these issues.

The United States will not change its system of government (although the idea of a new Constitutional convention is not without merit, nor is consideration of moving toward a quasi-parliamentary hybrid, bringing the executive and legislature more closely in alignment). Significantly reducing and streamlining the obscene number of rules and regulations, as well as the bloated organization of the government, and rationalizing the huge number of international organizations, conferences, and relationships aimed at making life better are worthy, critical, yet infeasible aims. America has "reformed" intelligence, defense, homeland security, and law enforcement. Those reforms are not working, as Hurricane Katrina proved. Big ideas that will change public attitudes and policy directions are critically needed.

If they take hold, big ideas have the promise of breaking the grip of the worst aspects of culture, crusade, and partisanship on government. For that to happen, developing a vision and means for engaging the public are the first steps to be taken. Greater public involvement, particularly at election time, will have profound political effect. Accountability within both branches (executive and legislative) will force elected leaders to behave more responsibly, from actually reading legislation before voting on it to submitting realistic and credible budgets and reliable spending estimates. Then changes in organization and structure, as well as incentives for public service, can follow in due course and reinforce these bolder actions. But it is ideas that count, and good ones are needed more than ever.

Peace, partnership, and prosperity (as well as reducing pandering) are my first proposal as a big idea, forming a vision that can rally broad support. In order to engage the public and counter the influence of interest groups usually reflecting more extreme views, universal voting and a system of nationwide townhall meetings and national referenda are offered as big ideas. To force government to become more functional, accountability is essential. The big idea is through a Sarbanes-Oxley–like solution. In addition, a few specific proposals and recommendations are offered for repairing other fault lines regarding people, organization, and enemy combatants.

Before laying out these ideas, several truths set an important context. In any society, certain problems are intractable and never fully solvable. The nation will fight, and never win, never-ending wars against poverty, drugs, disease, injustice, and social ills. Assimilation of minorities, absolutely essential to ensuring social cohesion and reducing the grounds for violence of the sort that swept through France in late 2005, very much remains unfinished business. Immigration policy is part of this difficult issue. Unless the United States can continue to assimilate minorities and minimize the extent of perceived inequalities, the grounds for civil unrest will ripen. As with crime, poverty, disease, and other social ills, they can never be eliminated, but they can be held in check.

Division of the nation into "red" and "blue" states, and the hardening of partisan lines around issues that are virtually awash in terms of public support, have made reconciliation difficult, if not impossible. Majority rule works when there is majority consent. However, when opinions are equally divided, the worst of the political angels, to borrow from Lincoln, will descend on the process, bringing gridlock and worse.

So, how can government be made to work and its dysfunctionalities reduced? A vision is the first step. The first caveat about a vision is that, lacking resources or public support, it becomes a delusion. Hence, a vision must be worthy of obtaining public consent. And a vision must have a clear understanding of who the adversary is.

Understanding the Adversary

That there is no Third Reich, fascist Japan, or Soviet Union to serve as an enemy is a mixed blessing. The obvious absence of dangerous foes is indeed a blessing. However, the absence of such a tangible enemy to rally against makes constraining the centrifugal properties of government more difficult, especially at a time when the potential danger may indeed be greater.

It is also a mistake to pick on more than one or, at most, a few adversaries at a time. Hitler guaranteed that Germany would lose the war when he turned east to attack the Soviet Union. The United States must be exceedingly careful not to duplicate that strategic blunder. For the foreseeable future, China and Russia are not adversaries, and indeed can be strategic partners. All three states share mutual interests that cut across strategic, political, economical, societal, environmental, and cultural issues.

As George W. Bush was leaving for his trip to China in November 2005, members of the Christian Coalition publicly reminded the president that China was not a democracy, and democracy needed to take root there. Evangelicals have had long experience in trying to proselytize in China. However, the simplistic view about the universality of democracy and the implied superiority of American values is the dangerous manifestation of the negative effects of culture and crusade.

There is a lesson to learn again, a lesson that we failed to understand in Vietnam and repeated in going to war in Iraq with such urgency. There were grounds for deposing Saddam; sadly, weapons of mass destruction were not the right ones.

Neither George Washington nor Woodrow Wilson got it exactly right. There is a balance between pragmatism and idealism. When the balance goes off track, the result is predictably bad for policy.

The United States is not at war against Islam. Yet, despite repeated reassurances to the contrary, continuing on the same path, with policies and actions that offend and alienate Arabs and Muslims, that is exactly what could happen. "War" is the wrong term. But alienation, hatred, and hostility are likely byproducts, if the United States does not learn this lesson and—more important—demonstrate that it is prepared to reexamine its policies and ensure that they are well explained both at home and abroad.

North Korea and Iran (and Venezuela) may turn out to be real enemies. But policy should be based on making *their* actions, not ours, the cause of regarding them as such. In looking at means to address irritants, bold actions such as recognizing Fidel Castro and Cuba as the best means to end that regime cannot be disregarded simply on the basis of pandering to the Cuban–American vote in Florida. If that inflexibility had applied decades ago, the Soviet Union might still be in existence and China might be a real enemy.

The danger is twofold. Flawed perceptions on our part can lead to making unnecessary foes. And failing to understand the potential threat posed by jihadist extremists will make matters worse. These jihadists, like Lenin and Hitler, are out to seize power. That their religion is used to camouflage and "legitimize" these aims does not diminish the intent or the danger. Whether some form of Taliban-like regime is formed in some remote part of the Greater Middle East, or there is an attempt to overthrow governments in Pakistan, Saudi Arabia, Iraq, Egypt, or Jordan, the danger is political. We need to keep reminding ourselves that we faced and defeated an earlier enemy who used suicide tactics against us.

The Vision

Peace, partnership, and prosperity are unobjectionable and commendatory aims. But they are also a slogan. As with all politics, what does any slogan mean, and how can it be translated into actual policies and concrete actions?

First, all three of these aims are interrelated. Peace cannot be obtained without partnership or prosperity. The aim of partnership is to secure peace and prosperity. And prosperity by itself is incomplete.

The international agenda is a good starting point. During World War II and the Cold War, victory was won through alliances. After 1945, the victorious Western alliance shattered, with former friends becoming adversaries divided into two armed camps. Sixty years later, that earlier system of alliances needs to be rejuvenated and expanded in the pursuit of peace. But what is meant by "peace"?

Peace must be more than just the absence of violence or war; it must signify an international commitment to stability, the rule of law, and the responsibility of governments—not merely for the well-being of their citizens, but also for issues that affect much or all of mankind. Environment; energy; trade and commerce; and the elimination or neutralization of terror, of crime, and of trafficking in drugs, weapons, and people—these all have no borders. A problem and a reality is that there are few good mechanisms for addressing these issues of global and national importance. A second problem is that beyond the UN Charter on Human Rights, there is no universal agreement on even the nominal definition of these objectives.

The United Nations is too large, divisive, and inefficient a body to take the leading role in the drive for peace, though it must play an important one. International conferences and treaties likewise require national consent. The Group of Eight, the World Trade Organization (WTO), the European Union, and alliances such as NATO and the Shanghai Cooperative Organization (SCO) each have resources to bring to bear, as well as countless non-governmental organizations (NGO's) from the Red Cross/Red Crescent to Doctors Without Borders. And there are countless other bilateral and multilateral organizations and groups dedicated to addressing one or more of these issues.

This reality creates an opportunity. An organization or network somewhere between the UN and the Group of Eight is needed. None exists. How can one be put in place? One answer offers great potential.

No one in the U.S. government has yet tried to rationalize, integrate, and coordinate this vast network of organizations to use them in a more practical and efficient way. The task is immense but not impossible. The first step is creating the charter and assigning the authority and responsibility for action. A combined executive–legislative task force is a good way to begin this process. That task force would begin by conducting a regional and global assessment of what needs to be, and could be, achieved in bringing about greater measures of peace, stability, and the rule of law through utilizing this global network. Part of this assessment would focus on enhancing public and preventive diplomacy.

Here is what such an assessment might look like, beginning in East

Asia. The major issues and points of potential confrontation and conflict are no secret. China's future, Taiwan, stability on the Korean peninsula, and Japan's role top the list. Free and fair trade, and protection of intellectual property, energy, and the environment are specific commercial issues of important mutual interest within a broader political and strategic context.

East Asia: The Six-Power Talks and Beyond

The goal in East Asia should be forging a regime of peace through partnership as the best means of contributing to stability and prosperity. This means creating a strategy that operates on the political-security, economic, and social levels. An anchor point for security is the Six-Power Talks on North Korea. These talks have had little success, producing only more meetings (which, at least, do keep the diplomatic process alive).

The purpose of these talks, from the perspectives of the United States, China, South Korea, Japan, and Russia, is clear: prevent North Korea from becoming or remaining a nuclear power. Pyongyang's agenda is less clear.

Kim Jung Il no doubt wants to gain legitimacy through these talks. A high-level delegation of British parliamentarians, led by former chief of defence staff general Lord Charles Guthrie, visited North Korea in the latter half of 2005. While the delegation did not meet with Kim, the impression was, as mentioned before, that North Korea believed that the United States was so preoccupied with the war in Iraq that any military action against North Korea by America was out of the question. Hence, North Korea had few incentives to negotiate.

The thrust of these talks can be expanded in two ways. First—and discussions I had in Beijing in 2004 confirmed this—Chinese interest is to connect North Korea's nuclear ambitions with resolution of the Taiwan independence issue. China has conducted bilateral talks with North Korea on the nuclear issue for some time. President Hu visited North Korea as recently as the fall of 2005. China no more wants a nuclear neighbor than does anyone else. And China does not wish any instability that would trigger a diaspora of North Korean refugees across its border.

China can become the broker for inducing North Korea to forgo its nuclear-weapons ambitions. Incentives would include: tightly monitored construction and use of new nuclear reactors (the light water reactor agreed to by the Clinton administration, on hold because of Pyongyang's unwillingness to honor the terms of the deal); a final peace treaty ending the Korean War; a formal non-aggression treaty with the South and America; and agreements on increasing trade and aid to the North. If China can deliver such an agreement, the quid pro quo is resolution of the Taiwan issue.

With an ironclad North Korean agreement, including inspection and verification guarantees in hand, the United States government would clarify its policy on Taiwan and independence. Should China attack Taiwan without provocation, the United States would still defend Taiwan. However, should Taiwan unilaterally declare independence without provocation, all "bets" would be off, meaning that automatic American response would not be forthcoming. Taiwan would understand that unilateral action on its part to declare independence was no longer an option.[61] China's leaders have indicated that such a condition would defuse the Taiwan situation indefinitely. And the United States could still continue to provide Taiwan with defensive weapon systems.

The second stage is to expand the Six-Power Talks in scope and membership. The broader—and initial—purpose is to prevent the use and spread of nuclear and other mass-destruction weapons. Beyond the original six, Britain, France, India, Pakistan, South Africa, Iran, Israel, Argentina, and Brazil should be included. Politics withstanding, the fact that at least several of these states are openly hostile to each other should not be disqualifying. If a state such as Iran chose not to respond, membership could remain open-ended.

This broader group might even be linked with the Shanghai Cooperative Organization, as preventing the spread and use of WMD is a major issue among those members. At a further point in time, some links with NATO and the EU might be appropriate. The aim is to construct a web of like-minded states and organizations with a common goal and interest. Talks and meetings might be the initial—or only—products. That is good enough reason for them to go forward.

Cynics will argue that there is already an excess of organizations and that this approach is akin to organizational littering. The telling point is that while there are many security and regional organizations, official and otherwise, beyond the NPT regime, the Proliferation Security Initiative,[62] and the UN, among others, a specific omnibus agency created for the purpose of preventing the use and spread of WMD is needed to draw together these disparate groups. This is one example of how these partnership arrangements can be created and would work. As noted, the CSCE, now the OSCE (Organization for Security and Co-operation in Europe), is an excellent model of how, over time, such organizations can be successful.

China and Russia

China and Russia are potential strategic partners, if not friends and potential allies. It is here that culture, crusade, and partisanship are doing their worst to distort these relationships. This is not the place to make all the arguments about why partnership, not provocation, is the only path to take. If one simply examines the changes in China from Mao to Hu or visits that country, it is clear that China is progressing on a largely positive track. Those who automatically would make China an enemy because of her size, her growing influence, or her military are making a big mistake. That becomes a self-fulfilling prophecy.

In Russia, democracy obviously is not the same as in America. Russia also has a far greater and real-time terrorist threat within her borders. If an American school were taken over by Chechen terrorists and hundreds of students slaughtered, the reaction to the perpetrators might make our recent treatment of enemy combatants look tame by comparison. This is not an argument that we should tolerate brutality; it is a call for some rationality in understanding the profound differences between other cultures and ourselves. The absence of this cultural awareness is a profoundly vulnerable fault line, one for which there is no easy—and maybe no—cure.

Southwest Asia and the Middle East

The Indo–Pakistani and Arab–Israeli–Palestinian conflicts by themselves are intractable without the expenditure of huge amounts of political and financial capital. Surely for the Israeli–Palestinian dispute, outside intervention is essential. (India and Pakistan may be able to reach a modus operandi on Kashmir that at least could foreclose on military conflict.) The Arab world must formally recognize Israel's right to exist, and Israel must allow a Palestinian state to flourish within its very bosom. And that does not get into the questions of the future of Jerusalem or the return to 1967 borders. Nor does it address the hostility of Iran, President Ahmadinejad's threat to "wipe Israel off the map," and Iranian support of Hezbollah.

The tectonic changes in the Arab and Islamic worlds may end up swamping these conflicts. In the former, the "new" seeks to wrest political power from the "old" leadership. Egypt and Saudi Arabia are cases in point. In Islam, Salafists, Wahabis, and other radical factions seek to turn the clock back to the seventh century and install radical and fundamentalist Taliban-like regimes. Both revolutions pit modernizers against reactionaries, though in opposite fashion.

There is no security structure for the Greater Middle East, which runs from roughly the eastern Mediterranean to the Bay of Bengal. The Arab League and Gulf Cooperative Council (GCC), even with fundamental transformation or expansion, are unsuited, since both are Arab-Muslim in character and do not have the mechanism or political clout to become long-lasting institutions in a broader context. It is not obvious that either would welcome or accept membership in an umbrella organization, unless that organization had powerful incentives to offer.

Iraq, however, offers a common linkage. Aside from the jihadists and possibly Iraqi Sunnis, who have no alternative if denied or cut off from power, it is in no one's interest for Iraq to explode in a civil war or a partition along ethnic and racial demarcations. The Arab League has made exploratory sallies into Iraq, in the event the United States should withdraw, as a possible replacement to assist in the transition by providing some measure of additional security forces. However, it is exceedingly unlikely that, given preoccupation with terror in each of these other countries, many rulers will be willing to dispatch their forces to Iraq, risking casualties and diluting their strength abroad.

What is needed is an ongoing cooperative security conference on Iraq, much like the contact group that worked so well in Bosnia. This group would consist of regional and outside powers. The function would be to work with Iraq to improve the security situation there and, more importantly, to prevent instability from spilling over.

The regional players are anything but cohesive and unified on anything except possibly that civil war in Iraq is in only the insurgents' and jihadists' interest. And perhaps linking the expanded Six-Power Talks with such a conference to take on the issues of preventing the use and spread of WMD might provide other avenues for mutual interest.

Beyond this group, Iran must be kept from obtaining nuclear weapons; and, if that fails, then it must be deterred from either threatening their use or actually using them. As of publication, Iran has stated that it is not intending to develop nuclear weapons. Most likely, it is hedging, wanting to have that option. The broad strategy should be to take Iran at its word. Having IAEA inspectors back on post to monitor Iran's nuclear programs and having Russia perform uranium enrichment outside the country are valid goals. Iran has so far rejected Russian reprocessing. An option is to commission a reprocessing plant in Iran controlled by a third party outside Iranian control to do the reprocessing. That is not the best alternative, despite the likelihood that IAEA inspectors would have full access. After all, as Iran physically occupied the U.S. embassy in 1979, the same thing could happen again. There are no guarantees, even with the threat of sanctions, that Iran will agree to any of these proposals. So what do we do if Iran breaks its word and proceeds to develop nuclear weapons?

Before that point, the nuclear powers—the United States, France, Britain, Russia, and perhaps China, India, and Pakistan—should reach a tacit agreement on Iran. A protective nuclear umbrella should be extended to the Greater Middle East, covering all of the states in the region including Israel. Should Iran break its word, develop nuclear weapons, and then threaten or use them, the nuclear powers will respond accordingly. The idea here is that the threat of a response will be sufficient. Otherwise, the danger of a regional nuclear arms race with Egypt, Turkey, Saudi Arabia, and others participating—not to mention that Israel reportedly has an inventory of possibly 200 weapons—will become real.

Europe

Europe already has a plethora of security, political, economic, and social organizations. NATO (and its Partnership for Peace [PfP] and the Russia–NATO Council), the EU, WEU, and OSCE are the most prominent.[63] There are several dozens more. The overarching problems are the degree to which the need for an economically united Europe can bring political unification, and the degree to which national sovereignty will impose limits on both. The vote in Europe in 2005 against the Treaty of Europe that would have moved in the direction of further unification indicates the difficulty of the issue.

The purpose here is not to craft a plan for a united Europe. That would be a waste of time. Instead, the purpose is show how the vision of peace, partnership, and prosperity can be used in Europe principally through NATO, the EU, and the Collective Security Treaty Organization (the CSTO joins Russia, Armenia, Belarus, Kazakhstan, the Kyrgyz Republic, and Tajikistan in coordinating and deepening military, security, and political cooperation).

With the end of the Soviet Union, NATO has made a determined effort to transform itself from a military alliance based on a real military threat to a broader military alliance able to deal with security problems beyond the borders of its neighbors. That NATO has been deployed to Afghanistan with over 20,000 troops and is in the process of assuming responsibility for the entire country over the next two years is a graphic demonstration of NATO's new reach. However, progress in Afghanistan still must cope with the growing narco elements and challenges, since well over half of the Afghan GDP comes from the drug trade. And, while NATO has a small training role in Iraq, divisions over the war there still limit it from playing a larger role.

The thrust for the current changes in NATO came from the Prague Summit in November 2002, which laid out an ambitious plan to change NATO's capability and charter to more expeditionary roles suited to the challenges and threats posed by the proliferation of WMD, terror, regional instability, and the need for nation-building types of capacities to prevent states from failing and to return failed states to functional status. The centerpiece of this new NATO is the NATO Response Force (NRF), ultimately to reach a level of about 20,000, that is capable of deploying rapidly and operating more or less continuously in areas of instability and of direct security relevance to the alliance.

The obstacle here is money to transform NATO's current forces and force structure, from the largely defensive and immobile capabilities that were required when the alliance had to counter the Soviet military threat of a potential attack directly into Europe, to agile, deployable, and flexible forces. Tanks, artillery, heavy equipment, and supporting logistics that could operate in the plains of Central Europe in the event of war, are not suited for rapid deployments or for the types of missions envisaged at the Prague Summit.

Meanwhile, the European Union is developing its own military capability and has established a European Defense Agency to coordinate and rationalize that effort. However, the forces that the fifteen members of the EU possess are the identical forces that would be assigned to NATO. This seeming contradiction is overcome by the understanding that the EU capability and the rapid-reaction force it is fielding complement

NATO and, over time, any conflicts and tensions can be worked out amicably. If NATO didn't have the track record of having survived for almost sixty years, such a compromise might seem unrealistic.

While the PfP has brought former East European states into NATO and Russia plays a key role through the NATO–Russia Council, it would be imprudent to rest the future on the triumphs of the past. The key dilemma is keeping a military alliance together when the military threat has become more diaphanous, broader, and probably more dangerous.

The substantial Muslim populations in Europe (and the past bomb attacks in London and elsewhere in Europe, plus the riots in France) and the potential linkage with jihadist extremists and al Qaeda franchises—all underscore the potential danger that lurks. While NATO has every reason to look beyond its borders for threats that can and will damage its members, internal violence and disruption can no longer be dismissed or downplayed—if it ever could be. The likely upshot is that members will be unwilling to put up the funding to transform the alliance along the agreed-upon Prague goals, given the combination of domestic security needs and economies that are stumbling. So NATO—too easily—will drift into less relevance.

NATO's pending demise has been predicted since its creation. But in the current era, NATO's relevance must be made credible if the alliance is to remain strong and militarily viable. There will be a need for a military relationship among the members, old and new. The key issue is how NATO might be configured to deal with these realities. The links should be with the EU and the CSTO.

NATO faces challenges from within and without. Population growth from the Maghreb will drive Arab-African-Muslims northward in greater numbers. On its eastern flanks, aside from the matter of Turkey (so far denied entry to the EU, in large measure on ethnic and religious grounds, although never so publicly stated), it abuts on the Greater Middle East and Central Asia and is irrevocably linked to those regions through trade, commerce, and the need for energy. Hence, the security picture has been turned completely upside down. Can the alliance follow suit and continue the transformation as the bedrock for Western security?

Using the vision of peace, partnership, and prosperity, one new focus for the alliance and the other security organizations in Europe is energy and infrastructure protection. Europe receives about three quarters of its oil and gas needs from the East. A handful of pipelines traverses the continent. If any or all were cut, disrupted, or destroyed, whether by the elements (virtually impossible) or by man in an attack, Europe's economy would virtually come to a halt. This is a further example of the vulnerability faced today by modern states.

Consequence management, the term of art for dealing with disasters after they occur, would become the key priority in Europe to cope with such a cataclysmic event. And there are others, from the spread of disease such as mad cow or avian flu to the disruption of electrical power. Every state has an interest in preventing and minimizing the effects of these disasters.

Because the EU is a broader organization than NATO, going beyond military needs to incorporate political, economic, and social relationships over time, it is probably better suited to assume the responsibilities for European consequence management. Military forces will play central roles, if only for providing additional support and security assistance if needed.

With American support, consequence management must be brought into play as a more important objective for each of these organizations. Linkages with the expanded Six-Power Talks that would embrace the spread and use of WMD are also possible. The intent is to build a web of interrelated organizations and real or quasi alliances that can coordinate, operate, and communicate with interested states on matters of extreme cross-border importance. Yes, there would be overlap and redundancy. It would have been far easier to start from a zero base and build from there. But that option is not possible.

Africa and the Americas

Alphabet-soup lists of multifaceted organizations crisscross both continents, from the Organization of American States to the African Union. These continents have profoundly different problems and opportunities. Engagement in both to bring peace, partnership, and prosperity has the same general goal and plan of action. However, the specifics for each country and sub-region or state will be very different. And public and preventive diplomacy are crucial.

Africa is a region where application of this vision can have a very positive impact.[64] Africa presents both great opportunity and great despair. It has huge resources. New oil and natural gas reserves have been found in the Gulf of Guinea, off Africa's west coast, beyond the large deposits that are already being tapped. Mineral and agricultural resources are vast, if they can be harnessed. And, because of the explosion in the north and the Maghreb, Africa's population is the fastest-growing of all continents. HIV/AIDS is rampant in south and central Africa. Poverty is endemic. Despite progress in democratic rule, there is far too much corruption and, in several cases such as Zimbabwe, despotic rule. Ethnic and religious pogroms such as in Sudan and Rwanda have claimed millions of lives. Terrorism is infectious. In a crucial state such as Nigeria with a large Muslim population and huge oil and natural gas deposits, the threat of a jihadist insurgency or revolution is not inconsiderable within the next decade.

There have been innumerable programs and initiatives for Africa. The Millennium Challenge Account, the G-8 Summit in Gleneagles, Scotland in the summer of 2005, and Live Aid are representative. And NGO's, private foundations, and global and regional organizations persist throughout the continent. Yet, despite the need, conditions in Africa are resistant to promoting long-term stability, peace, and prosperity.

The United States has some thirty-five different agencies involved in providing aid, support, and assistance around the world. But there are no formal means of coordinating those efforts. In Africa, about thirty U.S. agencies are involved, with about $5 billion in total program funding.

Regarding security assistance, about half a billion dollars of funding comes from Title 10 (Department of Defense), Title 14 (Coast Guard), Title 22 (State Department), and Title 32 (National Guard). But there are "handcuffs" on those funds that prevent any flexibility and fungibility. Defense funds may not be used for assistance. State funds cannot be used for operations. Title 10 covers military-to-military engagement and exercises on counterterror and counter-drugs. Title 22 covers military financing, military education, peacekeeping operations, border security, demining, and AIDS/relief.

It would of course be remarkable if the U.S. government (probably the NSC) could convene a "war cabinet" meeting to address Africa as a whole. Given the disparate participants and stakeholders, a football stadium would probably be needed. The point is that the vastness of the size of involvement and, indeed, the unknowables about which vital attendees were missing would probably make such an endeavor unworkable, unless there is a profound change in how we approach comprehensive solutions, revealing a measure of the dysfunctionality problem.

So, in the absence of directing such a coordinating meeting, what can be done?

The PfP and NATO are an excellent model. The PfP is the mechanism that aided former Eastern-bloc states in making the transition to democracy and free markets and to full NATO membership. Military-to-military engagement was crucial. The reason was not so much "training up" the armies of these states according to Western and NATO standards; more important was the democratizing effect that NATO military exchanges had on local armies and the impact in turn on governments. In a similar way, military-to-military exchanges and engagement in Africa can produce parallel effects.

Such engagements have been ongoing. That is not the problem; making them work is. That means recognizing and exploiting the potential of these engagements and their expansion. The inability to move money from account to account, with full oversight, is a further limitation. One example of how the vision of peace, partnership, and prosperity (and preventive diplomacy) can be applied is through the Gulf of Guinea initiative.

The Gulf of Guinea is that huge indentation in Africa formed when massive shifts in the earth's crust broke South America away from Africa. Nigeria, who dominates the region, Equatorial Guinea, Cameroon, and the tiny island-state of São Tomé share the rights to the new oil and gas resources discovered in international waters in the Gulf. At present, the oil and gas rigs in the Gulf, owned and operated by public energy companies such as BP, Shell, and Conoco, have no protection against attack. Nor do supertankers transiting the Gulf or hauling gas and oil from the embarkation terminals. Given the limited extent of the reserves and the potential vulnerability to terrorist attack, preventive measures taken now and funded by the local states seem both sensible and essential.

The initiative calls for a maritime protection regime that would be easy and inexpensive to establish and patrol. Systems such as radar and other surveillance means would cost very little. Establishment of a coast guard or gulf guard force of relatively small patrol boats and cutters, reinforced with helicopters and well-equipped and-trained troops, is not difficult. Political agreement among the local states and the concern over Nigeria's potential for dominating the region can be addressed. It turns out that Cameroon has some twenty U.S. Navy Swift boats stored ashore that could possibly be converted for these duties.

The aim would be to provide protection and defense of the Gulf against terrorist attack or environmental mishap. Local states, guided by the United States and other maritime states—and here NATO could play a role—would have the full responsibility for these missions. The external nations would provide training, advice, and support, and would occasionally sail ships of their navies to the Gulf as a signal of commitment and a means to conduct joint exercises.

The concept is clear, smart, and unobjectionable. But it has not been approved for implementation, even though it is clear to local and oil-importing states that such an initiative could bring obvious benefit. The key reason why it has not happened relates to the dysfunctionality of government and the difficulty of taking action where it makes most sense to do so.

In Latin America, the bulk of military-to-military engagement was largely conducted by Guard, Reserve, and Special Forces. These units are now in such high demand in Iraq that few can be spared for Latin America. New means of engagement, especially given the election of Evo Morales as the populist and socialist president of Bolivia, along with Chavez in Venezuela and Castro in Cuba, conjures up the specter of an "axis-ito of evil." Preventive and public diplomacy is essential here to ensure that the United States does not lose the battle of ideas in our own back yard.

The Second Big Idea—Engaging the Public: Universal Voting

The thesis of this book rests on the belief that that the nation faces a multitude of challenges and real and potential crises that its government currently is not up to handling. Reducing the excesses of culture, crusade, and partisanship is proposed as the most effective way of redressing this failure of government. And one key means for achieving this aim is to engage the public in demanding better governance. But how can that be accomplished?

Perhaps the most provocative of the ideas set forth in this book is the answer to this question. One of the most important, yet overlooked, responsibilities of citizenship is voting. However, Americans vote in relatively small numbers. In the eighteen presidential elections since 1932, the largest percentage of voter turnout was in the Kennedy-Nixon race of 1960, in which 62.8 percent of registered voters cast ballots.[65] Kennedy won by less than 120,000 votes. But suppose 70 or 80 or 90 percent of

American citizens voted. Would that not turn politics upside down? Instead of focusing on narrow "bases," both parties would be forced to expand their messages to attract the larger electorate.

To engage the public, why then not mandate universal voting requirements for presidential and national elections? Before critics and opponents cite the reasons and arguments why this is not a good idea, consider all of the other mandatory requirements that apply to citizens, from paying taxes to obtaining licenses and insurance for driving cars and flying airplanes, to registering for social security and the draft, to having to tell the truth to federal law officials or risk breaking the law. There are literally dozens of mandates citizens must follow. Is mandating some form of universal voting beyond the pale of reasonability, then?

Under this program, all American citizens eligible to vote would be required either to file an absentee ballot or to report to voting stations for national elections. Ideally, this would also apply to by-elections for Congress, but not necessarily to state and local elections. Once at the polling station, the only requirement is to submit a ballot. Citizens would not be required to cast a vote for a candidate or write one in, merely to show up and submit a ballot of some kind. An upper age cutoff, say seventy, with medical exemptions would be established. Including incentives such as a tax exemption of $100, suggested by General Brent Scowcroft, is one positive way to encourage full participation. The penalty for failing to vote could be mandatory hours of community service rather than a fine.

Universal voting would be implemented through law passed by Congress and signed by the president. That the law has in the past sufficed to regulate voting age and guarantee voting rights should be sufficient proof that nothing more is needed, such as a Constitutional amendment.

The overall rationale for universal voting registration is straightforward. By expanding the electorate by tens of millions of voters, many of whom represent the political center rather than the extremes, both political parties would be forced to concentrate on more than their narrow bases. On the plus side, this would theoretically dilute the influence of powerful and narrow interest groups. It would force politicians to appeal to a larger audience and hence alter their messages accordingly. And it would at least offer the opportunity for more citizens to take an interest in who governs and how they do so.

Some or many will object. Citizens, it can be argued, can have the right not to vote. Why then force them to the polls? Isn't this somehow undemocratic?

Others will suggest that universal voting may bring in the so-called underclass, who lack the knowledge or the level of responsibility to be allowed to cast a legitimate vote. With a larger turnout, fraud is indeed at least possible. Votes, particularly of an underclass, could too easily be bought or so the critics would allege. Of course, votes can be bought today, irrespective of the turnout—or of the "class" of the voter and many lower income individuals chose to exercise this basic right of citizenship.

It is also true that over time, politicians will learn how to game a system in which 70, 80, or 90 percent of the public shows up at the polls. However, in terms of reducing the influence of lobbies and other influence-serving groups and bringing national versus narrow-constituent interests into greater focus, an expansion of the electorate will have certain impact.

Expanding the electorate from 110 or so million in 2004 to numbers closer to 200 million will also have huge logistical, organizational, and scheduling problems. Fraud will not necessarily be reduced, particularly if absentee ballots and online voting are increased to keep up with the larger electorate.[66] Fraud might even become a larger problem if ways are found to tamper with electronic and E-mail voting. Obviously, means to curtail fraud would need to be put into place.

Perhaps the Founding Fathers would also object. After all, for more than a century, voters were restricted to white male property owners. Fortunately, the Constitution was changed. And, if universal voting were required, it would seem that grade and high schools would have the task of teaching students the duties of citizenship, including what voting meant and how people should learn to evaluate candidates and make their decisions. A well-educated public, particularly on the subject of politics and government, must be the best guarantee of preserving the democratic system based on one person, one vote.

Other states have in fact adopted this method. Australia and Brazil are two of the more prominent. Both find that it works well. Australia averages over a 95 percent voter turnout.[67] Clearly, politics in both nations are far different from here. Yet, if the United States is to over-come the pernicious effects of culture, crusade, and partisanship, re-engage the public, and break the vise-like grip of special-interest and narrow constituency-oriented groups, universal voting certainly offers one means. It will also be interesting to listen to how politicians react to such a proposal and who will rise up to oppose it and for what reasons. At the least, this idea should spark debate over governance and the role of citizens in playing greater roles in that governance, itself a virtue.

Engaging the Public—National Townhall Meetings and Referenda

Members of Congress are scrupulous in keeping constituents informed and listening to as many of them as possible. The exodus of so many law-makers on Thursday evenings, bound for their home constituencies, returning late Monday or early Tuesday—Congress is normally in full session only from Tuesday through Thursday—enables members to keep a finger on the local pulse. But presidents—aside from scripted press conferences, carefully managed speeches, and other public engage-ments—are too protected and isolated. Hence, the idea of "question time" was floated above, in large part tongue-in-cheek.

But some form of national townhall meeting is needed, above and beyond the Sunday-morning television talk shows and the carefully crafted presidential public appearances. FDR did this through his "fire-side" chats, even though the number of those chats was relatively small, and JFK did it with his dazzling press conferences. Presidents should commit to a televised quarterly national townhall meeting, broadcast during prime time.

The format can be determined by the nature of the questions and questioners and how much of each will be from the public and from the press. These cannot be "pep rallies" or staged events designed to make presidents look good. Unless tough and fair questions are asked, then the effort is wasted, will not work, and should not be implemented. However, that is not to say that it should not be tried. An informal version of the presidential debates, obviously with only one participant, is a good model to emulate. This will bring the president into closer contact with national audiences and force a certain discipline through the spon-taneity of the unrehearsed format. It also brings some risk, as no presi-dent wants to look foolish or be embarrassed. But those are risks that must be accepted.

States, famously California, often use referenda to decide important issues. California's governor, Arnold Schwarzenegger, put those to use—or tried to. In 2005, voters rejected four of his initiatives, handing the bodybuilder-turned-actor-turned-pol a major defeat. Even so, it is important on major issues to get a sense of the electorate.

National referenda could be non-binding and need not tie in only to election cycles. But that is the easiest and probably most tamper-resistant method. Imaginative use of Internet providers for secure voting deserves consideration for off-cycle voting. Congress and the president can agree to the topics or questions, and a non-partisan, distinguished panel could frame them in objective terms so there is no bias. The hue and cry over the notion of national referenda would be fierce, as the political implications and consequences of manipulation could be politically terminal. However, on a trial basis, national referenda should be tested to determine whether or not such an idea would work and work well.

Gaining Accountability—A Sarbanes–Oxley Law for Government

The year 2002 was a bad year for the corporate world. Scandals, from the collapse of Enron, the energy giant headed by friend of President Bush (known as "Kenny boy") Kenneth Lay, and WorldCom to misdeeds by CEO's such as Dennis Kozlowski of Tyco, resulted in Congressional action. The Sarbanes–Oxley Act, HR-3763, was enacted and signed into law in October 2002. Sarbanes–Oxley sought to make corporations, boards, and CEO's more accountable by imposing greater visibility and stricter requirements on disclosure, accounting, and accuracy of financial and related reports for publicly traded companies.

What is needed is an equivalent Sarbanes–Oxley Act for government to enhance and ensure fuller accountability. Three of those provisions are relevant to requiring greater accountability.

In Sarbanes–Oxley, chief executives had to certify that information in published financial reports did not contain any "untrue statement . . . or omit" material fact in "fairly presenting" the corporation's financial condition. Boards of directors were to impose much closer scrutiny, and a supermajority would be "independent,"—i.e., have no fiduciary or other direct linkages with the company. The Audit Committee became a full-time second job, to ensure that accounting was done accurately and promptly. Finally, the Public Company Accounting Oversight Board was established, terminating self-regulation of the accounting industry.

To many in the private sector, Sarbanes–Oxley went too far, in imposing demands that were excessive or unnecessarily expensive. The new oversight and accounting requirements have proven extremely costly, and at shareholder expense. It is not clear that fraud or malfeasance has been any easier to detect. Boards of directors, the representatives and guardians of shareholder interests, were the obvious center for oversight, and new legislation was not needed to change those responsibilities. The law did get directors' attention, however. That aside, the corporate world needed a wakeup call, and that is what it got. Government is no different.

Visibility, accuracy, reliability, and truthfulness are no less important for a prosperous private sector than for a healthy government. So if Sarbanes–Oxley was essential to prevent corporate misdeeds, why should there not be a parallel provision for government? Three areas—certification of reports, audits, and oversight—would form the basis of restoring accountability.

Certification would encompass budgets, fiscal requests, and required reports, whether compiled by the executive branch or Congress. And certification would apply both to factual and accounting veracity. Hence, supplying Congress with information on Iraqi WMD, for example, would have meant fuller disclosure and at least reporting the fact that additional classified material, not releasable for particular reasons, was available.

For budgets and fiscal requests, certification would mean that the figures and calculations are known to be accurate and are not so insufficiently documented as to be misleading. For example, if a supplemental request for defense spending sets a particular figure, that figure had better be an accurate representation of what was needed, not just a down payment. The Medicare Prescription Drug Bill of 2004 is a perfect case in point of why such certification is essential. That bill knowingly understated costs of the program by some hundred and fifty billion dollars, about a 50 percent increase. It was passed and signed into law. Only then did Congress discover the underfunding.

In a Sarbanes–Oxley for government, the senior official responsible for the program, budget, or report would certify that to the best of his or her knowledge, the material sent to Congress (or wherever) was accurate and complete. If it turned out otherwise, automatic provisions would kick in. Suppose the report or legislation under-or overestimated the costs by a threshold amount, say 30 or 40 percent or more in a defined time period of a year or two. Then that bill or report would be automatically resubmitted and corrected. If it had already become law, then

Congress would revote or revoke it. That is the only way to instill a measure of accountability.

Sarbanes–Oxley was sixty-six pages long. Appropriations and authorization bills can run into the thousands. One fact applies. Virtually none of these bills are read in their entirety—if at all—by members of Congress. This is even worse for so-called omnibus bills, used at the end of the fiscal year to pass budgets at the last moment, when all manner of pork and spending are crammed in.

Members, before voting, should affirm that they have read or that they at least understand the law on which they are voting. That requirement should become part of law. And adding amendments and resolutions after a bill has been passed must be stopped.

Some obvious caveats will limit the reach and scope of a Sarbanes–Oxley for government. The president has a justifiable claim of executive privilege. And some matters may be so sensitive and highly classified that they warrant being withheld.

Members of Congress have overloaded schedules, so reading legislation on which they must vote exacts a heavy price. Former Senator Ernest Hollings of South Carolina estimated that about a third of Congress's time is spent fundraising.[68] Turnover of senior people, as well as the size of government, have inherent constraints on accountability. These factors can be addressed. The key point is that government must be made more accountable in its process, in the information and reports it provides, and in carrying out its responsibilities. A Sarbanes–Oxley–like piece of legislation would go a long way in that regard.

Modernizing Congress

If only one wish were to be granted for overcoming the dysfunctional organization of government, it would be to reorganize Congress. Thirteen appropriations bills and hundreds of committees and subcommittees dominate the structure and organization of Congress. On top of that, three separate processes—budgeting, authorization, and appropriation—determine how spending bills become law. The budgeting process is supposed to set fiscal and dollar limits. The authorization process provides the authority for spending, and appropriations determines who gets what.

Committees and subcommittees are the fora for conducting business, from holding hearings to determining spending. One of the reasons for so many is the scope of responsibilities. A second is to provide leadership positions for the members: about 20 percent of them hold chairs or ranking-member assignments. Radically reducing the committees by consolidating them and collapsing the budgeting process into a single activity, along with going to a two-year budget, have been frequently proposed and rejected. The fact is that Congress is not going to reform itself, unless there is a crisis of incredible proportions or such powerful political pressure from constituents as to mandate reorganization. And even in those unlikely circumstances, the chance is slim to none that Congress will reform itself.

That does not mean that Congress has not changed over the years. Obviously it has, and this is where progress can be made.

Congress formerly did not have the capacity to deal with all of its budgeting responsibilities. So in the 1970s, the Congressional Budget Office was created. Congress also established intelligence committees to conduct oversight. Two further changes can have powerful impact:

First, Congress should establish a Joint National and Homeland Security Committee. This committee should be the equivalent of the NSC in the White House and liaise directly with that body. Membership should be the senior leadership of both parties: the Speaker, majority and minority leaders or their designees, and key chair and ranking members of appropriate committees, to number no more than ten people or so. The purpose of this committee would be to coordinate policy between the two branches. When differences arise over substantive or partisan issues, that body would be the basis for either reconciling the gaps or ensuring that the various sides of the arguments are ventilated. At the very least, the public good is much better served having this forum at the outset of policy deliberations, not after decisions have been made.

The second is for Congress to create a National and Homeland Security Office similar to the CBO. This office could either incorporate the appropriate assets in the Congressional Research Service or develop its own. This would give Congress an intellectual and research counterweight to the executive branch, in order to delve more deeply into these crucial issues and help Congress conduct its oversight responsibilities. Intelligence responsibilities could be folded into this office as well.

Closing the Gap Between Promises and Revenues

As economists are accused of having predicted hundreds of—instead of

the actual five—economic recessions that have occurred over the past
five decades, alarm over future imbalances between federal budgets and
projected revenues is always being sounded. But the future that lies ahead
is different, for all the demographic and programmatic reasons already
noted. More money will be needed for health care, retirement, and social
security at a time when a larger number of elderly Americans who will
live longer lives will be dependent upon smaller workforces for providing
remittances. The additional costs of the global war on terror, homeland
security, and Iraq, as well as promises to rebuild the Gulf Coast post-
Katrina, will add trillions of dollars of unanticipated obligations.

Between now and 2015, if CBO estimates prove accurate, the nation will
accumulate a cumulative total of about $163 trillion in GDP. The net asset
value of the United States is probably incalculable and resides in the scores
of trillions of dollars. But GDP and total net asset value are not fully fungible.
If budget and trade deficits are not narrowed, and if the tax cuts of 2001 are
made permanent, the gap between obligations and dollars will be huge.

The argument that the nation has been in similar tight straits and survived is true. A quarter of a century ago, the savings-and-loans crisis
loomed larger than life. So did the social security crisis of that day. Both
were fixed. But, in retrospect, those crises will pale in comparison to
what lies ahead in terms of the array of problems that have accumulated
and the failure of government in being able to resolve them.

The only solution is public recognition of the need for tough choices.
Since Americans are rightly interested in, not to mention transfixed
with, issues of the moment that directly affect their lives such as providing food, shelter, education, and health care for their families, finding
the forcing functions to broaden that aperture will not be easy. Universal
voting and national referenda may help. But this is the weak link.
Without broader public engagement, America will be at greater risk and
may be unable to extend its promise to the future.

Fixing the Interagency Process

The failure of government is reflected in how the executive branch con-
ducts its business through the interagency process. As noted, in 1986 the
Goldwater–Nicholls Act brought "jointness" to the Department of
Defense. The interagency process needs the equivalent act. The Center
for Strategic and International Studies has done yeomanlike work in producing recommendations to that end.[69]

Here, and as the 9/11 Commission recommended, the walls between departments restricting the flow of information must be abolished. The only way for this to happen rests with the president. The president must assign specific responsibility, authority, and accountability to individuals who then can be empowered to work across departments. That will require the loyalty and agreement of cabinet secretaries, something that has not happened before. However, unless significant change is made, the nation will never be safer or more secure.

Unless the White House is willing to recognize the need for major change and act on that need, the massiveness of that branch will resist even the legislation of Congress. The Department of Defense, by comparison and despite its hugeness, could be made accountable to implement the law. The executive branch cannot, unless the president leads. Failure will retain, not repair, a dangerous fault line that continues to impede the nation's ability to protect itself and provide for a safer, more secure future.

The Main Battery: People

The nation's best asset is people. Outside of a few notable exceptions such as the Department of Defense, government does not do a good job of educating and training its workforce, particularly regarding national security. One big idea to correct this fault line and to facilitate interagency jointness rests in transforming the current National Defense University and military service academy system into a broader national security university–oriented system, to both recruit and educate this professional cohort. Enrollment of the four service academies (Army, Navy, Air Force, and Coast Guard) could be greatly expanded, even doubled, with curricula concentrating on the broader subject of national security. Graduates would receive reserve military commissions. However, a number of these graduates would be permitted to complete obligated service in designated national security billets across government, beyond the three military departments.

The president of a new National Security University would be given broad authority for educating, across the entire government, about national security in this new environment. War-college students would come from beyond the traditional Defense, State, and CIA constituents and include more Congressional staffers. To demonstrate the importance of this position, the president of NSU could hold cabinet rank and serve on the National Security Council. And, on a regular basis, a short refresher course conducted by this university would be mandatory for senior government officials as well as key Congressional staffers, as the Defense Department's current CAPSTONE course is for advanced education of all new flag and general officers.

As the danger from jihadist extremists who use terror to advance a political cause becomes more sophisticated and menacing, the nation must respond. In the rush to correct the problems that produced September 11 and the mishandling of post-war Iraq, the nation cannot forget that people are its most important resource. The nation must embrace this understanding and, in so doing, guarantee that more than a few good men and women enter and stay in the ranks that are crucial to safeguarding the nation.

Removing the Stains: Getting the Treatment of Enemy Combatants Right

Because the administration genuinely believed that, in order to protect the nation at large, the handling of terrorists could be conducted separately and distinctly from the judicial process, and because it chose to conduct its deliberations in secret, the result proved to be disastrous for America's standing and reputation worldwide. The administration finally and grudgingly accepted that criticism, a form of advanced political cognitive dissonance, and agreed to accept legislation sponsored by Senator John McCain with remedial safeguards to prevent "cruel, inhuman, and degrading" treatment. Those laws are necessary but not sufficient.

During the Korean War, many American prisoners of war, under abusively harsh conditions of captivity, were broken by their captors. As a result, after the war the Code of Conduct for American Fighting Men was drafted and learned by every uniformed member of the military. A code of conduct for treating enemy combatants is needed today, not just for the military but throughout government. That code should be based on four points:

First, rules of engagement must be specified and approved by legal authority in the form of the courts. The British, for example, did that in drafting rules of engagement for Northern Ireland, directing when soldiers could open fire and when they could not.

Second, those rules must have the force of law and must be approved by a federal judge or federal court.

Third, if there are to be exceptional conditions for aggressive interrogation and techniques that may approach torture, these must be approved by a senior court or group of judges and oversighted by a reviewing body with appropriate clearances and complete independence from the agency conducting the interrogation.

Finally, Congress must conduct frequent and thorough oversight of all detainees held as enemy combatants.

Unless or until such action is taken, the stain of America's treatment of enemy combatants will never be removed.

Balancing Liberty and Security

Had September 11 not occurred, much of this discussion would have been deferred to a future crisis. That debate is crucial, provided culture, crusade, and partisanship do not turn it into diatribes and angry exchanges between Republicans and Democrats unwilling to listen to each other.

The USA PATRIOT Act became a lightning rod for the debate over protecting individual rights and defending the nation against attack. The risk, as with Lincoln's suspension of habeas corpus and FDR's internment of Japanese-Americans, is overreaction. The administration's mishandling of enemy combatants, to say the least, does not mitigate these concerns.

Analysis of the PATRIOT Act is well done elsewhere. There is one area under the PATRIOT Act that must be corrected now. The 9/11 Commission recommended establishing a senatorially confirmed board charged with ensuring that civil liberties were not abused. That board has not been formally convened, and it is not senatorially confirmed.

Congress must act to correct this flaw to afford the nation protection. The intent to defend the nation is noble. But as history shows, the possibility for excess is irresistible. And if, one day, the unimaginable happens and terrorists attack the nation with nuclear or biological weapons, unless safeguards are in place, a crackdown on civil liberties on the grounds of re-establishing public safety in crisis could ultimately do more harm to the Constitution than WMD. The controversy over terrorist surveillance and whether or not Bush 43 bypassed the law or exceeded his Constitutional authority as commander-in-chief is still unsettled. Appendix III summarizes the debate and the legal and Constitutional arguments on both sides of the dispute. Virtually all Americans agree that the nation should conduct surveillance of potential terrorists. However, drawing firm lines to prevent that surveillance from becoming "domestic spying" is crucial. These are not easy lines to define.

In the questioning of Attorney General Alberto Gonzalez before the Senate Judiciary Committee in February 2006, Senator Lindsey Graham posed a question that illustrated the difficulty of resolving this debate over what was legal and what was not, demonstrating just how tough the issues are that must be resolved. Graham asked Gonzalez what he, the attorney general, would advise a soldier in the field regarding interrogating an enemy combatant. Graham pointed out that the soldier was bound by the Uniform Code of Military Justice, a law passed by Congress that prohibited torture; by the Convention Against Torture; the Geneva Convention; and the recent law forbidding "cruel, inhuman, and degrading" treatment. Then Graham launched his bomb. Suppose the commander-in-chief ordered or directed the soldier to conduct extreme interrogation in violation of those laws. What would the attorney general tell the soldier to do?

Gonzalez answered that he did not know. This answer was shocking on two levels. First, it appeared that the attorney general had not even considered this possibility. Second, the answer is not easy to give and could be impossible, given the fundamental conflict between the extent of the law and presidential powers. Which trumps which? The only solution is thus oversight. Another branch of government must have oversight of the executive if there is to be a balance between civil liberties, the law, and presidential power. That oversight can rest either with Congress or the courts. However, there must be some. Otherwise, this fault line will remain and could provoke a Constitutional crisis.

Will The Public Engage?

On the simple answer to this simplest of questions rests the future of the nation. It is impossible to prove beyond a reasonable doubt that business as usual will guarantee a nation that is less safe and secure, at greater risk. Many Americans will be convinced that the nation is not at risk without further terror attacks. Complacency remains the enemy.

A focus on immediate matters that directly affect families and individuals will understandably override issues of broader consequence to the nation. The paradox is clear. A globalized world is more interconnected. Yet, as this happens, many Americans are turning inward, perhaps a return to historical characteristics wrongly associated with George Washington.

Raising big ideas may help. The biggest of those ideas is universal voting. Whether it is taken seriously or not, the idea should arouse controversy. And that controversy may cause more Americans to consider these matters and realize that the Declaration of Independence was right: When government is not working, it is the duty of the people to change or to fix that government. What worked in 1776 may perhaps have some utility in 2006.

A Plea for the Reader

YOU WILL MAKE UP YOUR own mind as to whether America today is at greater or lesser risk; whether America is safer and more secure or not; and whether America's promise is in jeopardy. My wish is that a profound sense of concern, if not outrage, with the failures of government will persuade you to take a more active role in matters of personal and national importance and of governance. But no matter what conclusion you draw, you will agree, I hope, that the public needs to be more intimately engaged in its governance if the nation is to emerge from the crises and challenges it faces with its values and expectations for the future relatively unscathed. In my view, limiting, not totally avoiding, damage is the best case possible. Less salutary ones are more likely.

As it was impossible to predict what the United States would have been like ten or twenty years after the Revolution, the ratification of the Constitution, or the Civil and world wars, the same uncertainties hold today. On the one hand, there is no theoretical reason why the United States cannot be the strongest, wealthiest, most influential, and most secure nation in the world in 2015 or 2025. On the other, there are practical reasons for envisaging a far gloomier view.

The array of problems America faces is accumulating faster than the solutions that can be implemented. Many of these solutions, given the current state of government, will be incomplete and temporary, and possibly will make matters worse, not better. One reason is the inherent intractability of finding solutions that will muster widespread consent and approval, whether inside our borders or, to use a quaint term, overseas.

Second, the nature of checks and balances and divided power has led to a structure of government in which responsibility, authority, and accountability have become extraordinarily diffuse, stretching across an obscene number of departments, agencies, and institutions. As a result, the only really accountable individual is the president. It is certainly unfair to hold that one individual responsible for the activities of a government, when those activities are vast and impossible to monitor in a timely fashion.

Third, powerful interest groups, lobbies, and constituencies skew the governing process. Narrow, rather than national, interests shape and set policy, from the number of warships the Navy needs to tax credits to incentives for the private sector that stimulate economic growth.

Fourth, the best and worst of culture, crusade, and partisanship have enormous impact on governing. Since the end of the Cold War, these effects have been largely harmful and indeed reflect historical trends that have been part of the nation's fabric since 1789.

Consider some of these linkages. Culture and crusade produced active American involvement in addressing both domestic and international issues. The demarcation point was 1898, after which the United States sought to expand its values and perceptions of liberty, freedom, and democracy to others. What drove McKinley into war with Spain was not substantially different from what motivated Wilson, Kennedy, and Bush 43. Another was American post-war planning.

In 1865 and 1918, the United States dismally failed to anticipate the post-war conditions. Reconstruction in the South was unduly harsh and unfair. That legacy still persists today, albeit in a far more moderate form than the past racial animosities and anger on the part of Southerners against the North. The post–World War I peace in Europe, in which the Central Powers were laden with reparations and war debt, sowed the seeds that led to World War II. Fortunately, the post–World War II period was a triumph of internationalism, magnanimity, and common sense in not repeating the disaster of 1918. But it took decades for real democracy to emerge in the defeated Axis powers.

Post-war Iraq resembled at first what happened after 1918, not 1945. At least half a trillion dollars has been spent in Iraq by the United States, and tens of billions were supposed to have been remitted from Iraqi oil revenues. Unfortunately, the lion's share of that money has gone into attempts to make Iraq more secure, not rebuilding it after three wars and five decades of Baathist rule. Germany and Japan after 1945 of course had no such security problems and had been so thoroughly defeated by the Allies that the task of establishing democracy and open markets was infinitely easier. And both Germany and Japan were largely homogeneous societies with some prior experience in democratic rule.

But worse, Iraq became, for the United States, the surrogate for waging the war on terror. That strategic flaw has enabled jihadist extremists means, opportunity, and motive for empowering and refreshing their cause. In some ways, if Iraq fails, America's strategic miscalculation mirrors that of the Japanese high command in attacking Pearl Harbor. The Bush 43 administration's assumption that democratization would work not only in Iraq but in the entire Greater Middle East will prove no sounder than Tokyo's assessment that the destruction of the U.S. fleet would force Washington to the negotiating table.

As a result, and from the analysis presented earlier, despite the strong protests of the administration to the contrary, the United States is certainly not winning the war on terror and indeed has not provided any calculus or formula to determine how well or badly it is faring, beyond promises and expectations that, after "staying the course," we "will and must prevail." However, the decline in America's relevance and influence abroad, the continuing vulnerability of its society to massive disruption through attack or its threat, the failure to understand the nature of the adversary, seeming indifference to or arrogance about making further enemies, and what appears to be a continuing influx of jihadist recruits—all indicate that the balance has swung against us.

In that context, confronted with a dangerous, cunning, ruthless, and clever adversary who does not need a conventional army, navy, or air force and who uses ideas, ideology, and terror for political ends and an array of hugely different and quickly accelerating problems along the way, American government is overloaded by these tests. Furthermore, based on its record of performance, from reforming various departments and agencies to responding to disasters such as Katrina to allocating budgets and adjudicating social tensions, overall, our government is dysfunctional. There are a great many dedicated and able elected and governmental officials trying to do their best, even at a time when many are discouraged from service. But the process of government not only limits their effectiveness; too often, it neuters it.

As we have seen, cronyism dating back to the spoils system of political patronage has reached a new level of ubiquity. The revolving door of government to industry and especially to lobbying is spinning faster than ever. And too many officials have been appointed to important offices based not on experience and qualifications but on political friendships, debt, and other favors.

No list of specific reforms, however detailed, can correct these ills. Big ideas that motivate people to act differently are what is needed. The vision of peace, partnership, and prosperity is one. And engaging the American public is another.

Universal voting will provoke, one hopes, a healthy debate. Because such a change will upset the current political balance of power and prove so threatening to the multitudes of special-interest groups and constituencies and act as a dagger pointed at the throats of many elites and others who are comfortable and successful in working the political process for personal gain, the opposition will be enormous. It will prove ironic that if a popular movement to implement universal voting is sparked, then the battle will resort to war rooms on *both* sides spinning attack ads and negative campaigns to make their case. Such could lead to a Pyrrhic victory.

Finally, it is wishful thinking to hope or to expect that a "great" leader will emerge. We have had forty-three presidents. Only a few were great. The nature of the nominating and electing process and the conduct of politics almost guarantee that winners of the Oval Office will have very real limitations in experience and ability to cope with the multitude of problems and issues. Of course, a Washington, Jackson, Lincoln, Roosevelt, or Truman *could* emerge. However, hope for that is neither a plan nor a strategy.

In lieu of the great leader, Americans must redress those issues that are correctable. The worst excesses of culture, crusade, and partisanship are the only targets that can be affected for the better. The accumulation of crises and problems, the difficulty in reaching practical solutions, and the overall organization of government based on a balance of power remain constants, and are relatively immutable to reform or immediate correction.

America's relevance and influence abroad and its promise at home are in severe decline. The consequence will be a continued erosion of our way of life and our safety and security. The erosion could be accelerated, should jihadist extremists be allowed to achieve their ambitions for seizing political power. In that circumstance, the nation and its friends will be at severe risk politically, strategically, culturally, and economically.

Left unanswered is the basic question raised by this book. Can a political system designed by the best minds of the eighteenth century withstand the rigors of the twenty-first? If we cannot answer this question in the coming decade, generations of our children and our children's children will bear that burden. And it could be an oppressive one.

March 15, 2006

IN THE THREE MONTHS SINCE the final draft of this book was completed, the symptoms of what ails America have taken even more vivid and visible form. Despite the $500 billion the United States has so far poured into the war and its aftermath, Iraq is still struggling to form a government. The basic contradictions and tensions over power sharing; ethnic, religious, and tribal factions; the role of women; division of oil revenues; reduction in corruption and cronyism; and establishing a viable security force have not gotten better. In many cases, they have deteriorated. And the trial of Saddam Hussein has turned into a perverse spectacle, with the deposed despot making a mockery of the proceedings and the court seemingly incapable of restraining him or his antics.

The destruction of the Golden Mosque in Samarra in February 2006 may not have set off a truly bloody civil war. However, it was close. "In extremis" is, among its other definitions, a nautical term, which means that two or more ships are about to collide and only the most extreme maneuvers can prevent that collision. Iraq is surely in extremis in this context.

Despite the hundreds of billions of dollars that have been poured into homeland security, the House of Representatives presented a devastating critique of the response to Hurricane Katrina, conclusions that were predictable and predicted. The White House released its findings and recommended corrective actions in late February 2006, also on Katrina. Why such an evaluation was not performed *before* such a crisis, in order to assess the ability of the Department of Homeland Security to carry out its duties, is inexplicable. However, this is the nature of government.

Congress and the White House are still at loggerheads over terrorist surveillance and the balance of power between the two branches of government. That balance was tested by the controversy over the transfer of management of six U.S. ports to Dubai Ports World, a corporation owned by the government of the United Arab Emirates. The firestorm came over the emotional response to having U.S. ports "controlled" by an Arab state. The fact that the security of the ports was unaffected by whomever held the management contract, and the continuing vulnerability of U.S. ports and infrastructure, and the failure to take corrective action, were obscured by the politics of the controversy with both Republicans and Democrats assailing the administration, in part for the wrong reasons.

The combination of the failure of response to Katrina, the bombing of the Golden Mosque in Samarra, and the brouhaha over the managing of U.S. ports demonstrates issues beyond the reach of government to solve and the failure of government to extend its reach to cope with these pressing and vital matters.

The Federal budget for FY 2007 posits a deficit along with the trade imbalance that will jointly exceed a trillion dollars this year, and no steps have been taken to address the yawning gap between expectations, obligations, and revenues that seem only to grow larger and larger.

Iran looms as a further crisis over its nuclear ambitions. The election of Hamas to power in Palestine and the incapacitation of Israeli Prime Minister Ariel Sharon (and possibly his death, as he still lingers in a coma as this goes to press) have derailed what was left of the peace process. Egypt and Saudi Arabia appear to be sliding back from modest experiments with democracy. And Pakistan faces growing unrest and violence in Baluchistan amidst all of its other problems.

The twin revolutions in the Islamic and Arab worlds have been fueled by continuing stories of maltreatment of enemy combatants by the United States long after the abuses occurred. And the dozen cartoons in the Danish press last fall set a large part of the Arab and Islamic worlds into fiery protest, some with extreme violence. That reaction is a frightening precursor of what could come next if or when demagogues and jihadists chose to exploit this weapon of violent protest for their own political ends. Nigeria is experiencing increasing violence and attacks against oil facilities and, most recently, insurgent threats to attack tankers. Nor is Latin America or Africa emerging on a positive track. Evo Morales's legitimate election in Bolivia is another setback for the United States and for the notion of democracy and freedom as the best ways to ensure peace, stability, and friendship.

Meanwhile, it is too early to tell whether Congress's awakening to its oversight responsibilities is real or temporary.

The Bush 43 administration and its supporters of course reject these points of reference and trends. Whether that is denial, hardheadedness, or a view that will ultimately prove correct is in the eye of the beholder. But most Americans are concerned, many are worried, and some are plainly frightened.

The proof or rejection for the thesis of this book will play out over the coming months and years. If the array of seemingly endless and tough problems diminishes and if government somehow takes charge and brings a measure of rationality to resolving these challenges, then I will happily admit to profoundly flawed analysis. However, the reader can judge what he or she thinks will happen.

This is a time not for revolution, but for restoration of America's promise. And, if the analyses prove correct, then only we the people can make that happen.

Appendix I

THE ARGUMENTS IN *AMERICA'S PROMISE Restored* are clear and stark.

- Driven by the worst of culture, crusade, and partisanship, our political system has grown dysfunctional. Examples are rife. How we have dealt with Iraq before, during, and after the 2003 war is but one glaring indicator of this dysfunctionality. Congress's performance is another.

- The formidable list of hugely complex and profound challenges that cannot be indefinitely deferred includes stemming cascading economic debts, deficits, and liabilities; finding sensible energy solutions that address conservation and environmental concerns; protecting pensions, social security, and health-care programs during the graying of the population; ensuring a viable homeland defense; waging the Global War on Terror; and much more. Each represents a real or potential fault line. Muddling through the items on this list will be a fool's mission, if the nation's future depends upon competent and smart decisions and actions by government. And expectations promised by government exceed likely revenues by as much as 50 percent, probably more.

- The external enemy will not be contained solely by traditional, comfortable, and familiar means that have worked in the past. Lacking an army or navy, this enemy employs ideas, ideology, and terror as the means to win political power. Worse, this enemy targets the very openness of our society, compounding the difficulties of containing the danger and of reducing our fault lines and vulnerabilities.

- Because of a combination of our foreign and domestic policies, the end of an era dominated and restrained by two superpowers, and tectonic changes occurring around the globe, by almost every metric America's relevance and influence abroad are in free-fall. The United States is viewed with cynicism and scorn abroad, reflected by virtually every opinion poll conducted among foreign audiences.

- As a result, visible and hidden "fault lines" embedded throughout our society are in danger of failing, possibly catastrophically, from the onslaught of these external and internal forces and pressures. The key question is whether or not our system of government, and those we elect to run it, are up to the tasks ahead.

- And we are largely ignorant, indifferent, or unwilling to confront these realities.

Will we act? That is up to us, the public of the United States.

Appendix II

Pros and Cons for Universal, Mandatory Voting

AUSTRALIA IS A COUNTRY THAT ALREADY practices compulsory voting, which means that every Australian citizen (18 years or older) is required by law to enroll and vote. If a person does not vote and is unable to provide a "valid and sufficient" reason, a penalty is imposed. Compulsory voting is a distinctive feature of the Australian political culture. Because it is instructional to our case for compulsory voting in America, we present the following data.

History of compulsory voting in Australia:
- Compulsory voting was advocated by Alfred Deakin at the turn of the twentieth century.
- Compulsory enrollment for federal elections was introduced in 1911.
- Compulsory voting for state elections was introduced in Queensland in 1915.
- Compulsory voting at federal elections was introduced in 1924.

Arguments used in favor of compulsory voting in Australia:
- Voting is a civic duty comparable to other duties citizens perform (e.g., taxation, compulsory education, jury duty).

- Voting teaches the benefits of political participation.
- The elected parliament reflects more accurately the "will of the electorate."
- Governments must consider the total electorate in policy formulation and management.
- Candidates can concentrate their campaigning energies on issues, rather than themselves having to encourage voters to vote.
- The voter isn't actually compelled to vote for anyone, because voting is by secret ballot.

Arguments used against compulsory voting:

- It is undemocratic to force people to vote—an infringement of liberty.
- The ill-informed and those with little interest in politics are forced to the polls.
- It may increase the number of "donkey votes" (in Australia, the practice of numbering the boxes on ballot papers sequentially from top to bottom. Donkey votes are typically cast by uninterested or ignorant voters.)
- It may increase the number of informal votes.
- It increases the number of safe, single-member electorates—political parties then concentrate on the more marginal electorates.
- Resources must be allocated to determine whether those who failed to vote have "valid and sufficient" reasons.

Appendix III

Terrorist Surveillance or Domestic Spying—An Overview

TO MANY OBSERVERS, THE CONTROVERSY raging in Washington, D.C.'s governing classes over what the Bush administration calls "terrorist surveillance" and critics label "domestic spying," is very difficult to understand. For those unfamiliar with this story, last December, the *New York Times* broke the electrifying news that the National Security Agency (NSA) had been conducting super-secret surveillance of Americans at home in apparent violation of the law. NSA is America's electronic spying agency, and it is forbidden by law to conduct surveillance at home of U.S. citizens.

To many outside the United States, the reaction was, what was the issue? Governments have the right to protect their citizens. In much of the world, such intrusive acts of eavesdropping and wiretapping are to be expected, even if unwelcome, in the name of public safety and security—especially if a nation is engaged in a Global War on Terror.

But the fact is that domestic surveillance inside the United States has explosive potential. The conflict is constitutional in character, impinges on protection provided citizens against unlawful search and seizure, and pits the power of the presidency against that of Congress. The only good news is that this conflict, for the moment, is less one of partisan politics—with Democrats taking on Republicans and vice versa—than a clash of authority between two major branches of government over the Constitution and what constitutes unjust search. Understanding how and why a dangerous collision could occur provides a critical insight in better understanding America and its system of government.

The Story

Shortly after the attacks of September 11, 2001, President Bush authorized the NSA to begin a highly secret, covert program of surveilling communications either from abroad to the United States or from within the states to phone numbers and E-mails of individuals suspected of being members, associates, or people otherwise involved with al Qaeda. Eight members of Congress were briefed: the leaders in both the Senate and the House and the ranking members of the two intelligence committees. Until the *New York Times* story, the program's existence was unknown.

Immediately, critics saw this program as suspending the protection against search and seizure that is guaranteed by the Fourth Amendment to the Constitution, as well as bypassing or violating the Foreign Intelligence Surveillance Act of 1978 (known as FISA). FISA specified that no domestic surveillance or spying on Americans could be conducted without a court-approved warrant. FISA grew out of the excess of an earlier era.

In the 1960s, President Lyndon Johnson relied on extralegal wiretaps, as did his director of the FBI, the infamous J. Edgar Hoover, all or most in direct violation of the law. In the 1970s, the Nixon administration carried on the practice by wiretapping several of Nixon's own key staff members, and also conducted the break-in of the Democratic Party Headquarters in the Watergate Office Building in central Washington, D.C. that ultimately led to his resignation.

After disclosure of these and other covert intelligence activities, the Church Committee, named for the late Democratic senator Frank Church of Idaho, investigated the CIA and produced a long list of reforms. From those investigations, FISA was passed and signed into law by President Jimmy Carter, who wrote as a "signing statement" attached to this law that FISA was the ultimate authority on how domestic surveillance would be conducted, meaning only with court-approved search warrants.

FISA created a special and secret FISA court, with eleven federal judges hand-picked by the chief justice of the Supreme Court. All domestic wiretaps and electronic surveillance of American citizens categorically required warrants issued by this court. (Warrants could be obtained retroactively within twenty-four hours of beginning the surveillance.)

The Bush administration rested its decision to authorize this surveillance on four reasons. First, it argued that the Constitution gave the president virtually unlimited power in his capacity of commander-in-chief in time of war, superseding FISA and the Fourth Amendment.

Second, it argued that the Congressional Resolution of September 2001 to "use all necessary and appropriate force" in responding to al Qaeda attacks applied to all forms of electronic surveillance.

Third, it cited the Supreme Court case *Hamdi v. Rumsfeld*, in which an American citizen captured in Afghanistan fighting with the Taliban could be detained as an "enemy combatant" and thus not be afforded his Constitutional safeguards, as evidence that the president possessed extended powers under the resolution authorizing force to authorize this surveillance.

Fourth, the administration argued that technology in the form of cell phones, the Internet, and fiber-optic transmission lines rendered FISA obsolete, which, they claimed, meant that the surveillance ordered was not covered by FISA. And what they did not say publicly was that about a third of all international calls are routed through the United States, raising the question of whether tapping into these sources was also outside FISA.

A further justification for its policies on domestic surveillance was derived from the premise that in certain circumstances, such as when a detainee or suspect had information that could prevent an attack that could kill tens or hundreds of thousands, extreme methods were necessary. Those methods pertained to surveillance and eavesdropping. Yet, in 1978 when FISA was enacted, the threat of the Soviet Union included the possibility of a thermonuclear war in which the United States would have been obliterated. Extreme methods were not deemed necessary then, when the absolute risk was catastrophic.

Finally, the president and his leading intelligence and law-enforcement officials claimed that proper oversight was already being conducted by lawyers in the Justice Department, the White House, and the NSA, and that the president re-approved the surveillance program every forty-five days. However, no outside oversight by another branch of government was sought, and only the head FISA judge was aware of the program.

The Senate Awakens

Meanwhile, a Congress that had largely downplayed oversight of the administration showed signs of finally waking up. The controversies over "torture" and the ill-treatment of enemy combatants captured in the Global War on Terror and detained at Guantánamo Bay and Abu Ghraib and other prisons, and over the continuing violence and chaos in Iraq, as well as the disastrous response to Hurricane Katrina that devastated three southern states on the Gulf of Mexico, brought Congress into direct confrontation with the White House. Senator John McCain, himself a Vietnam War prisoner of war who suffered torture, and a few others literally forced the White House to sign into law a statute barring "cruel, inhuman, and degrading" treatment of prisoners—grudgingly. And long-absent Congressional oversight, from monitoring post-war reconstruction in Iraq to the mishandling of hurricane recovery, appeared to be stirring.

But it was the domestic-surveillance issue that engaged both Republican and Democratic members of Congress. The Senate Judiciary Committee, chaired by Arlen Specter, summoned Attorney General Alberto Gonzalez for a full day of grilling in early February. Four Republican senators of the committee joined all eight Democrats in registering great concern and worry that the authorization to surveil domestically bypassed—and possibly broke—the law and the Fourth Amendment.

Their arguments were based in large part on fundamental disagreements with the presidential interpretation of FISA and the resolution authorizing force. FISA had been amended five times after September 11, including extending the twenty-four-hour deferral to seventy-two before needing to obtain a warrant. The USA PATRIOT Act had been passed by overwhelming majorities and provided the president with further latitude in surveilling suspected terrorists. If the White House was not satisfied with those actions, why was Congress not asked to make further changes?

Regarding the resolution authorizing the use of force, members of Congress voting at the time did not believe that surveillance was covered. The majority leader, Senator Tom Daschle, in fact deleted reference, in the White House's proposed resolution, to any domestic authority to conduct surveillance. Hence, in the view of a number of members of Congress, the presidency exceeded its authority based on this resolution.

What Next?

With Congress still debating what to do, it is difficult to know what lies ahead. The White House has exerted significant pressure on the Senate Judiciary Committee not to take further action on terrorist surveillance. At the time this book goes to press, after being more extensively briefed on the program by the administration, Congress seems to have had its appetite for overhauling the NSA surveillance program curtailed.

The most sensible solution is for Congress to pass a law that gives the oversight responsibility to the FISA Court for day-to-day matters regarding surveillance, and to the two Congressional intelligence committees for broader review. So far, the White House has resisted this compromise, preferring to remain committed to the broader view of presidential power. If the impasse remains, it is possible that the president will claim that FISA is unconstitutional and an undue infringement on presidential authority. Should that occur, the case would presumably go to the Supreme Court (who, after all, are the only party who can actually determine that a law is unconstitutional).

Any number of "fault lines" persist within the fabric of American society. As with all states, vulnerability to terrorist attack can never be reduced to zero. There are growing economic concerns over rising debt and deficits. Iraq does not appear to be growing more stable or safer. Iran is challenging the international order regarding the Non-Proliferation Treaty and pursuing nuclear weapons. Any of these, as well as other fault lines, could fail or shatter.

Now is not the time to provoke a Constitutional crisis. But if the White House views this strictly as a test of wills and Congress sees it as a threat to its authority and responsibility, as it should, then this fault line could become the most exposed of all. Those from abroad with interests in better understanding the politics of this nation should recognize the potential that domestic surveillance has for engulfing the United States in further political gridlock, while remaining sufficiently objective to recognize that this issue could simply melt away because it is too difficult to handle head-on.

Endnotes

Introduction

1. To avoid confusion between the two Bush presidents, George H. W. Bush, the forty-first president is noted as Bush 41 and his son, George W. Bush, the forty-third president, as Bush 43.

2. See David Broder, "Time for A House Cleaning," *The Washington Post*, December 8th, 2005, p. A33 as one of too many examples of how Congress circumvents its rules and responsibilities. Regarding "earmarks" that are spending add-ons usually inserted without any oversight or review, the number has swelled in 2005 to over 15,000 up from about 4,000 a decade ago. Interestingly, Ronald Reagan vetoed a transportation bill in his first administration largely because it contained less than 200 "earmarks."

3. That the United States Government could not agree on a definition of torture is a further indication of government's dysfunctionality. The White House line that we do not use "torture" was unconvincing given the many reported cases to the contrary. The spectacle that accompanied a call for a new strategic approach to Iraq by the prominent, pro-war and decorated Democratic Congressman, Representative John P. Murtha of Pennsylvania, shows we are in trouble

and is discussed later. The intensity of the reactions and the amount of venom that spewed forth from both Republicans and Democrats is indicative of how partisanship is limiting rational debate and discussion. And the decision to allow surveillance of Americans may prove the administration's undoing. These explain in part why the president and Congress have such low opinion ratings in the polls.

4. There is a fourth and silent "p" that is taken up in the recommendations—pandering to special interest and other groups—and how public engagement can mitigate the effects of this "p."

Part I: The Fault Lines
Chapter One: Why We Are at Risk

5. What we call the adversary is important. If Islam is used in any form such as Radical Islamists, it suggests a condemnation of the religion. The word terrorist misses the larger political motivations. The term I use is jihadist extremist, realizing the word "jihad" can also imply an unwanted legitimacy to the adversary's cause, a lesser of two evils.

6. The American Dream encapsulates what most Americans believe America is and what it stands for—the collective view of values and aspirations and indeed the "promise." Culture reflects the general mood and political perceptions of Americans—what Alfred Thayer Mahan called "national character." Crusade is the expression of idealism that has always been in tension with pragmatism in defining American foreign policy—the clash between Washingtonian and Wilsonian views of the world and, in a broader context, has been influenced and tainted by religion and occasionally imbued with a missionary spirit. Partisanship reflects the degree of political polarization and factionalism that are becoming dysfunctional or worse.

7. Pat Robertson, an evangelical Christian leader, founder of the Christian Brotherhood (television) Network and former presidential contender, is a prime example of these extremes, calling for the assassination of Venezuelan President Hugo Chavez and predicting God would take revenge on a community for recognizing homosexual rights. The reality is that tens of millions of God-fearing Christians take Robertson very seriously.

8. The resignation of Michael Brown as Head of FEMA ("You're doing a heckuva job, Brownie" said the president) had been tendered before

Hurricane Katrina and the demotion of Brigadier General Janice Karpinski, commander of Abu Ghraib prison, are token actions.

9. The confirmations of Supreme Court John Roberts as Chief Justice and Samuel Alito as an Associate Justice and the withdrawal of White House counsel Harriet Miers are indicative of the destructive sides of this form of political discourse. Roberts was wrongfully smeared over a position he did not take on right to life. Miers was in over her head but still the attack ads distorted her record, too. And Alito's hearing turned into partisan and often childlike bickering that revealed strikingly little about the nominee except his level-headed temperament and coolness under fire.

10. The foreign press carries on a daily basis, reports of the declining stature and increasing opposition to American policies. Following allegations of secret U.S. detention centers in Europe in the war on terror, headlines abroad repeatedly pointed to American hypocrisy over human rights. See also Chris Patten, *Cousins and Strangers— America, Britain and Europe in the New Century,* a tough critic of U.S. policy and the negative reaction abroad. Patten is a former British politician and diplomat.

11. On the other hand, consider the experience of the unsuccessful candidates for president. Gerald Ford, who lost in 1976, was highly capable as was former Senate Majority Leader Bob Dole, defeated in 1992. Former vice president and senator Walter Mondale had the credentials for office in 1984. Michael Dukakis, former governor of Massachusetts lacked the experience, losing in 1988. And Senator John Kerry's twenty years in the Senate prepared him for high office when he lost in 2004. Vice President and former senator Al Gore is the anomaly. With a highly credentialed résumé like the first George Bush, Gore won the popular vote in 2000 and lost in the Electoral College.

12. On November 1, 2005, Senate Minority Leader Harry Reid called for a rare "closed session" of the Senate under Rule 21 to debate what Democrats saw as inaction by the Republicans to complete the second part of the investigation of the intelligence failure over WMD. Republicans called this a "stunt" and Majority Leader Bill Frist complained that for the rest of this session of Congress—because of this ploy Frist took as a "slap in the face"—he no longer could place any trust and confidence in Senator Reid.

13. This argument was made in my last two books and particularly in

Finishing Business—Ten Steps to Defeat Global Terror (Naval Institute Press: 2004), 246p.

14. See Appendix III for a thorough analysis of this issue.

Chapter Two: History Matters: Past Fault Lines

15. In summary these points were: 1. Abolition of secret diplomacy; 2. Freedom of the seas; 3. removal of economic barriers among nations (free trade); 4. reduction of armaments; 5. readjusting colonial claims 6: restoration of Russia; 7. return of Belgium to her people; 8. Return of French territory seized by Germany in 1870; 9. readjustment of Italy's frontiers; 10. autonomous development of Austria Hungary; 11. Restoration of the Balkan nations; 12. protection of Turkish minorities; 13. independent Poland; and 14. a general association ("League") of Nations to guarantee independence and territorial integrity.

Chapter Three: Unchecked and Unbalanced—The Enemy from Within: Dysfunctional Government and an Exposed Nation

16. James Garfield issued no veto but only served for six months before dying in office.

17. See William A. Galston and Elaine C. Kamarck, "The Politics of Polarization," The Third Way Middle Class Project, October 2005, 64p.

18. Ibid, page 4.

19. Northrop owns Newport News, the only yard capable of building nuclear aircraft carriers; Ingalls; Avondale; and Gulfport. General Dynamics owns Electric Boat, Bath Ironworks and National Shipbuilding.

20. Routinely, hazardous materials criss-cross the United States without fanfare or security. In the nation's capitol, rail lines as well as truck routes run directly through the city. Suppose a truck bomb were exploded under the railroad bridge at the intersection of Second and E Streets SW in Washington, D.C., just as a chlorine tanker passed overhead. Estimates suggest 100,000 people would be killed or injured. These vulnerabilities persist throughout the United States as well as every other country.

21. About a decade ago, George Soros bet against the pound, made a fortune and nearly collapsed the British currency.

22. "An Assessment of the Vulnerability of the Port of New York and New Jersey" conducted through a generous grant of the Smith-Richardson Foundation and released in September 2004. The co-chairmen of the study were the Hon. Jerry M. Hultin, now president of Polytechnic Institute in New York, and myself.

23. In 2004, the BBC produced a movie called *Dirty War*. The movie was an accurate portrayal of how terror cells operated, in this case to explode a dirty bomb in London. Ironically (or cause and effect), ground zero in the movie for the explosion was the Liverpool Street Underground station, the same spot extremists hit on July 11, 2005.

Chapter Four: The Enemy from Without

24. When President Bush declared that in this war, "you are either with us or against us," had Britain used the same standard in battling the IRA, it would have forced a confrontation with America—the source of strong financial and political support for the IRA.

25. Beginning with the Proclamation of 1763 that restricted where the colonists could settle, the Revenue Acts (1764) that raised taxes; The Stamp Act (1765) that brought new levies; the Townsend Act (1767) that imposed further revenue demands; the Boston Massacre of 1770 in which British soldiers killed eleven rock throwing Yankees; and the "Intolerable Acts" (1774) that closed Boston Harbor until restoration of the damage from the Boston Tea Party of the previous year was made good, all managed to galvanize the colonies into a show of unity against arbitrary British rule that led to the revolution.

26. Ayman al-Zawahiri, *Knights Under the Prophet's Banner*, translated by Foreign Broadcast Information Service, document FBIS-NES-2001-12012.

27. Letter from al-Zawahiri to al-Zarqawi, published by the Director of National Intelligence, October 11, 2005.

28. Ibid, p. 3.

29. Interview conducted by Dr. Scott Atran on August 13 and 15, 2005, from Cipiang Prison in Jakarta, Indonesia and reprinted in "Spotlight on Terror," Volume 3, Issue 9 (September 15, 2005), provided by Dr. Atran to the author.

30. Ibid. All subsequent quotes come from the article and are not footnoted.

31. See *Finishing Business*, Chapters 7, 8, and 9.

Part II: Crusades Abroad

32. In early 2005, Europe was considering breaking the embargo on certain arms sales to China. U.S. intervention changed their minds and the sales were never consummated.

33. Ibid, *Unfinished Business*.

Chapter Five: The World As It Is, Not As We Wish It

34. Several years ago, the head of NSA, the world's most advanced electronics surveillance agency, received a call from his physician, an expatriate Pakistani. Worrying that his health was the issue, the general was surprised to hear from his doctor that former Pakistani prime minister Benazir Bhutto was being arrested in Islamabad by Pakistani authorities. The general, with all of America's best surveillance equipment at his fingertips, asked how the doctor knew. The reply puts globalization in perspective. On his other cell phone was a cousin in Islamabad, sitting three cars behind Bhutto watching the whole affair play out.

35. Harlan Ullman, *Unfinished Business: Afghanistan, the Middle East and Beyond—Defusing the Dangers that Threaten America's Security* with a Foreword by Senator John McCain; New York: Kensington Press, 2002), 300p. and *Finishing Business—Ten Steps to Defeat Global Terror* with a foreword by Newt Gingrich and an Afterword by Wesley Clark (Naval Institute Press, Annapolis: 2004), 246p.

36. The commission reported in the fall of 2005 that the FBI and other intelligence agencies "have made little progress in key areas they must reform." And see Commissioner John Lehman's column "Getting Spy Reform Wrong," in the *Washington Post*, November 14, 2005, that "Since September 11, there's been no real action to fix our government's most glaring failure: the dysfunctional intelligence bureaucracies whose incompetence exposed us to surprise attack."

Chapter Six: The Chinese Puzzle and the Russian Enigma

37. Extraterritoriality was a sore point for America. In 1821, in the Terranova case, an Italian crewman and a U.S. ship had caused what was likely the accidental drowning of a Chinese woman. The hapless sailor was convicted in a Chinese court and then strangled to death. The Treaty of Wanghia, signed on July 3, 1844, codified these agreements.

Chapter Seven: Vietnam and the Greater Middle East

38. Press Conference Number 2, February 1, 1961.
39. The Tonkin Gulf incident is well documented. At the time, the United States had been conducting as series of covert attacks against the North called Operation 34 A. The attacks were carried out by U.S. "Nasty" class PT boats sailing from DaNang and were highly unsuccessful covert attempts to coerce the North from operating in the South. North Vietnam had file diplomatic protests citing that these covert attacks violated the Geneva Agreement. Washington was intimately aware of what happened and Johnson deliberately manipulated the incidents to gain the authority to broaden the war.
40. See Justin Frank, *Bush on the Couch: Inside the Mind of the President* (New York: Harper Collins, 2004). Discussions with several psychoanalysts reinforced the view that Bush was dyslexic.
41. See the *New Yorker* Scowcroft interview on October 31, 2005, the address of Lawrence Wilkerson to the New America Foundation on October 19, 2005 and Melvin Laird in *Foreign Affairs* Nov/Dec 2005.
42. Among the members of the Defense Policy Board were former Vice President Dan Quayle; former Speakers of the House Newt Gingrich and Tom Foley; former Secretary of State Henry Kissinger; and a number of former defense secretaries including James Schlesinger and Harold Brown.
43. See Tommy Franks, *American Soldier* (New York:Harper Collins, 2005).
44. For a complete description, see *Finishing Business.*
45. Private discussions with participants at that meeting and the author.
46. For their service, General Tommy Franks, George Tenet and Coalition Provisional Authority head L. Paul Bremer all received the Presidential Medal of Freedom.
47. See Larry Diamond, *Squandered Victory* (New York: Times Books, 2005) 369p. and George Packer, *Assassin's Gate* (New York: Farrar, Straus and Giroux, 2005), 467p.

Part III: Restoring America's Promise

48. Creating solutions for social security (reducing benefits and increasing revenues), health care, pension funds and other obligations can be done. But as the President's Commission on Tax Reform demonstrated, the trick is implementation.

49. The Savings and Loan crises of the 1980s are forgotten. In its interest to preserve these banks, Congress expanded the authority to make more low-interest loans in areas where the management had no competence and then provided government guarantees in the event the loans went bad. The S&L's responded recklessly and promiscuously in making uncollateralized or insufficiently collateralized loans. As loans came due, they could not be paid. Many of these banks failed and tens of billions of dollars of government backed guarantees came directly out of taxpayer pockets. Government was the cause, however and the banks were merely the delivery instruments for paying the bills.

Chapter Eight: Partisanship and Paradox at Home

50. When queried by the White House why the students had not been rescued yet, the operational commander Vice Admiral Joseph J. Metcalf signaled back the reason. In his view, they were not in immediate danger. That story, fortunately for the administration, never got out.

51. Ambassador Joe Wilson was sent to Niger by the CIA to investigate whether or not Iraq has sought to purchase Uranium "yellow cake" for its nuclear program. Wilson returned with ambiguous information. Later, memos would surface debunking the allegation. In mid-2003 after the Iraqi invasion, Wilson wrote an op-ed piece in the *New York Times* arguing that the charges against Iraq were wrong and politically motivated. Wilson's wife, a former covert agent, was then working at Langley. A column written by Robert Novak asserted (wrongly) that Plame had gotten her husband the assignment and exposed her as a covert operative, beginning this sordid saga.

52. Discussions between the author and members of Congress held between 2003 and 2005. As these were private, names are not disclosed, although the subjects could be discussed without attribution.

53. Fortunately, the relationships between chairmen and ranking members of the Armed Services, Appropriations, Judicial, and Foreign Relations Committees for example do not reflect this bitterness. However, should the "nuclear option" be taken over judicial appointees and the filibuster ended, it would be a tragic day for the Senate and the nation.

54. The religious composition of the Supreme Court could prove interesting as there are five Catholics, two Protestants and two Jews on

the court, giving Catholics a majority for the first time in American history. For those fixated on the growing impact of religion, this will be cause for concern perhaps as JFK was the first Catholic to become president. More than likely, this will prove to be an anomaly with little consequence. It is worth noting, however.

55. Larry M. Bartels, "Partisan Politics and the U.S. Income Distribution," February 2004.

56. See Georgetown University Long Term Care Financing Project Fact Sheet, July 2004.

57. See Statement by CBO Director Douglas Holtz-Eakin to the House Committee on Ways and Means, May 19, 2005.

58. See Exxon Mobil Third Quarter Estimates, October 27, 2005 published on its homepage. By comparison, milk ($4 per gallon), bottled water ($8 per gallon or more) and Starbucks coffee ($160 per gallon) cost far more per gallon than gasoline and the profit margins are often larger.

59. Bing West, *No True Glory—A Frontline Account for the Battle of Fallujah* (Bantam Books: New York, 2005), 380p.

Chapter Ten: Big Ideas

60. The pending sale of a company that manages major U.S. ports from a British to a Dubai/United Arab Emirates corporation has provoked a strong negative reaction in Congress. While such acquisitions are screened and monitored by the interagency Committee on Foreign Investment in the U.S. (CFIUS) and are carefully controlled regarding all elements of security, the perception of a Gulf state overseeing U.S. ports in the eyes of many Americans is troubling and even unacceptable. That perception does not reflect reality. However, it is likely to carry the day. And the reaction in the Gulf and among Arab and Muslim friends of the United States will no doubt be highly negative and critical, doing further harm to the status and standing of America abroad.

61. U.S. supporters of Taiwan and democracies in general and those distrustful of China would profoundly object. However, Taiwan would still remain autonomous and the threat of war would be largely eliminated— not a bad tradeoff.

62. A separate volume could be written on initiatives and bi- and multilateral arrangements. There are about a dozen or so maritime initiatives in play from the Proliferation Security Initiative, Container

Security Initiative, Regional Maritime Security Initiative, Malacca Straits Coordinated Patrol, International Ship and Port Security Patrol to counter-proliferation efforts, including the Missile Technology Control Regime, international code of conduct against ballistic missile proliferation, and Wassenaar Arrangement, and not to mention intelligence and law enforcement regimes.

63. Here is a partial list: The European Union (twenty-five members); NATO (twenty-six members); Western European Union (ten members, six associates, five observers, and seven associate partners); European Free Trade Area; European Economic Area; European cooperative committees on coal and steel; spaced, rivers, seaports; and the Council of Europe.

64. Many of these views reflect my participation on the Senior Advisory Group of Commander, European Command (EUCOM) from 2003 onward, several visits made to the region under EUCOM's responsibility, and attendance at numerous SAG meetings.

65. In 1992, the turnout was 55.9 percent; it was 49 percent in 1996; 51.3 percent in 2000; and 53 percent in 2004. With a larger turnout, politics could be stood upside down.

66. On the subject of voter fraud, see Tracy Campbell, *Deliver the Vote— A History of Election Fraud, An American Political Institution— 1724-2004* (Carroll & Graf: New York, 2005), 453p.

67. Australia began mandatory voting in 1924. Before then, voter turnout was comparable to America's—50 to 55 percent. In the past twenty years, average turnout has been above 95 percent. Failure to vote results in a fine and the process is overseen by the Australian Elections Commission (see its Web site https:aec.au.gov and Appendix II for a list of pros and cons for universal voting). The total costs for the last election were $161 million Australian dollars.

68. Ernest Hollings, *The Washington Post*, Outlook Section, February 19, 2006.

69. See CSIS study by Clark Murdock and Michelle Flournoy, "Beyond Goldwater-Nicholls: U.S. Government and Defense Reform for a New Strategic Era–Phase II Report," July 2005.

Index

'Abduh, Muhammed, 94–95
ABM Treaty, 126, 146
abortion issue, 57
Abu Ghraib, 227–28, 254
accountability. *See* governmental accountability
activists, nature of, 205–6
Afghanistan: Bush 43's crusade in, 13, 62, 180; NATO commitment to, 132; and nuclear weapons (scenario), 102–4; Soviet invasion of, 88, 95, 203; as springboard to Iraq, 180; the Taliban, 180–81, 250, 299; tribal warlords' control of, 135, 181; vanishing promise for, 250
Africa and the Americas, 266–69
African Americans, 30–35
al Qaeda: bin Laden, 71, 82, 88, 92, 96–100, 232, 233–34; intent of, 69, 71, 239–40; Internet utilization, 71; motivation of, 88–89, 233–34; and 1993 World Trade Center bombing, 105; as primary international adversary, 14; retaliation against, 180; and Sunni clergy, 93. *See also* jihadist extremists
Al-Afghani, Jamal as-Din, 94
Alaska purchase, 154
Alito, Samuel, 305n9
al-Zawahiri, Ayman, 88, 92–93, 98–99
American Dream: current threats to, 11, 14–15, 214–16; distribution of wealth in America, 210, 217–18; historical view of, 12, 21–25, 47–48, 304n6
American Dream, current need for, 15–16
American Revolution, 5, 25–30, 86, 307n25
Angleton, James Jesus, 161
Arab League, 262
Arab world. *See* Islam and Islamists; jihadist extremists; Middle East; *specific countries*
Argentina, 213
Armed Forces. *See* Department of Defense
Asia, 19–20, 122–23, 259–61, 261–63. *See also specific countries*

Asian tsunami, 67, 187, 236–37, 238–39
Assessment of the Vulnerability of the Port of New York and New Jersey, 73, 306n22
Australia, mandatory voting in, 271, 295–96, 312n67
axes of evil, 21, 84, 235–36, 269

Ba'asyir, Abu Bakar, 100
Bay of Pigs fiasco, 159, 161–62
beliefs. *See* culture
Berlin Wall, 24
bin Laden, Osama. *See* al Qaeda
Blair, Tony, 183, 223
Bolsheviks, 38, 87, 92, 154–56, 248
Boxer Rebellion, 142
Bremer, L. Paul "Jerry," 185, 220
Brezhnev, Leonid, 54
Britain: and American Revolution, 26; and Blair, 183, 223; and China, 140; Downing Street Memo, 223; and Falkland Islands, 237–38; London transport bombings, 77, 130, 231; and Middle Eastern oil, 155, 265–66; political process in, 245
Brown, Michael, 220, 304n8
Brzezinski, Zbigniew, 13
Bundy, McGeorge, 161
Bush, George H. W. "Bush 41": 24, 147, 204, 237
Bush, George W. "Bush 43": agenda of, 126, 174–76, 176; from alcoholic to born again Christian, 176–77; authorization of domestic surveillance, 298, 299; axis of evil, 21, 235–36; campaign promises and results, 206–8; and China, 133, 147–52, 228, 279; crusades of, 13–14, 113–14, 152, 178–82, 207–8, 285; intelligence manipulation question, 184; and Iraq, expectations, 13, 165, 182–83, 304n6; and Iraq, reality, 188–89; Kennedy compared to, 165–66; mandatory question time for, 245, 246–47, 272; "mission accomplished"

Revolutionary War (American), 5, 25–30, 86, 307n25
Rice, Condoleezza, 175, 178
Roberts, John, 304n9
Roberts, Pat, 129
Robertson, Pat, 213, 304n7
Roe v. Wade ruling, 57
Roosevelt, Franklin Delano (FDR), 20, 22, 41, 43, 55–57, 157
Roosevelt, Theodore "Teddy," 36–37, 38, 154
Rostow, Walt, 144–45
rules of engagement, 279–80
Rumsfeld, Donald, 124, 149, 174, 175, 178
Russia, 138, 152–56, 163, 261. *See also* Cold War; Soviet Union

Sadat, Anwar, 95
Saddam Systems takeover by USA Inc. (scenario), 221
Salafist ideology and ideas, 88–89, 92–96, 98–99, 105–6, 262
Sarbanes–Oxley Act (2001), 221–22, 273–74, 275
Sarbanes–Oxley Act for government, 194, 273–75
Saudi Arabia: and al Qaeda, 93; and bin Laden, 88, 232; Bush 43's plans for, 178–79; current political direction, 134, 290; and Islam, 95–96; Khobar Towers bombings, 178; speculation about jihadist takeover of, 91–92, 106
Savings and Loan crises of the 1980's, 310n49
Schneider, William, 212
Schwarzenegger, Arnold, 272–73
Senate Judiciary Committee, 300, 301
September 11, 2001, terrorist attacks: and American Dream, 24; Americans' reaction to, 82; and Bush administration, 126, 176, 177; symbolism of targets, 71; transformation of DoD due to, 66; U.S. response to, 178–80; and USA PATRIOT Act, 280, 300; use of commander-in-chief title, 54–55. *See also* al Qaeda; enemy combatants; Jihadist extremists; 9/11 Commission
1789 and the election of Washington, 25–30
Shanghai Cooperative Organization, 260
Shia Islamists, 96, 101, 186–89
Sinclair, Upton, 36
Sistani, Ayatollah Ali al, 186
Six-Power Talks on North Korea, 101, 132, 236, 259–60, 262, 266
slavery in America, 30–31, 32–33
social and entitlement programs: current financial condition of, 3, 4, 197, 276–77, 293; and implementation of solutions, 194–95, 309n48; political complications from, 55–56
society: assimilation of minorities, 255; effect of fault lines cracking, 60; nonresponse to Global War on Terror, 72; politicization of issues, 12, 55, 57–58; psychology of vulnerability, 76–78; rigors and contradictions of modern, 24–25; and television, 59–60; voter turnout in U.S., 269–70, 312n65; vulnerability of, 49–51, 67–69, 78–80, 123–24, 244. *See also* culture; public involvement
Soros, George, 306n21
Southwest Asia, 261–63
Soviet Union: Cuban Missile Crisis, 162; and Eastern Europe, 46, 157–58; history of, 153–56; implosion of, 60, 162–63, 233; intent

of nuclear buildup, 159–60; Lenin, 38, 87, 92, 154–56, 248; and Loyalists in Spain, 42, 155; military open press, 160–61; nuclear bombs in, 47; political parties' agreement on, 55; as Russia, 138, 152–56, 163, 261; and United States, 153–56, 157–63. *See also* Cold War
Spanish Civil War, 42, 155–56
Spanish-American War, 36, 47
special-interest groups and lobbies: dysfunctional government from rise of, xiii, 284, 304n4; increase in, 56; nature of activists, 205–6; polarization of issues due to, 198; political action committees, 60; quantity of, 60–61; and social issues, 57–58; and universal vote, 271
Stalin, Joseph, 43, 91, 144, 156–57
Stanton, Edward, 34
Stevens, Thaddeus, 32–33
strategic analyses: Bush 43's, 20–21, 117, 118, 177–78, 179–80; components of strategy, 249–50; demonizing enemy as counterproductive to, 82–83; of enemy designation, 85–86; of failure in Iraq, 285; of jihadist Extremists, 90–92; of motivation of terrorists and revolutionaries, 76, 77–78, 86–89, 121; need for, 11–12, 21, 135, 163–64, 240–41
strategic and historic analyses: of American Dream, 12, 21–25, 47–48; of Bush 43 administration, 174–76; of China, 139–47; of Civil War and its aftermath, 30–35, 40; of Iraq and Middle East, 173; of Japan's attack on Pearl Harbor, 19–20; 1918 and the end of World War I to the Great Depression, 35–41; 1935, the Great Depression, fascism, and communism, 41–44; of Russia, 153–63; 1789 and the election of Washington, 25–30; of terrorism, 76, 77–78, 86–89, 121; of U.S. involvement in Vietnam, 167–72; of World War II, 41–47
strategic communication, 212, 213
strategic damage paradigms, 70–71
Strategic Hamlet Program, 170
Sumner, Charles, 32–33
Sun Tzu, 119
Sunni Islamists, 92–96, 103, 188–89, 197, 262
Supreme Court, 57, 206, 209, 227, 246, 299, 310n54
surveillance of Americans, 14–15, 280–81, 297–301, 303n3

Taiwanese independence issue, 150, 259–60, 311n61
Taliban, the, 180–81, 250, 299
Tarbell, Ida, 35–36
technology and conduct of war, 121–22, 279
television and politics, 59, 202
Tenet, George, 175, 219, 220
Tenure of Office Act, 34
terrorism: examples of, 76–78, 77, 130, 178, 231; financing for, 106–7; future forms of, 123; history of, 76–78, 121; nature of, 294; as ongoing threat in U.S., 239–41, 253–54; rectifying causes versus attacking symptoms, 102, 125, 134–35, 233, 242–44; strategic and historic analysis of, 76, 77–78, 86–89, 121. *See also* Global War on Terror
terrorists: advantage in imposing costs, 80, 105; applying labels to, 304n5; disruptive potential